The Princeton Review

PrincetonReview.com

L

A COMP   N,

GAY, BISE   TS

                                                                    ES

John

a

The Princeton Review, Inc.

2315 Broadway

New York, NY 10024

E-mail: bookeditor@review.com

ISBN 978-0-375-76623-7

Publisher: Robert Franek

Editor: Adrinda Kelly

Designer and Production Manager: Scott Harris

Production Editor: Christine LaRubio

Printed in the United States of America.

9 8 7 6 5 4 3 2 1

2008 Edition

Acknowledgments

Thanks to Coleen O'Shea for your perseverance and to Fiona Hallowell for believing in my project. Thanks to Margaret Gee for the first round of attempts all those years ago and for discovering the title. Gratitude to all my early readers for suffering through the first drafts: Dan, Susan, Susanne, Cynthia, Julie, Wolf, Jill, Vaunceil. Special thanks to yogini ninja Jennifer Amman for emergency management services.

Gratitude to Sean and Tania for laying the foundations. And to Brent Hyde for helping me get the whole thing started.

AUTHOR BIOS

John Baez received a MA in English and Critical Theory from the City University of New York and is an active arts educator, writer, and producer. He is one of the founding partners of the NYC-based Punkmouse queer media group and is the Co-Executive Director of the annual Queer Media and Entertainment Conference.

Jennifer Howd is a writer, producer, director, and queer visibility activist living in NYC. She is the founding partner of Punkmouse, a media and entertainment group dedicated to developing, producing, and marketing lesbian, gay, bisexual, transgendered, and queer inclusive media.

Rachel Pepper is the Coordinator of Lesbian and Gay Studies at Yale University. An award-winning journalist and freelance writer, Pepper is the author of *The Ultimate Guide to Pregnancy for Lesbians* (Cleis Press) and is a long-standing book columnist for Curvemagazine."

ACKNOWLEDGMENTS

Thanks to my partner Simon Spelling for being there whenever I needed support; to my loving mother Violeta; to my ever-supportive in-laws Barrie and Marie; and to Kristen Bremner, Joe Baranello, Brenda To, Julie DeMaio and Michael Lopez for always believing in me.

Extra-special thanks go out to Roberta Sklar and Inga Sorensen at the Task Force, Paige Schultz at Soulforce, and Shane Windmeyer at Campuspride.org for all of their help in getting this book written.

—John Baez

Thank you to Adrinda Kelly, Robert Franek, and the entire Princeton Review team for their vision in seeing the need for creating this groundbreaking book. My sincere acknowledgments also go out to the myriad out-and-proud LGBTQ college students across the country who each took a stand to help the readers of this book by sharing their personal quotes and photos. Special thanks and appreciation to James Babbin for bringing this book to my attention and for opening the door to John and me. A very special thank you to Debbie Bazarsky and Cathy Renna for their assistance in coordinating and securing our amazing team of contributing authors. Thanks, also, to Rachel Pepper and to the members of the National Consortium of Directors of LGBT Resources in Higher Education for their tremendous guidance, cooperation, and contribution. Sincere appreciation to Jennifer Cuenot and Tony and Diane Howd for their loving support and enthusiasm. Special thanks to Sandra Madsen, Reid Mihalko, and Alina Wilczynski for their continued friendship and encouragement. And, lastly, recognition to my "brother," business partner, and best friend, John Baez to whom I am eternally grateful to have had by my side throughout the process of creating this book—and to whom I am forever beholden for being my personal superhero.

—Jennifer Howd

I would like to warmly thank everyone who shared their experiences and knowledge with me during research for this book, including the professors, college students, and graduates quoted, as well as the administrators from the National Consortium of Directors of LGBT Resources in Higher Education. In particular, I would especially like to thank PFLAG parents from all over the country who answered my questions so honestly about their LGBTQ children. Your belief in this project and your trust in me is a great honor. Finally, I would like to thank my coauthors John and Jennifer, The Princeton Review, and especially our fine editor there, Adrinda Kelly.

—Rachel Pepper

FOREWORD

LGBTQ student life has burgeoned with an increase in programming, support services, and visibility on college campuses nationwide. The face and experience of LGBTQ college students is dramatically different than it was ten—or even five—years ago, which is what gives space and interest for a book such as this. In 1997, Ellen DeGeneres came out on national television to the great controversy of companies pulling advertisements, people condemning her, and the show being canceled. Today there are numerous gay and lesbian characters on television, and the controversy seems like a distant memory for those entering college today.

So, who are today's college students? For the majority of their lives, they have always known "out" characters on television; they have been aware of out musicians, athletes, and politicians. They have only known the same-sex marriage debate as one over civil unions, marriage, and domestic partnership (versus no rights at all); they have gay/straight alliances in their high schools and friends, as well as family members, who are out. They have numerous examples of ways to be queer in an incredibly diverse community with a growing openness to a wide range of labels and flexibility of identity; and some have been out since childhood, with no memory of the closet in the same ways it has been constructed in the past.

In what sociologist Steven Seidman refers to as the post-closet era,[1] LGBTQ college students come to the table with a different outlook on college life than those who paved the way before them. In addition, straight students have grown up with many of these same experiences and arrive at college with openness and understanding for their LGBTQ peers. With allies showing greater support and involvement and a larger number of out LGBTQ students, life on campus is increasingly open and integrated.

Support services for LGBTQ students have also dramatically changed. Eighteen years ago, there were eight schools with LGBTQ offices. Now there are over 100, and they range from small private colleges to large public universities in over 36 states and several provinces in Canada. LGBTQ offices provide a home and community for students on campus. These centers offer programming, advising, support, and advocacy and give students the space to explore their identities, gain leadership opportunities, and have a better overall college experience.

In addition, most colleges and universities have at least one, and sometimes many, LGBTQ student organizations. Increasingly, schools are offering support and social groups for LGBTQ students of color, transgender and genderqueer students, LGBTQ athletes, bi and fluid students, and many others. Also, many schools offer regular programming for LGBTQ students through student life and academic departments. Notably, some schools support students through their multicultural office, women's center, or student activities offices. These are all things to keep an eye on during your college search.

Whether you are in rural Tennessee, a large city in Ohio, the Southwest, or anywhere in between, being LGBTQ, you are likely considering college with an additional layer of concerns and expectations. Throughout the book there are numerous references to LGBTQ centers and resources; however, a vast majority of schools do not have this level of support, and at these universities there are often amazing students like you who are challenging the system, advocating for more rights, and building support from the ground up. There are also LGBTQ students at schools that have a plethora of resources and vibrant communities who still feel like they are the only ones, fear rejection, and worry about being misunderstood or misrepresented. As much as things have changed, there are still challenges to being out in college and a need for more resources to help students like you in the journey of LGBTQ identity exploration.

Parents and students alike are factoring LGBTQ issues into their selection of colleges and universities, and if you are picking up this book, you probably are too. For prospective LGBTQ students, this book has numerous suggestions about how to find community, be safe, and have fun during your undergraduate years. From navigating the residence halls to finding the right summer internship, this book can be a resource for you to help make the most of your college experience. For parents and guidance counselors, this is a great place to start thinking about ways to offer support for LGBTQ college students, as well as figuring out how to guide them through the college experience. There are numerous quotes from parents throughout this book that offer insights into what their experiences have been. Take the resources here, but also reach out to other parents and students, either online or in person, to learn how they have dealt with the transition to college life.

College is a time of great transition and growth. It is a time when many LGBTQ students begin to understand their identities in deeper and more holistic ways. Looking for the right fit and making the most out your LGBTQ experience is important. This book will help you think about some of the things you should be considering, as well as some of the important questions you should be asking. College is a great time to find your way and your place in the LGBTQ community both on your campus and on the national stage. There are so many different ways to engage with LGBTQ life on campus today. Have fun with the process and good luck with your in*queeries*!

Debbie Bazarsky serves on the Executive Board of the National Consortium of Directors of LGBT Resources in Higher Education and is the Lesbian, Gay, Bisexual, Transgender Center Director at Princeton University.

1   Steven Seidman. *Beyond the Closet: The Transformation of Gay and Lesbian Life.* New York: Routledge, 2004.

CONTENTS

A MESSAGE FROM JUDY SHEPARD, OF THE MATTHEW SHEPARD FOUNDATION

Speaking to college audiences is one of the most gratifying parts of the work I do on behalf of the Matthew Shepard Foundation. The foundation seeks to "Replace Hate with Understanding, Compassion, and Acceptance" through its varied educational, outreach, and advocacy programs, and by continuing to tell Matthew's story. Encouraging young people to get involved in the political process is an essential element in making that change. College and university campuses are the ideal locations to do this work.

I am invited to a variety of schools—big, small, religious, conservative, progressive, and every type of institution of higher learning in between. Being a witness to collegiate activism has been informative from a work standpoint, and, at the same time, has helped me grow as an activist. I don't have a crystal ball, but from what I am seeing on campuses, this country is moving forward, and it gives me immense hope for the future of the lesbian, gay, bisexual, transgender, queer, and/or questioning (LGBTQ) community.

The real personal joy for me is speaking with students. I find that young people are no longer satisfied with being told who they are by others. They understand that they have a voice. They understand that they have power, and they want to use it. They are more motivated, active, and knowledgeable politically than the LGBTQ community was a generation ago. It's being with those people—who come to hear me speak, who share their own stories, and who get involved—that inspires me and gives me hope.

A couple of thoughts for any parents reading this book. First of all, thank you! The fact that you are taking the initiative to educate and inform yourself about the LGBTQ community means more to me than you can imagine. Secondly, as you begin this new part of life's journey with your child, please, please listen to what your children say. They know what they need and want. Their dreams and aspirations are the same as those of any other young person. Perhaps, most importantly of all, make sure your child knows that you will be there for them, unconditionally, as they reach for their dreams.

The world is very different now for LGBTQ people. The LGBTQ community is a far more accepted part of everyday life than it was for our generation. Your children are aware of that change, but they may still face prejudice, discrimination, ignorance, and even hate. Face it with them, support them, and be involved as much as you can in making a difference in their world. The LGBTQ community cannot do this alone; they need the support of their families and friends as allies. If we all work together, we will win this struggle for equality and respect—for everyone.

INTRODUCTION

When I first told my mom I was gay, she said she was fine with it, but just don't tell your dad. My mom could've used this book. Then again, so could I. Come to think of it, my dad could've used it as well. Also, my guidance counselor, freshman year roommate, sibs—you're getting the picture, right?! Our efforts and goals in creating this book were simple—to provide no nonsense info and guidance to students who are queer or questioning. The additional challenge was to provide that same info to their families, friends, counselors, and allies. I'm unapologetic in stating that I believe we've succeeded in achieving that goal.

The Princeton Review has been a long-time supporter of lesbian, gay, bisexual, transgender, and queer/questioning (LGBTQ) students on campus. Each year, we publish an annual ranking of the nation's most and least gay-friendly campuses in our *Best Colleges* series. As with all of our college rankings and guidebooks, our goal is to provide prospective students with the information they need to make sound educational choices—information they're likely not to find in college admissions view books or on a website.

In 2001, the National Gay and Lesbian Task Force conducted a survey of 1,669 students, faculty, and administrators across the country to gauge the level of LGBTQ acceptance on college campuses. According to their findings, 43 percent of the respondents rated their overall campus climate as homophobic; 23 percent feared for their physical safety because of their sexual orientation or gender identity/expression; and 41 percent said their college/university was not addressing issues related to their sexual orientation/gender identity.[1] Clearly, our ranking of gay-friendly schools did not tell the whole story. There was a need for a resource which would offer advice and guidance to LGBTQ students on how to deal with experiences of homo/bi/transphobia, how to evaluate campuses in terms of their safety needs, and how to find out about administrative policies related to LGBTQ student life. While the publication of *The Advocate Guide* in 2006 was an excellent step in providing school-specific LGBTQ info, there still remained the need for a book that

1   Rankin, Susan R. *Campus Climate for Gay, Lesbian, Bisexual, and Transgender People: A National Perspective.* New York: The National Gay and Lesbian Task Force Policy Institute. 2003. www.ngltf.org.

would treat, in a substantive way, the many efforts schools are making—and sometimes not making—to ensure that *all* students are valued and encouraged to participate fully in their undergraduate community.

In keeping with our philosophy that students are the real experts about their schools, we surveyed over 1,100 students at colleges and universities across the country about LGBTQ student life. Their quotes, interviews, testimonials (and even a few photos!) fill these pages. Their willingness to speak openly and candidly about their experiences has truly been inspiring. When reading these stories, remember there is no such thing as a single "LGBTQ" experience, and that multiple experiences—both positive and negative—may be reported by students at the same college. It's up to you to take a look at the big picture, and use these testimonials to find *your* "best fit" school.

Student experiences are the centerpiece of this book, but we have also reached out to parents and college administrators for tips and advice on how LGBTQ students can make the most of their college experiences. To do that, we partnered with two national organizations whose expertise and insights have been an enormous value to us throughout the development of this book. The executive director and regional chapter directors of the PFLAG (Parents and Friends of Lesbians and Gays) Association were instrumental in helping us reach out to the parents of LGBTQ students across the country whose insightful comments fill these pages. PFLAG has also provided a number of tips in the book specifically for parents on everything from dealing with an empty nest to safeguarding students from peer and administrative homo/bi/transphobia. The National Consortium of Directors of LGBT Resources in Higher Education was instrumental in helping us develop this project in a way that was inclusive of the concerns of the "B" and "T" in LGBTQ. In the "Speaking Out" sections of the book, members of their executive board offer essential guidance on various topics related to LGBTQ college life from an administrator's standpoint. There you will find advice on everything from how to evaluate college nondiscrimination policies toward LGBTQ people, to finding safe zones on campus. Counselors and advisors of LGBTQ students, in addition to parents, allies, and the students themselves, will find this advice to be invaluable as they work toward implementing change on their respective campuses. Campus Pride and Soulforce are just two of a number of LGBTQ organizations that have supported this project throughout, and have contributed quotes and essays peppered throughout these pages.

A word about the language used in this book. GLBTAU, LGBTAQ, GLBTQA, GLBT, LGBT, GLBTQSA, GLBTPIQA, non-straight, queer, gay, LGBTQ, homosexual, and many more combinations of identities appear in the following text. Each has its own history and meaning in the context of a campus and the speaker or author. We learned that the labels so often applied to the LGBTQ community only imperfectly reflect the broad spectrum of identities that it encompasses. So often, the "B" and "T" in LGBTQ gets silenced or ignored, and the "Q" is often left out altogether. Our choice to use the acronym LGBTQ to refer to the community of students whose experiences are profiled in these pages, is an effort to help lend visibility to students who challenge conventional conceptions of gender and sexuality at every turn. The "Q" in this acronym—which stands for queer and/or questioning—is there in recognition of the fact that college is a time of self-exploration and self-discovery for many students, and their fluid experiences are a major part of this book.

That said, we recognize that it is not possible to write a text that is inclusive of all LGBTQ identities, relationships, and life experiences. Our readers may self-identify in many different ways and these identities may change over time. In fact, many individuals identified as LGBTQ may choose to use other self-identifying terms or none at all. The National Gay and Lesbian Task Force's Campus Climate Survey suggests that not all respondents wanted to place themselves in LGBT identities. Many would prefer choices such as "same-gender loving," "gender-queer," "pansexual," "woman-loving-woman," etc. Some considered the "gay," "lesbian," "bisexual," and "transgender" categories to be rigid social constructs of identity that are not relevant to their personal experiences. Moreover, using the term LGBTQ while discussing sexual orientation may not represent transgender people. A transgender person's sexual identity is not necessarily connected to his or her gender identity. Some transgender people may identify as queer, heterosexual, bisexual, gay, lesbian, fluid, asexual, etc. Bisexual communities may also face marginalization and misunderstanding in the LGBTQ—as well as heterosexual—community. This book seeks to acknowledge and support people of complex gender identity who may have a physical and/or emotional attraction to people of different gender expressions and/or sexual orientation.

We use the term "queer" throughout this book to refer to the collective community of LGBTQ students. In the past, the term "queer" has been used in a derogatory manner, but today, it has been reclaimed by many in the LGBTQ community as a term of empowerment and inclusiveness. Finally, much of the advice in this book is written from the perspective of students who can expect to receive the support of their families throughout their college years. We know that not all LGBTQ college students will have emotional and/or financial support from their parents, or a home to go home to. To those students, we hope you will use this book to connect with a supportive community of LGBTQ people and allies who can help guide you during your college years.

The opportunity this book has given us to provide a resource for an amazingly diverse and unique community of students has truly been phenomenal. So many folks have come to us saying, "If only there had been a book like this around when I was applying to college. . ." —we are glad to be able to say "Now there is." Whether you're lesbian, gay, bisexual, transgender, queer, some combination of these, or none of the above, we hope you will use this book as a resource throughout your time at college. Remember, that above all, college is a time of growth and discovery. No matter how you may choose or not choose to be open about your sexual identity and/or gender identity expression on campus, know that, starting here, there is a fine community of people out there who will support and appreciate you just the way you are.

Robert Franek, Vice President—Publisher

The Princeton Review

Nota Bene: The National Consortium of Directors of LGBT Resources in Higher Education changed its organization name in July 2008, after this book had already gone to print. While we refer to the organization by the old name throughout this book, please note that the organization's new name is the Consortium of Higher Education LGBT Resource Professionals. Please visit them online at lgbtcampus.org.

CHAPTER 1
OUT OF THE CLOSET AND COLLEGE-BOUND

However near or far, if you are picking up this book, college is on the horizon—and as a lesbian, gay, bisexual, transgender, queer, or questioning student, picking the right school—the right place to spend the next four years of your life—requires serious thought, careful research and planning, and focused determination. Whether you're "out," "in the closet," "questioning," or totally on the "down low," being queer will most certainly affect and influence your collegiate experience, and while the transition to a college environment can certainly be exciting, it can also be extremely challenging for LGBTQ students.

But before we jump into the nitty-gritty of queer college life, we want to spend some time talking about your precollege queer experience. Why? Students are coming out earlier and earlier across the United States. According to a national survey of 1,752 college students conducted by the authors of *Sex on Campus: The Naked Truth About the Real Sex Lives of College Students*, Forty-eight percent of self-identified gay and bisexual college students became aware of their sexual identity in high school, while 26 percent found their true sexuality in college.[1]

Let's face it: This isn't your parents' coming out party. Times are a-changin', and many of you—whether lesbian, gay, bisexual, transgender, or questioning—felt empowered enough to come out to your friends and family while you were still in high school.

> "My high school GSA helped me learn how to network with LGBTQ people, as well as be a safe person to come to when in need."
>
> Doug, Sophomore,
> University of New England

This chapter will go over your high school queer experience, discuss the support networks in place for queer high school students and their parents, and give you a brief primer in queer labels and how best (and how not) to use them. Consider this chapter a college prerequisite course you have to take in order to truly understand and benefit from the fun stuff afterwards. And the "fun stuff" you have to look forward to is college life as a happy, vibrant, and involved queer student. But let's not get too ahead of ourselves. First, let's turn our attention to your high school queer experience.

1   Leland Elliot and Cynthia Brantley. *Sex On Campus: The Naked Truth About the Real Sex Lives of College Students*. New York: The Princeton Review, 1997.

AM I THE ONLY ONE?

Despite the major strides this generation of students has seen in society's perceptions and treatment of LGBTQ people, at some point, all queer or questioning teens have felt like they were alone in the world. You may have felt that no one understood what you were going through or the challenges you faced. But the truth is, you are not alone; many others have faced, and continue to share, similar experiences. Whether you're completely out or still sorting things out, it's comforting to know that there is support out there—and lots of it. Even high school students who live in a rural area, don't have a local LGBTQ Community Center in their city, or aren't out to their parents, can still find lots of support. Today's high school students are able to tap into a large network of LGBTQ youths on the internet who are dealing with similar issues, get advice from people who have already gone through what they are currently facing, and even get information about colleges and universities that will be supportive of their needs. Of course, as with any online community, it is important to protect yourself by going onto safe and established youth forums. One popular online network for youths is Youth Guardian Services (www.youth-guard.org), which operates *for youth only* e-mail lists that serve as discussion and support forums for youth. Their lists include support groups for LGBTQ youth who are 17 years old or younger, between the ages of 17 and 21, between the ages of 21 and 25, as well as lists for friends and family members of LGBTQ students.

Many high school students have taken advantage of the support network offered by their school's Gay-Straight Alliance (GSA). GSA is a student-run club that provides LGBTQ students with a safe place to meet, support other students, talk about issues related to sexual identity, and work to end homophobia in their school. Josh, a junior at Georgia State University and former GSA President of his high school explains that "While the activities of GSAs vary, the mission and goals are primarily the same—to foster academic and social growth to LGBTQ students, and to promote tolerance and understanding of LGBTQ students to non-LGBTQ students."

In addition to support and providing social outlets for LGBTQ students and their straight allies (such as gay proms and GSA-sponsored dances), GSAs can provide students with ample opportunities for working on educating themselves and the broader school community about sexual identity and gender identity issues. Participating in a GSA also creates resources for lobbying to get LGBTQ issues represented in your school's curriculum. GSA activists from high schools across the country have successfully gotten LGBTQ-related books placed in their school's library, and have organized "Teach the Teachers" staff development days that focus on teaching school staff how to be better allies for queer students. Whatever their individual initiatives might be, participating in a GSA provides students with an important opportunity to hone their public speaking and event planning skills, and can help boost their self-assurance as they transition onto the college LGBTQ scene. Visit the Gay Straight Alliance Network (www.gsanetwork.org) to learn how you can create a GSA in your high school.

QUEER & CANDID

COLLEGE STUDENTS REFLECT ON THEIR EXPERIENCES WITH HIGH SCHOOL GAY STRAIGHT ALLIANCES

"I was involved with the GSA all 4 years of high school and was president my senior year. The hard work raised my confidence level and allowed me to gain information about LGBTQ issues of today."

Lizette, First-year, University of Illinois at Chicago

"I was in my high school's GSA. It didn't necessarily provide me with any particular skills, but it did allow me to discover my community and realize that I wanted to be a part of a queer community wherever I decided to go to college."

Marcus, Senior, Brandeis University

"I went to a private high school in Connecticut that was rife with heterosexism, and even more transphobia. The GSA in my school was started with good intentions by one of the only openly gay students and the only openly gay teacher at the school. I attended the first few meetings, where a lot of icebreaking work was done, but the group, unfortunately, almost immediately was transformed into a token organization that did little more than chalk things like 'Michelangelo was gay,' or '1 in 10 people are queer,' on the school walkways now and then. The next year the GSA itself had members who used heterosexist language to joke and insult, except for in GSA meetings. It was at that time that I stopped attending the GSA meetings. From that experience I learned when to speak up, and how to speak out against a crowd of people, even when you are a lone voice. Since I graduated, I have visited my high school on two occasions and educated students about transgender and genderqueer issues and awareness."

"Robbie," Sophomore, University of Vermont

THE "COMING OUT" CONTIMUUM

At their best, GSAs offer high school students a safe space in which to discuss issues of sexuality and gender identity, and mount campaigns to educate their peers and improve tolerance in their school communities. For high school students who are considering coming out, GSAs can offer an important support system in which to explore the benefits and challenges of the decision to be open about one's sexuality. The fact is, coming out is a unique experience that each and every individual engages with differently. For some, the decision comes earlier and more easily than others. But it's important to remember that whether you're 16 or 60, the decision to be open about your sexuality and/or gender identity/expression to your parents and friends is one that is not taken lightly. Fear of alienation, compromised safety, and isolation are all reasons why some students may not come out as proudly or loudly as others. The process of sexual coming-of-age is a relatively simple (albeit angst-laden) experience for non-queer students, but for LGBTQ students it is much more complex. For queer students, news of a first crush or a first kiss is often compounded by fears of being judged, ostracized, and made to feel deviant, simply for being oneself. Coming out is not a static process; some students will come out to their closest high school buddy long before they ever consider the possibility of coming out to family members or other friends. Others may have families who are liberal and likely to take the news well, or have even anticipated it. Still others will receive no support from their families and may face repercussions such as being financially cut off. There is no prescribed experience, and this fear of the unknown is what keeps many students in the closet.

Trans students considering coming out to better express their gender identity may face additional obstacles. Students who are "coming out trans" should know that they will be affected by federal, state, institutional, and local policies that specifically exclude the medical, emotional, and support needs required to express their gender. Lesbian, gay, and bisexual people may choose to be "out and proud" while others are less "in your face," and a trans person can experience and/or choose the same variance in visibility. Some trans folks want to be visible and take on the advocacy and educational role of being the one trans person a particular school, group, or workplace knows while others strive to "pass" as their expressed gender or live "stealthily" under the radar of other people's perceptions of them as gender variant. Again, there is no right way to "come out trans," and students must carefully consider all their options.

Many students wait until they arrive at college to be fully open about their sexuality/gender identity, and even then some will continue to be closeted at home. Tom Bourdon, the Assistant Director of UCLA's Lesbian, Gay, Bisexual, and Transgender Campus Resource Center notes that "coming out can be a life-long process. After the huge step of coming out to oneself (which often involves reconciling with internalized homophobia and heterosexist beliefs), there is still that never-ending task of coming out to friends, roommates, family members, classmates, teammates, coworkers, and even that person who has a crush on you that could never result in anything . . . ever . . . *seriously*." Bourdon also contends that "by speaking with people or even reading literature that deals with coming out, not only will you get invaluable advice, but you will also feel a lot less alone in the process. Eventually, you will become more comfortable in your own skin, and have more support as you go through some of the scary, exciting, and even fun steps of coming out. Don't forget, if you come up against problems when coming out (or with other orientation/identity issues in general), LGBTQ Centers are there to help and support you."

Certainly, many colleges offer a safe and empowering space for students to explore their sexuality and gender identity. But for high school students, who haven't yet had a chance to reinvent themselves on a liberating college campus, the process of coming out can be fraught with extreme anxiety about not fitting in, being an embarrassment to their loved ones, or being ostracized by the local community. These anxieties are compounded by all the stresses every adolescent faces, from the highs and lows of a first crush to the pressures of acing the SATs and getting into a great college. Fortunately, most students who come out find that most, if not all of, these worries were unnecessary, and are immediately embraced by a supportive network of family and friends. Even those who aren't so lucky have access to some amazing resources to help them go though the coming out process. Students should realize that family support for the coming-out process varies greatly and prepare themselves financially, socially, emotionally, and spiritually for the worst-case scenario. Trans students should also note that their families and university health services will not always be equipped to support them through the transition process, and should prepare themselves for that contingency. Whether you're contemplating coming out as a high school or college student, or on a case-by-case basis, The Human Rights Campaign (HRC) provides a wealth of information about this process. HRC believes that coming out is "a journey that we make every single day of our lives" and that "there are three broad stages that people move through on the coming out continuum." These three stages include:

- **Opening Up to Yourself:** The period when your journey is beginning—when you're asking yourself questions, moving toward coming out to yourself and perhaps the decision to tell others.

- **Coming Out:** The period when you're actively talking for the first time about your sexual orientation or gender identity with family, friends, coworkers, classmates, and other people in your life.

- **Living Openly:** The ongoing phase after you've initially talked with the people closest to you about your life as an LGBTQ person, and are now able to tell new people that come into your life fluidly—where and when it feels appropriate to you.

According to HRC, "For each person it is a little different, and you may find that at times you move backward and forward through the phases all at once." Visit HRC's website (www.hrc.org) to get more information about their Coming Out Project.

Coming Out: The Parent Factor

For many students, whether in high school or college, the hardest part about peeking out of the closet is building up enough courage to tell their parents about their sexual and gender identity. According to a 2001 Horizons Foundation National Survey of 1,000 American parents[2]:

2   Sexuality Information and Education Council of the United States (SEICUS). "Lesbian, Gay, Bisexual and Transgender Youth Issues." SIECUS Report, Volume 29, Number 4, April/May 2001. www.siecus.org/pubs/fact/fact0013.html.

- Seventy-six percent of parents nationwide would be comfortable talking to their child about issues related to people.
- Sixty-seven percent of parents nationwide favor teaching children that gay people are just like other people.
- Fifty-five percent of parents nationwide favor allowing openly gay teachers to teach in middle schools and high schools.
- Sixty-two percent of parents nationwide would be comfortable talking to their child's teacher about issues related to gay people.
- Sixty-one percent of parents nationwide said that queer sexual identity is "something I would discuss with my children if they asked me questions, but not something I would raise with them on my own."
- Fifty-six percent of parents nationwide favor allowing groups or clubs on school campuses to promote tolerance and prevent discrimination against gay and lesbian students.

These statistics would seem to suggest that most American parents are prepared to be supportive of their openly gay child. But the truth is that many parents find it difficult, especially initially, to be fully okay with their child's announcement that he or she is gay. Some parents may be at odds with the child's sexual orientation or gender identity expression due to religious affiliation or beliefs. Other parents may have preconceived notions about what being gay means and struggle with stereotypes that they have about queer people. Some parents may be fine with the idea of their child being gay, but may fear for their safety and health. And some may even blame themselves for how their child "turned out." Just as each LGBTQ person's coming out experience is unique, so is each parent's reaction to learning about or acknowledging his or her child's sexual and gender identity. Fortunately, parents of LGBTQ students have access to a great support network, to help them deal with the unique privileges and challenges associated with having an LGBTQ child. PFLAG (Parents, Families and Friends of Lesbians and Gays) is a national nonprofit organization with over 200,000 members and hundreds of satellite chapters around the country. PFLAG offers these suggested dos and don'ts for family and friends of queer youth:

DO:

- Do listen to what your loved one's life is like, and what kind of experiences he or she has had in the world.

- Do take the time to seek information about the lives of LGBTQ people from other parents of LGBTQ people, friends of your loved one, literature, and, most of all, directly from your loved one.
- Do get professional help for anyone in the family, including yourself, who becomes severely depressed over your loved one's sexuality or gender identity.
- Do accept that you are responsible for your negative reactions.
- Do help your loved one set individual goals, even though these may differ drastically from your own.
- Do try to develop trust and openness by allowing your loved one to be who she or he is without pressure.
- Do be proud of your loved one's capacity for having loving relationships.
- Do look for the injured feelings underneath the anger and respond to them.
- Do defend him or her against discrimination.
- Do respect your loved one's right to find out how to choose the right person to love and how to make relationships last.
- Do say, "I love you."

DON'T:

- Don't blame your feelings on your loved one.
- Don't rush the process of trying to understand your loved one's sexuality or gender identity.
- Don't assume that your loved one should see a professional counselor or encourage "reparative therapy."
- Don't criticize your loved one for being different.
- Don't expect your loved one to make up for your own failures in life.
- Don't try to force your loved one to conform to your ideas of proper sexual behavior.
- Don't blame yourself because your loved one is lesbian, gay, bisexual, or transgender.

- Don't demand that your child (or loved one) live up to what your idea of what a man or woman should be.
- Don't discriminate against your loved one.
- Don't try to break up loving relationships.
- Don't insist that your morality is the only "right" one.[3]

QUEER-TIP: PFLAG—A SUPPORT NETWORK

PARENTS

The idea for PFLAG began in 1972 when Jeanne Manford marched with her gay son in New York's Pride Day parade. After many gay and lesbian people ran up to Jeanne during the parade and begged her to talk to their parents, she decided to begin a support group. Over the next several years, through word of mouth and in response to community need, similar groups sprang up around the country, offering "safe havens" and mutual support for parents with gay and lesbian children. In 1981, the national organization was officially launched, and PFLAG has continued to be a source of valuable information for parents, friends, and allies of LGBTQ students. PFLAG's website (www.pflag.org) offers a wealth of resources, including answers to questions that often come up when students come out to a family member or friend (or if a family member or friend comes out to you).[4]

Queer students' decisions on how and when to come out have been known to challenge parent-child relationships. On the other hand, many parents may eventually become staunch supporters and defenders of their child's choice—or at least come to terms with it on some level. In fact, many parents are not just supportive of their child's decision, they are downright proud of it. This is extremely heartening for students who

3   Parents, Family, and Friends of Lesbians and Gays (PFLAG). "Do's and Don'ts for Families and Friends." www.pflag.org/Dos_and_Don_ts_for_Family_and_Friends.do_dont.0.html.
3   Parents, Family, and Friends of Lesbians and Gays (PFLAG). "History." www.pflag.org/History.history.0.html.

are worried that coming out to their parents will jeopardize their relationship and cause them to be cut off, cast out, or rejected. We asked a number of PFLAG parents what made them most proud of their LGBTQ children. "Deanne," a mom in Iowa, says she is "Proud that even when I was timid about telling people [my daughter] was not." In fact, more than one parent said they were proud of their child's bravery in choosing to be open about their sexual identity/gender identity: "What makes me most proud is my child's courage in telling me. It is a huge thing to tell your parents that you are gay," explains "Etta," mother of a gay son in Indiana. "Holly," mother of a transgender son in New Hampshire says, "I am most proud of the strength and patience she has. To suddenly start presenting as female is something I cannot even imagine. But she is the same person and we have always respected her."

Other parents admire their children for their passion and involvement in LGBTQ activism. "Alina," a Massachusetts mother of a lesbian daughter, says that she is "proud that [my daughter] held a press conference at the state capitol when she was 16 and she continues to evoke change." "Ingrid," a Virginian mother of a transgender son says: "Our son is perfect in every way! He is kind, patient with everyone he meets, and also happened to be his high school valedictorian, but we are most proud of him for the way he gives back to his community and his world through his many volunteer efforts. He also started his high school's first Gay/Straight Alliance as the first openly gay student."

Other parents are more conflicted about their child's choice to be open.

"I am embarrassed about her being a lesbian, but I am very proud of her and her accomplishments," says "Patrice," a mother in Texas. "Alona," a mother in New York, says of her openly gay son: "I always take pride in what he does, no matter how we may disagree on some matters."

The bottom line is that no family is going to have the same experience when it comes to dealing with a loved one's decision to come out. Initial reactions—whether positive or negative—almost always end in closer, more honest, and staunchly supportive family relationships. For most families, the "coming out" part of the process is the hardest. Organizations

> "Our son knew he was gay at 11 and came out to us at 13. Our son, our only child, is our whole world and his being gay did not matter to us at all."
>
> "Tracey," Rhode Island

like PFLAG are there to help parents through what becomes a lifelong process of learning. They can give advice on how to acknowledge that loved one to other friends and family members while still being respectful of their loved one's privacy, and dealing with homophobia from both expected and unexpected sources. To find a PFLAG chapter near you, visit: PFLAG.org.

PFLAG Parent Tip: Acknowledging Your Openly LGBTQ Child

It's always a process for parents to figure out how best to introduce their LGBTQ child—and their potential friends and partners—to friends and family. Some people may find this an agonizing exercise, while to others, the process isn't a big deal. It all depends on your comfort level, your family's religious beliefs (or those of your extended family), the general political tone of the state or province where you live, and the size of your town or city.

You will first need to ask yourself honestly whether you find the fact that you have a LGBTQ child shameful, and whether you assume others will too. If you do find it shameful, you will have a hard time convincing other people that this is not a problematic issue. As one mother of a lesbian daughter said, "I'm not comfortable addressing her sexuality because my family would not understand it." This can be complicated further if your child is transgender or transitioning. One parent says, "We sent off a lesbian to school, and a trans kid came home."

Yet family members and friends may indeed be more supportive than originally imagined. A parent of a gay son wrote that, "For the first couple of years after he came out at 13, we said nothing to immediate family. This was possible because all our family lived thousands of miles away. I waited until my elderly parents came to visit before I told them in person, with our son in attendance. I had library books and PFLAG literature at the ready. But the conversation was one of immediate love and total acceptance."

Most families fall somewhere in the middle, as this mom of a lesbian daughter points out, "I suppose we usually use the word 'gay' when the subject of sexual orientation comes up. Her grandfather, upon hearing, used to say 'her situation'. We taught him to say 'her sexual orientation' instead."

Another mom found that discussing this subject pointedly with her daughter was the best way to find a solution comfortable for everyone. She says, "My daughter and I worked out together how I would discuss her relationship with friends and family. I tell people that my daughter is 'in a relationship with another woman' instead of saying she is a lesbian. The identity label is my daughter's to apply as she wishes; the relationship facts are mine to report as a parent. This allows for whatever changes may occur and avoids the whole labeling practice."

Family friends can be a whole other matter. Although it can be assumed these days that most people in the United States and Canada have by now met at least a few openly gay men or lesbians (and no doubt a few transgender folks too, but perhaps not as knowingly), stereotypes and prejudices remain. One mother writes of her family's experience: "With some friends we would wait until the gay issue came up in a conversation. Generally it was in a negative context and we didn't know how to respond. We usually tried to softly suggest that we might have a different viewpoint on the matter, but unfortunately this would usually progress to a very uncomfortable place. We would then end up stating our son was gay, which would cause our friends to be embarrassed and create an awkward situation for everyone. After this scenario played out a few times, we specifically told our closest friends during a special conversation and that went very well. Now when the conversation heads in 'that' direction with people we don't know so well, I just tell them right away. Generally forthright honesty is the best approach."

Parents of transgender students need special support in dealing with a child's coming out and ensuing physical transformation. One mother said, "I think it's very important for parents of trans kids to have a specific support system. We have to really understand that there's nothing wrong with our kids—they're just different. I belong to an online support group and get good suggestions from them about dealing with extended families, neighbors, etc. And for those really distraught parents, it's an absolute requirement to hear from other people in the same situation that everything will be okay. There are also referrals to doctors, therapists, surgeons, and just plain old fashioned camaraderie."

THE PROBLEM WITH LABELS: FIGURING OUT YOUR QUEER IDENTITY

Identity is a loaded concept that involves far more than your style of dress or who you choose to hang out with. Your identity has many different dimensions—you can have a sexual identity, a gender identity, an ethnic identity, a religious identity, even a context-specific identity. Sometimes, the different dimensions of your identity may be in conflict with one another, such as when LGBTQ students have a difficult time reconciling their spiritual beliefs with their sexual identity/gender identity (see Chapter 8 for more information on how to deal with this). At no time is your identity fixed. As a high school student especially, your identity is constantly transforming, and the labels used to discuss your sexual identity/gender identity—just a small component of who you are—are often hot topics of discussion and debate. Remember that childhood rhyme: *Sticks and stones may break your bones but words will never hurt you?* Yeah right. While words may not have the same impact as a physical blow, we all know that they can be used in hurtful and harmful ways. As a queer student you have a right to be addressed with respect and sensitivity and to not be restricted by labels that only inadequately describe who you are. In order to discuss the multifaceted aspects of queer identity, it is necessary to expand the traditional terminology. In addition to the more well-known labels of "gay" and "lesbian," there are now dozens of terms that have begun to be utilized in order to more fully represent the myriad identities and expressions that make up the queer community. For example, "queer," once a term of scorn for all gay people, has been reclaimed by many as a term of empowerment.

As you start thinking about colleges, remember that your identity is multiple and shifting—you are under no obligation to remain the same person tomorrow that you are today. College can be a liberating time of exploration, in which you can invent and re-invent your queer identity. The National Consortium of Directors of LGBT Resources in Higher Education is an organization that, among other things, works to make sure your rights as a queer college student are respected. This includes your right to be addressed with respect by administrators, faculty, and students on campus.

QUEER-TIP: NATIONAL CONSORTIUM OF DIRECTORS OF LGBT RESOURCES IN HIGHER EDUCATION

The National Consortium of Directors of Lesbian, Gay, Bisexual, and Transgender Resources in Higher Education is an organization for professionals who provide support and services to lesbian, gay, bisexual, transgender, and queer/questioning (LGBTQ) students, staff, and faculty who seek to educate campus communities about sexual orientation and gender identity issues.

Since its inception in 1995, the Consortium has provided a forum for LGBTQ professionals in higher education to address the challenges facing LGBTQ people at colleges and universities. The Consortium offers useful information to those who work with LGBTQ students, faculty, and staff and provides a vehicle for institutionalizing LGBTQ issues and concerns in the academe. Currently, the Consortium has over 250 members from more than 100 colleges and universities in the United States and Canada.

Visit LGBTcampus.org for more information.

Consortium Tips on Labels and Identifying LGBTQ Students

by Terri Phoenix, Assistant Director of the LGBT Center, The University of North Carolina at Chapel Hill

Gay. Lesbian. Bisexual. Pansexual. Queer. Transgender. Transexual. Genderqueer. MTF (male to female). FTM (female to male). FTDG (female to different gender). MTDG (male to different gender). Asexual. Intersex. Butch lesbian. Boi. Each and all of the preceding terms are in use today by people to describe themselves in terms of their sexual orientation, gender identity, and/or gender expression. Youth are "coming out" earlier (average age now is 13–17 years as compared with 18–23 years in the 1990s) and they are finding communities online and in person to talk about their experiences, bodies, gender identities, gender expressions, and sexuality. While it is still true that part of the coming out process involves recognizing what one is not (e.g., heterosexual or cisgender) and discovering what one is (e.g., gay, transgender, or lesbian); the terms and labels in use today are more numerous and more multifaceted than even five years ago. In many respects these differing labels are somewhat related yet there are tensions within and among the various communities represented by them. Sometimes the same term can have several different meanings depending upon who is defining the term and how it is being used. "Queer" is a good example of this. Some people still use queer as an insult or a derogatory term. Others use it as a broad term to describe people who are lesbian, gay, or bisexual. Still others use it to denote that they are a person who challenges the cultural norms around sex and gender without necessarily saying anything about their own sexual orientation, gender identity, or gender expression. Then there are those who reject the idea that they can be summarized using *any* label, and many use the term queer to connote this rejecting of labels.

People use labels to create communities of "people who are like me." Even though labels are problematic and incomplete pictures of the people they attempt to describe, they are still useful in finding, creating, and sustaining communities. The labels in use today will be different 2, 5, 10, and 20 years from now.

The important thing for folks who might be seeking a community of "people like me" is to find out what people mean by the labels they are using. Talk to people, ask questions, and avail yourself of the wealth of information available on the Internet or in other media. Assess whether that particular use of the label matches with your experience. If so, you may be at the beginning of finding a community in which you feel comfortable and supported. Similarly, if you are a parent, friend, or family member of someone who is using some of the above labels to describe their lived experience or their identity, you too may have some research to do. Be respectful and ask the person what they mean by that term or ask for resources to help you understand their experience better. There is a wealth of information available from a variety of organizations whose mission is to educate people about sexual orientation, gender identity, and gender expression. Educate yourself not for the purpose of being able to put a label on someone else, but in order to understand better those who are using labels to describe their lives.

PFLAG PARENT TIP: IDENTITY 101

For many parents, the terminology that their LGBTQ children use to describe themselves and their identity may be a bit perplexing. Gone are the days of using the word "homosexual" to describe anyone with an attraction to someone of the same sex. Even the words "gay" and "lesbian," historical benchmarks in the LGBTQ equation, are not inclusive enough to cover everyone. To more fully understand your child's world, it is important to speak some of the same language. As a parent, knowing the key terms that you are likely to hear from your child will go quite a long way towards bridging any gaps in understanding. Your child will also appreciate your efforts to understand his or her world.

So here's an identity primer, written just for the parents of LGBTQ students:

- **Ally:** A person, though usually not gay themselves, who is a supporter of LGBTQ people and their rights. Parents of LGBTQ children often become staunch allies of their children.

- **Bisexual:** A man or woman with a strong sexual and often emotional attraction to both men and women. Traditionally, bisexuals have had a hard time finding a place within the gay and lesbian movement, as they were seen as "sitting on the fence" about their sexuality. It was thought that bisexuals just needed to decide if they were gay or straight, and they have been accused of having "heterosexual" privilege. While it is true that bisexuality can sometimes be a transitional safety zone during the coming out process, it's now believed that bisexuality is indeed a valid, authentic sexual and emotional category of identity. If your child comes out to you as bisexual, accept their identity as the full one that it is. Because many younger people consider sexuality fluid, keep an open mind if possible about all these definitions and wait for your child to take the lead in how they wish to be defined.

- **Coming out:** This term can either mean a process of self-identification and acceptance as a LGBTQ person, or may be used to define the act of revealing this identity to others.

So someone can come out over a period of years, or come out in a single act of disclosure. In other words, when your child came out to you, he or she had most likely been going through the process of coming out for some time.

- **Dyke:** Historically a derogative term for lesbians, it has been reclaimed as a term of familiarity and empowerment by lesbians. Primarily used by younger women as a term of self-identification. Parents and allies may find this term harder to hear and use.

- **Fag, or Faggot:** Historically a derogative term for gay men, it has been reclaimed by some as a term of familiarity or empowerment. Parents may be surprised to hear their son describe himself or friends using this term, but it is mainly used as slang and is not common in ally usage.

- **Gay:** A term primarily used to describe men attracted to other men, emotionally and/or physically. Can also be an umbrella term for gay men and lesbians.

- **Genderqueer:** LGBTQ folk who challenge society's more rigid definitions of what it means to be male, or even more often, female, often mixing various attributes of all genders and sexualities. Examples are femme queen, butch boi, and the usage of non-traditional language for gender, including terms like "hir" or "ze."

- **LGBTQ:** An abbreviation that stands for Lesbian, Gay, Bisexual, Transgender, and Queer and/or Questioning. Describes the overarching community and includes everyone. Sometimes A is also added at the end—for Ally. As a parent, you would then fit into this end of the equation. LGBTQ is the term most often used now by gay or gay-friendly organizations to describe themselves, unless their target group is just one component of the entire community.

- **Lesbian:** A woman who is physically and/or emotionally attracted to other women. Many younger women do not use this term, preferring dyke or queer, but the common ally term is still lesbian.

- **Questioning:** A man or woman unsure of their sexuality or same gender attractions. These feelings may lead to a self-identification of being LGBTQ, or they may not. Parents of students who are questioning may be dealing with many of the same feelings and issues that parents of students who have definitively come out are dealing with. Thus, parents of questioning young people may also find groups like PFLAG helpful both for support and as a place to find relevant resources.

- **Queer:** Represents "Q" in the LGBTQ acronym, and can be used to refer to lesbian, gay, bisexual, and transgender people, but also to people who are questioning, allies, intersex and other gender non-conforming people (like drag queens and drag kings) and anyone else who wants to be included. A term of choice for younger LGBTQ activists, reclaimed by early 1990s direct action political groups like Queer Nation. Sometimes used as "genderqueer" to describe those who don't want to identify with a rigid definition of identity. Many parents may find it difficult to use and/or hear their children use this term because of its history as a derogatory slur.

- **Transgender:** Transgender is an umbrella term for all people whose identity crosses gender lines from the body they were born into. Among transgender people, sexual orientation can range from heterosexual, gay, lesbian, or bisexual. It should be regarded as a term that describes gender identity and expression, and not primarily one of sexual orientation. Thus, a girl who grows up feeling male, and transitions towards becoming a man as an adult (F to M), can be physically attracted to men, women, or transgender people, and still be considered transgender. Common terms are also transsexual (a person who, for example, feels like and dresses like the opposite sex), F to M (female to male), and M to F (male to female). For many parents of transgender students, learning about these issues is a crash course in matters they have never before heard of or considered. Luckily, the Internet has become the research tool of choice and connection for parents of transgender students.

Consorteum Tips on Understanding the Experiences of Transgender and Genderqueer Students

by Brett-Genny Janiczek Beemyn, Director of the Stonewall Center at University of Massachusetts— Amherst

More and more college students are coming out as gender non-conforming or transgender (a general term for people whose gender identity and/or expression differs from the gender assigned to them at birth). Many identify as genderqueer, seeing themselves as neither female nor male, as both, or as somewhere in between. Although genderqueers describe and express their identities in a wide variety of ways and may or may not consider themselves to be transgender, they commonly understand themselves in ways that challenge binary constructions of gender and traditional images of transgender individuals.

In the past, it was expected that individuals who felt themselves to be a gender different from the one assigned to them at birth would seek to express that different gender by changing their bodies completely and by presenting unambiguously as that gender. But transgender and other gender diverse students today often call into question this binary way of thinking about gender. Some do seek to transition entirely to a gender different from their birth gender through hormones and gender reassignment surgeries, but many more only take hormones, or present as a different gender without hormones. Some alter their bodies in other ways, such as by having electrolysis or by body-building. Others do not change their bodies at all, but dress and present in ways that destabilize gender categories, such as by wearing a combination of "men's" and "women's" clothing or by completely cross-dressing. There are countless methods by which people express a transgender or genderqueer identity.

Transgender and other gender diverse students today are able to turn to a rapidly growing number of resources to understand and accept themselves and to educate their friends and family. They can find information and communicate with other young transgender people on the Internet, see themselves reflected in an ever-expanding body of transgender books and films, attend transgender and trans-inclusive events and conferences, and join national and, in many places, local transgender and trans-supportive organizations. As a result, young people coming out today as trans, unlike many transgender people in previous generations, are often able to find immediate support and do not feel that they are "the only one."

To Sum Up . . .

In case you haven't gotten the point by now, being LGBTQ and going to college is not a journey into the wilderness. If you want further proof that there is a thriving network of students out there just like you, check out some of the photos interspersed throughout this book. LGBTQ teenagers aren't a new phenomenon, and that every present-day gay, lesbian, bisexual, transgender, and queer and/or questioning adult was once an adolescent (and survived the experience). Moreover, LGBTQ youth aren't just statistics, but individuals. Whether the numbers you think of are "10 percent of the population is gay," or "28 percent of LGBTQ teens drop out of school," behind those numbers are faces and yours is one of them. So get ready to slap on that tie, tiara, or lip ring— your senior yearbook photo is just the beginning of a whole new and exciting world.

CHAPTER 2
THE PERFECT FIT: FINDING THE RIGHT SCHOOL

Choosing the right college isn't a science; don't take anyone's advice—including ours—without considering all your options and resources. In fact, you might have a few schools in mind already. Your father wants you to go to Ohio State; your mother went to Hamilton College; someone once told you nice things about Tulane; and your counselor thinks you should look at NYU. On the other hand, you may feel less sure of potential college choices, and maybe even completely clueless, lost, and alone in this whole college search game.

Before you jump the gun and get into the trenches of finding a school and all the things you should look out for, it's important to know that each campus is different and each student will face a unique set of experiences. Some schools, particularly ones that are located in more conservative areas of the country, might not be as welcoming or as supportive as you might need them to be, and some might be down right hostile. But, that doesn't mean *all* of them are that way. Instead of jumping to conclusions or stereotyping, do your homework and *investigate*. Finding the right school for you will take time and some legwork on your part but will be well worth it in the long run. This chapter will give you some things to consider and help guide you in your search.

HOME OR AWAY?

Some of you might be looking to stay close to home because of family obligations or financial pressures. Others of you might be looking to explore a new part of the country or might desire to get as far away from your families as possible to find the needed space to come out and explore your sexuality or gender expression on your own. As one senior at Smith comments, "It's a lot easier for me to be out at school than at home. In fact, I'm not out at home." The fact is, not all of us have the most open and understanding family members. By choosing to either live at home or even staying close by, you might have to deal with oppressive, restrictive, or overbearing family members and/or suffer from a lack of privacy, making it difficult to develop and explore your sexual orientation and gender identity expression. Living at home or close to it might mean that your parents will feel as though they have a right to control your comings and goings, as well as your academic affairs and involvement in social activities. If your home-town environment does not support you, the already-difficult process of coming into your own will be that much more complex.

But maybe your hometown or city is already host to your dream academic institution. Or maybe the thought of the money you'll save on tuition and living expenses is more than enough to keep you close to home for another 4 years. Either way, if you're lucky enough to have a network in place that provides a supportive environment, then staying close to home might just be the way to go.

On the other hand, the pros of going away to college are multifold. First off, you'll begin to develop your independence by being away from your parents, siblings and high school friends. This physical distance can also act as an emotional buffer to explore your sexual orientation and/or gender identity expression. Going away also gives you ample opportunities to meet a diverse range of people from a wide cross-section of the country.

Going away to college can present some difficulties as well. There are no guarantees that you will adjust smoothly to a different setting, and there's a chance that you might not have an immediate support system in place that meets your specific needs—especially as a queer or questioning student. Furthermore, money is always a factor when you consider living away from home. And although there are always options for subsidizing your education, the expense involved can be prohibitive, depending on your particular set of circumstances and the institution to which you're applying. But even if you think you can't afford going away—don't rule it out. There are plenty of work-study programs, financial aid, and scholarships out there to help you figure out how to make it work (see Chapter 3 for information on scholarships reserved especially for queer students).

Either way, the final word is yours. You have a unique set of issues surrounding your college choice, and the decision to attend a local university or jet off to another state or city is just one of many factors that will help you narrow down your options to find the "best fit" institution for you.

SIZE MATTERS

Let's face it, sometime size *does* matter. But bigger isn't always better—at least when it comes to choosing a college. There are benefits and disadvantages to going to either large or small schools. Large schools often offer top-notch research facilities, well-stocked libraries, cutting-edge labs, and may employ noted scholars working in a variety of fields of research and scholarship. Large schools also have large student populations—this means that there are tens of thousands of students to meet through a variety of activities, classes, and living arrangements. Odds are heavily in your favor that you'll find more LGBTQ students at a large university than you will at a small one. Plus, larger universities usually provide a wider variety of housing or dorm options that might be of interest to queer and transgender students.

Although it's true that larger institutions might offer you Starbucks coffee 24 hours a day, the chance to live in a spacious suite with your three best friends, and take part in loads of activities, it will also have some drawbacks that you should carefully consider. Larger institutions, along with all the libraries and dining halls, typically have lots of graduate students. This often means that the faculty will be heavily involved in graduate thesis projects and dissertation advising, in addition to their own research, academic writing, and departmental obligations. All this can add up to your professors having less time to give their undergrad students. Additionally, large universities often have large classes. Class sizes for required core or lecture courses can be upwards of 200 students, and graduate students and teaching assistants often teach introductory courses. Many students enjoy this environment; however, if you're the kind of student who needs to be in a small class or you'd be afraid to raise your hand and say, "I don't understand this week's assignment" or even, "I have a question about so-and-so," you need to think carefully about attending a large institution.

In contrast to large universities, small colleges often boast smaller class sizes and are more likely to be taught by faculty and tenured staff, giving you a greater chance to get to know your professors. Smaller colleges also often provide you with the opportunity to design your own course of study, or complete a creative project for your senior thesis. These are usually teaching institutions with few or no graduate students. These colleges are dedicated to providing undergraduates with a strong sense of community and a first-rate academic experience and often have strong advising systems that can offer tremendous assistance to students. This kind of school can often protect you from being one of those students who "slips through the cracks."

However, attending a small college can also present certain disadvantages. Diversity among students at smaller colleges might be less prevalent, and a smaller student body means fewer people. Translation: The queer social network is probably going to be small (or at least smaller). Think about that for a second. It may mean fewer events, activities, and resources designed or targeted for LGBTQ students as well as a smaller dating pool.

It's important to spend some time thinking about the kinds of opportunities you'd most like to have, and seek out schools that can meet your needs. A large school that has 62 majors will not necessarily allow you to coauthor research papers with professors or design your own interdisciplinary course of study or write a play or film a short movie for your senior thesis. But a small school may not have the extensive queer social network you're looking for. Decide what's most important to you, and weigh your options carefully. Remember, there are large schools out there that can provide highly personalized academic experiences, and small schools with a vibrant queer social scene. Do your research before ruling any options out.

PICKING THE RIGHT ENVIRONMENT

For some students, the issue of location is clear. You know that big cities make you feel energized and connected, or that quiet and beautiful "outdoorsy" surroundings allow you to focus more easily. Many others students experience mixed and conflicting feelings about which kind of college environment makes the most sense. Do you crave the hurried pulse of the big city? Or does the ability to commune with nature, go hiking, or engage in outdoor activities rank high on your list? Maybe you prefer a little bit of everything. Big city adventures, rural campus retreats, or suburban sprawls are all possible. It's up to you to ask yourself what environment makes you most comfortable. Following is a description of what different college environments have to offer:

- **Rural Retreats**

  Some students prefer the relaxed atmosphere that rural campuses offer. Easy access to outdoor recreational activities and the serenity that comes with the sounds of birds chirping outside your dorm window are pretty much sure bets if you decide to attend a school far away from it all. The down side of secluded schools is obvious—there's nowhere to go. When things are tough either with your roommate, your advisor, or best friend, there's nowhere to hide. If you're the kind of person who thrives on anonymity, think carefully about selecting schools that are in rural settings. It will either be a great challenge for you to stretch into new behaviors, or it will leave you feeling trapped and isolated. As an LGBTQ student, you might find yourself without a heck of a whole lot of activities/events specifically tailored to you.

- **Big Cities**

  The polar opposite of the slow and steady rural pace, city living is fast and furious. Urban universities offer a bevy of cultural and learning endeavors, both on and off campus. Cities also generally offer a greater diversity of people and activities, meaning LGBTQ resources are likely to be more readily available (and in some cities, actually abundant). An added bonus in an era of high gas prices and depleting ozone layers includes prolific public transportation. Not to mention that big cities mean big companies—which means if you're interested in internship opportunities, you will find plenty of them right outside your dorm-room door. Of course, living in the city isn't cheap, although being surrounded by a bevy of activities is often a good thing, it can also be a major distraction from your studies. Security can also be more of an issue at a city school where highly guarded, gated campuses are less prevalent. Certain cities are bigger—and more queer-friendly—than others, so don't automatically assume that just because it's a thriving metropolis, you'll be able to go out to a different club each night and paint the city pink. As one Binghamton University student aptly put it, "Generally speaking, I have found Binghamton University to be a very warm and accepting place. The city of Binghamton isn't quite the same fairy tale. 'Townies,' as we affectionately call them, are not always receptive to the gay community, but then again, they aren't too accepting of 14,000 liberal intellectuals either. The university and the city are truly two different worlds."

- **The 'Burbs**

  Suburban schools usually offer a taste of both the city and country life and are often fairly close to both, giving you the best of both worlds. Like colleges in rural areas, suburban schools tend to form their own communities within the confines of their respective campuses. However, they do offer more integration than rural areas, drawing in aspects of the city nearby. The added expense of a car is generally a key factor to consider when contemplating a college in the 'burbs. In some areas, public transportation might be limited or unreliable. So if you're looking to actively explore life in the city outside the suburban sprawl you're probably going to need a car.

- **College Towns**

  College towns are a comfortable alternative for students looking for some of the cultural and political amenities of a larger city but offered on a much smaller, more accessible scale. College towns tend to be liberal and arts oriented. Their economies tend to be stable, boosted in large part by the local college or university within its boundaries. Most college towns boast bookstores, coffee shops (many with wireless service), theaters, restaurants (including a good mixture of pizza, diners, high-end spots, and international food choices), boutiques and gift shops, night clubs, museums, and plenty of other things to do while you're not in classes. Touring musical acts, including LGBTQ performers, will stop in college towns, since they assume they can attract students and town residents alike to their performances. College towns also draw LGBTQ staff and faculty looking for a welcoming, affordable place to live and raise their families. Many college towns are also within commuting distance of larger cities, providing an escape for students on the weekends and breaks.

The best way to approach the issue of location is ultimately to find the colleges that are best suited for you, whether they're smack in the middle of New York City or tucked away on a lake in Minnesota. After you've found the schools, identified the programs that interest you, and looked into any other attributes that attract you to the school, go for a visit. The location may be surprisingly tranquil or bustling, but the main point is to be in an academic and social environment that leaves you feeling ready for the world. Find the right school for you—then worry about the location.

QUEER-TIP: WOMEN'S COLLEGE COALITION

Founded in 1972, the Women's College Coalition (WCC) is an association of women's colleges and universities—public and private, independent and church-related, 2- and 4-year—in the United States and Canada whose primary mission is the education and advancement of women. Led by Executive Director Susan Lennon, WCC makes the case for women's education to the higher education community, to policy makers, to the media and to the general public. Additionally, the Coalition collects and disseminates information relating to the education of women and gender equity in education. Other priority areas are the issues of recruitment and retention of women in math, science and engineering, and the development of women's leadership. For more information, including a comprehensive list of women's colleges, log onto WomensColleges.org.

ALL GIRLS, ALL THE TIME: THE PROS AND CONS OF WOMEN'S COLLEGES

While their numbers may not be as great as they once were, women's colleges have experienced a new popularity over the last several years. Competition is fierce at the most selective women's colleges, with many students choosing single-sex education not because it is the only option available to them, but because of the opportunities an all-women's college offers them. According to the Women's College Coalition, students at women's colleges "report greater satisfaction than their coed counterparts with their college experience in almost all measures—academically, developmentally, and personally."[1] In addition, the WCC states that women's college students "continue toward doctorates in math, science, and engineering in disproportionately large numbers."[2]

For queer students, choosing to attend this type of learning institution can be an empowering experience. You may feel a stronger sense of community and freedom to explore your identity as well as your sexual orientation. For others, attending a women's college can result in an isolating experience lacking in more integrated social activities inclusive of all genders and sexual orientations. The decision is a personal one. If you are thinking of a women's college, you probably already have a plethora of reasons why you want to apply. Do your research and find out what that school's attitude is towards queer students.

Interestingly, transgender or genderqueer students who have undergone some, if not all, the transitioning to a different gender are beginning to change the landscape of single-sex colleges. If a person is female by birth but decides to transition, even partially, does that mean that they would be violating certain admissions policies that are geared towards "women?" And how does the college administration deal with and support trans students, and students whose gender identity/expression fall outside of established norms? If you are transitioning or thinking of doing so while attending a specific women's college, make sure to protect yourself and find out everything you can about your school's policies to help make this an easier process.

MILITARY ACADEMIES: DON'T ASK, DON'T TELL. . . . DON'T APPLY?

United States Military Academies are notoriously tough to get into. Students who manage to get the congressional nomination required for the application, and are one of the lucky few to receive an acceptance letter in the mail, can look forward to receiving a top-notch education absolutely free in exchange for an officer appointment and military service requirement after graduation. Sound like a good deal? It is—for the right person.

1 Barnard College. "About the College."
   www.barnard.columbia.edu/about/why.html.
2 Ibid.

Queer students considering military academies should note that the United States currently prohibits openly lesbian, gay, and bisexual men and women from serving in any of the armed forces. And it doesn't look like it's a policy that is about to change anytime soon. Unfortunately, that means if you are planning on applying to one of the nation's military academies, you only have one option: to remain silent and discreet about your queerness and adopt their "Don't Ask, Don't Tell" policy.

Here are some organizations (operated by current and former LGBTQ service people as well as their advocates) that may be of assistance and can provide you with some valuable information if you are seriously considering the military academy option:

- **The American Veterans for Equal Rights**

  www.aver.us

  The American Veterans for Equal Rights is a grassroots, volunteer-based nonprofit organization of gay, lesbian, bisexual, transgender, and straight veterans and military personnel providing social and professional networking and support, as well as advocating for the fair treatment of—and end of discrimination against—LGBTQ members of the Armed Forces.

- **Service Academy Gay & Lesbian Alumni (SAGALA)**

  http://sagala.webexone.com

  This organization's mission is to provide a professional and social network for gay, lesbian, transgender, and bisexual Academy alumni; provide support to any service member under investigation or being discharged as a result of their sexual orientation; and encourage greater understanding and tolerance of gay people in the military and their contributions to our nation's defense.

- **Servicemembers Legal Defense Network (SLDN)**

  www.sldn.org

  Servicemembers Legal Defense Network (SLDN) "is a national, nonprofit legal services, watchdog and policy organization dedicated to ending discrimination against and harassment of military personnel affected by "Don't Ask, Don't Tell" and related policies."[3]

3   Servicemembers Legal Defense Network. "Our Mission." www.sldn.org/templates/about/record.html?section=10&record=15.

Consortium Tips on Figuring Out the Queer Climate at Your School of Interest

by Jeremy Hayes, Assistant Director, Office of Diversity Services, Suffolk University

During your college search, you will be considering many different qualities of your schools of interest, ranging from notable academic programs to the atmosphere of the surrounding area. But figuring out just how gay-friendly the schools are that you are looking to attend is just as—if not more—important as some of the other specifics you are considering, and should be looked at as an essential factor in your final decision. The questions you have may be limitless. Are there schools where LGBTQ students feel unwelcome or unsafe? Are there really academic havens for queer students? How do you know if the campus atmosphere is welcoming? And what do students, straight and queer, *really* have to say about LGBTQ issues?

Don't underestimate the value of knowing what the queer climate is at *all* of your top school picks. Some queer students are more comfortable being in a mixed environment; one in which sexual orientation and gender identity expression are as diverse as the racial, social, and religious backgrounds of the members of the campus community. However, some students need larger built-in support networks that supply an added sense of security, queer visibility, and on-campus activism. There are tons of campuses that go out of their way to address the needs of their queer students and provide the resources and support systems that they may require. Lis Maurer, the Coordinator of the Center for LGBT Education, Outreach and Services at Ithaca College, believes that "the current climate is mixed." Like many individuals working with LGBTQ college students across the country, Maurer believes that "against a backdrop of legislative and cultural uncertainty (and sometimes overt hostility), LGBTQ and Allied students are making their needs and interests known, and using their well-honed leadership skills toward positive change!"

The key to finding a school that will meet your individual needs is to be informed. While resources like *The Advocate Guide's* listing of the 100 most LGBTQ-friendly schools are helpful for giving you an idea of what the queer climate might be like on a particular campus, it's still important to do your own research. Even if you are shy, unsure, or "in the closet" about your sexual orientation, you can take advantage of the relative anonymity of the internet to get the scoop on the campus climate. Here are some tips for investigating the campus atmosphere from home:

- **Surf the School's Website.** Spend time on the websites of each school on your short list. See what information they post on LGBTQ campus resources, academic programs of queer interest, and what their nondiscrimination policies state about queer students. You may find out early on in the process that your choice of school is not as welcoming to LGBTQ students as you might need.

- **Make Peer-to-Peer Connections.** Call or e-mail LGBTQ Resource Centers and Queer Studies departments at each university or college you are considering, and ask to be connected to queer students. Currently enrolled students can give you valuable insight into the overall queer climate on their particular campus and usually love to talk about the pros and cons of their school's efforts with prospective undergraduates. Getting in with the individuals in the queer spaces on each campus will also help you make a quick transition to campus life if you decide to attend that school.

- **Cruise the Web.** Check out chatrooms, electronic mailing lists (listservs), and online groups dedicated to LGBTQ college students on sites such as AOL, Yahoo, and Google. Message boards and internet-based information portals are effective and interactive ways to get a wide ranging sample of insights about the schools you are looking into, as well as the atmosphere of the communities in which they are located.

- **Tap into Online Networks.** Use your blog, Facebook, or Myspace networks and other online social circles to ask queers out there in the cyber-universe about their experiences during college. You may find that some of the people in your network have a lot to say (both good and bad) about the schools they attended. They might also lead you to learn more about schools to which you might not have previously considered applying. Chances are if they read your blog or are in your network, they might be people whose opinions you should take into consideration about colleges to put on a short list.

PFLAG Parent Tip: Helping Your Child Pick the Right College

What can parents do to help their students pick the right college? Most experts recommend that parents play a backseat role. Remember that this is your child's college experience, not your own, and that the final decision is theirs to make. Additionally, parents stressed the importance of finding a college atmosphere that was openly accepting of LGBTQ students.

"The only 'right' college is the one where your child feels comfortable and can follow a course of study that's interesting and meaningful to them."

"David," Washington, DC

"Be clear about your child's sexual preferences or sexual identity issues in advance of the college search if possible, so you can clearly take that into account in the college selection process."

"Annabelle," Ohio

"Forget about labels, names, and reputations; they're meaningless if your kid's going to be unhappy."

"Trudy," Colorado

"We did have some conflicts over this, as I needed to be very conscious of finances and financial aid packages. I needed her to choose from a very short list of colleges."

"Della," Connecticut

"One school we visited seemed like such a good match to me, and I kept bringing it up in our discussions but my daughter just was not interested. It took a while before she admitted that it was the apparent lack of other gay people there that turned her off. On the other hand, she decided after much thought that she did not want to attend an all-female school with a reputation for having many lesbian students. The hardest part was letting go and just trusting her instincts."

"Patricia," Maryland

"My daughter initially picked a university in our hometown, but soon discovered she would rather be at a smaller, funkier school in a large town, than be in a large, impersonal university in a smaller town. So after two academically successful, but not entirely happy years at a large university, we are now helping her do a real college search."

"Jean," Oregon

"The student really does know best. I wanted my valedictorian son to choose an Ivy League college instead of the local state school. He resisted and applied to only one college---the one he wanted to attend. He had spent some time there as a high school student and felt very comfortable with the liberal campus and the professors. He is absolutely thriving now that he's in college there."

"Leigh," Maine

States of Concern: Discrimination in the U.S. and the Impact of Anti-Gay Statutes and Laws on Queer College-Bound Students

Where you go to college is a highly personal decision informed by several factors including cost, academic reputation, location and resources, but for LGBTQ students, the decision can be even more difficult. In many states where many well-respected academic institutions are situated, basic human rights are being denied to queer citizens. Though you may not be involved or even interested in politics, you should be comfortable that the institution you wish to attend, and its surrounding geographic area, will be a welcoming place for you. Here are some things you need to know before you make that call:

PFLAG PARENT TIP

- **First . . . the Good:** These 17 U.S. States prohibit discrimination based on sexual orientation: California, Connecticut, Hawaii, Illinois, Maine, Maryland, Massachusetts, Minnesota, Nevada, New Hampshire, New Jersey, New Mexico, New York, Rhode Island, Vermont, Washington, Wisconsin, and District of Columbia. Of these, the following states also ban discrimination based on gender identity/expression: California, Hawaii, Illinois, Maine, Minnesota, New Jersey, New Mexico, Rhode Island, Washington, and District of Columbia.

- **Now . . . the Bad:** According to the 2001 Henry J. Kaiser Family Foundation's *Inside-OUT* report on the experiences of lesbians, gays, and bisexuals in America, 74 percent of gay, lesbian or bisexual individuals have been the victims of prejudice and discrimination based on their sexual orientation.[4] In the following 33 states, individuals can *legally* be fired from their jobs, denied access to housing, refused admittance to educational institutions, and denied credit and public accommodations because they are gay, lesbian, bisexual, or transgender: Alabama, Alaska, Arizona, Arkansas, Colorado, Delaware, Florida, Georgia, Idaho, Iowa, Indiana, Kansas, Kentucky, Louisiana, Michigan, Missouri, Mississippi, Montana, Nebraska, North Carolina, North Dakota, Ohio, Oklahoma, Oregon, Pennsylvania, South Carolina, South Dakota, Tennessee, Texas, Utah, Virginia, West Virginia, and Wyoming.

4   The Kaiser Family Foundation. *Inside-OUT: A Report on the Experiences of Lesbians, Gays and Bisexuals in America and the Public's Views on Issues and Policies Related to Sexual Orientation.* 2001. www.kff.org/kaiserpolls/3193-index.cfm.

What does this mean for you? Well, you need to be very cautious about where you end up for the next four years. When picking a school, remember that figuring out the queer climate on your campus will take time. It is important to figure out if your school will be supportive *before* you get there, and this often means investigating the queer climate on campus as well as off. You should also try to keep in mind that just because a university is in a state or city with unwelcoming policies toward LGBTQ people, it doesn't mean that the school is unwelcoming. On the other hand, you could discover through some preliminary research that a school in a liberal state or city is quite conservative and even hostile toward queer students. Do yourself a favor and do your homework on *all* the schools on your list. You may be surprised at what you can dig up.

Consortium Tips on LGBTQ-Inclusive Campus Nondiscrimination Policies

by Brett-Genny Janiczek Beemyn, Director, The Stonewall Center, University of Massachusetts—Amherst

In the 1970s, LGBTQ students and allies on campuses across the country began lobbying their colleges and universities to add "sexual orientation" to their nondiscrimination policies in order to protect the rights of lesbians, gay men, and bisexuals. More than 550 colleges and universities, including most of the country's large state universities, have since amended their policies.

The inclusion of "sexual orientation" in nondiscrimination statements does not necessarily cover transgender people, who often face discrimination because of their gender identity/expression, rather than their sexual identity. Similarly, the reference to "sex" in such policies has historically not been considered to apply to transgender people. To protect the rights of transgender and other gender non-conforming individuals, colleges and universities, beginning with the University of Iowa in 1996, have added "gender identity and expression" to their nondiscrimination policies.

As of the end of 2006, more than 75 colleges and college systems have implemented trans-inclusive nondiscrimination statements. These institutions include many large public universities (such as the University of California, the University of Wisconsin, and Ohio State University), small liberal arts colleges (such as Colby College, Kalamazoo College, and Williams College), and all eight Ivy League schools (a complete list can be found on the Transgender Law and Policy Institute website: transgenderlaw.org). The number of colleges and universities with "gender identity" in their nondiscrimination policies more than doubled from 2005 to 2006 and will likely continue to grow tremendously, as institutions increasingly recognize the importance of serving the needs of their transgender students.

Here are some suggestions for college administrators, LGBTQ students, and student allies who are trying to add "sexual orientation" and/or "gender identity or expression" to their school's nondiscrimination policy:

- Learn the steps for changing the nondiscrimination policy.
- Identify the key decision makers at each step of the process.
- Educate these decision makers and other important administrators about trans/bi/homophobia and the experiences of LGBTQ students.
- Decide what arguments will work best with different decision makers (such as arguing that it is an important student need, a human rights issue, inline with peer institutions, or inline with state and/or city laws).
- Involve as many LGBTQ students, staff, faculty, and alumni as possible.
- Identify and cultivate influential allies (student leaders, administration officials, deans, department chairs, etc.).
- Seek resolutions of support from the student government, faculty senate, staff council, diversity committees, and other institutional organizations.
- Anticipate possible questions and concerns (such as the argument that you are "promoting homosexuality" or that the policy change would lead to someone who appears male using a women's bathroom or locker room) and be prepared to respond.
- Turn to people who have successfully changed the nondiscrimination policies at other colleges and universities for advice when needed.

Trends in Campus Nondiscrimination Policies

Another good way of assessing whether the university you are looking to attend is supportive of the LGBTQ community is finding out about their employee work policies. According to a 2006 study conducted by the Human Rights Campaign, 562 colleges and universities have written and put into place nondiscrimination policies that include "sexual orientation." In addition, 74 of these institutions have also included "gender identity and/or expression" in their policies.[5] While this is certainly a step in the right direction, this represents only a small percentage of the approximately 3,500 college and universities found in the United States.

Figure 2.1: Growth in number of campuses with "sexual orientation" and "gender identity and expression" nondiscrimination policies or offering domestic partner health benefits, by year.[6]

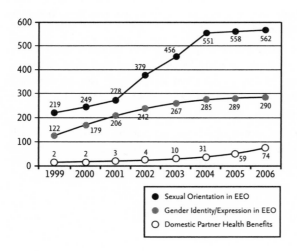

5   Human Rights Campaign Foundation. *The State of the Workplace for Gay, Lesbian, Bisexual and Transgendered Americans.* 2005–2006. http://www.hrc.org/Template.cfm?Section=Get_Informed2&CON-TENTID=32936&TEMPLATE=/ContentManagement/ContentDisplay.cfm.
6. Ibid.

You should also inquire whether or not the university offers domestic partnership benefits to LGBTQ employees and staff with same-sex partners. If they don't support their own staff, then they may not be progressive in providing resources and protection to their student population. The Transgender Law & Policy Institute regularly updates a complete list of colleges and universities with nondiscrimination policies that include gender identity/expression. Visit TransGenderLaw.org/college/index.htm#policies for more information.

Figuring out the queer climate at your schools of interest is no easy task. However, the information we have provided you is a good way to get started. But don't just stop there. In addition to thinking about whether to stay close to home or fly the nest and going online to research the queer climate at your schools of interest, you should also take advantage of other resources that can help you decide on a short list of schools to which to apply.

QUEER-TIP: FINDING AN LGBTQ-FRIENDLY CAMPUS

The Gay, Lesbian, and Straight Education Network (GLSEN) has produced a brochure that provides some questions to think about when trying to find an LGBTQ-friendly campus. Log onto GLSEN.org for more information. In addition, Jeremy P. Hayes, Assistant Director, Office of Diversity Services at Suffolk University, says that "There are also a variety of factors that you can research . . . that can give you some insight into the queer culture":

- Review the school's nondiscrimination and anti-harassment policies to see if they include sexual orientation and gender identity and expression.

- Find out if the school provides benefits to same-sex domestic partners of their employees.

- Does the campus offer health and counseling resources that are sensitive to the needs of queer students?

- Are the campus facilities (i.e., restrooms, locker-rooms, residence halls, etc.) trans-friendly?

- If themed housing options exist, is there an LGBTQ option?

- What other resources are available to support queer students and to ensure their needs are being met?

- Is there an LGBTQ or queer studies program? Even if you're not interested in studying this field, the fact that the school offers these courses indicates their level of commitment to the academic contributions of the LGBTQ community.

USING YOUR GUIDANCE COUNSELORS

According to the 2001 National School Climate Survey released by the Gay, Lesbian, and Straight Education Network, "fewer than 20 percent of guidance counselors have received any training on serving gay and lesbian students."[7] That means that you, as a queer or questioning student, may or may not have allies in your school who can help you with some of the issues that you face when it comes to finding a college that will have the resources and environment that you may need.

But things are looking up. In fact, the educational community has recently rallied behind LGBTQ student rights and the need to employ sensitive guidance counselors trained in handling queer issues. The American School Counselor Association (ASCA) believes that school counselors should "work to eliminate barriers that impede student development and achievement and are committed to academic, personal/social and career development of all students." The ASCA encourages counselors to work "with all students through the stages of identity development and understands this development may be more difficult for sexual minority youth. It is not the role of the professional school counselor to attempt to change a student's sexual identity but instead to provide support to [LGBTQ] students to promote student achievement."[8]

7 Smith, Ramona L. *Diversity in Public High Schools: A Look at the Experiences of Gay and Lesbian Students.* www.glsenco.org/Educators/gayandlesbianadolescents.html.

8 American School Counselor Association. *The Professional School Counselor and Gay, Lesbian, Bisexual, Transgendered and Questioning Youth.* 2005. www.schoolcounselor.org/content.asp?contentid=217.

What does this mean for you? It means that you have the right to expect your school counselor to counsel you throughout your high school experience, and especially during your college search. According to ASCA, they might:

- Assist you as you clarify feelings about your own sexual orientation/gender identity in a nonjudgmental manner.
- Advocate for equitable educational opportunities for you.
- Address inappropriate language from students and adults.
- Promote sensitivity and acceptance of diversity among all students and staff.
- Provide LGBTQ-inclusive and age-appropriate information on issues such as diverse family structures, dating and relationships, and sexually transmitted diseases.
- Use language that is inclusive of sexual orientation/gender identity and encourage policies that address discrimination against students.
- Promote violence-prevention activities to create a safe school environment that is free of fear, bullying, and hostility.[9]

When it comes to your college search, your counselor should understand your needs, and do his or her best to provide you with information and resources on schools that will be compatible. If your school counselor isn't equipped to help you articulate your needs as a queer college-bound student or help you find colleges that will address those needs, you can turn to a variety of other sources to help you with your search. The Princeton Review's website, Campus Pride, and *The Advocate College Guide* are all great places to start your search for an LGBTQ-friendly "best fit" school.

9   Ibid.

ATTEND AN LGBTQ COLLEGE FAIR

LGBTQ college fairs and similar events are burgeoning across the country, as colleges begin to recognize the need for providing safe spaces where queer high school students can come together and meet college admissions representatives. Over the past 5 years, there has been a noticeable movement in colleges' open and targeted recruitment of LGBTQ students. More and more, colleges across the country (including some conservative schools you may not consider very queer-friendly) have begun to actively scout out and court gay, lesbian, bisexual, and transgender youth as potential undergraduates at their institutions.

In 2003, the Massachusetts Governor's Commission on Gay and Lesbian Youth, in conjunction with the state's annual gay-straight youth pride celebration, organized the first large-scale LGBTQ college fair. Over 1,000 prospective students and 40 colleges and universities took part in this event. In 2005, dozens of colleges and hundreds of students participated in LGBTQ college fairs in Washington, DC and New York City.

These events are growing but are still relatively infrequent and may only occur in a few metropolitan areas across the country. Surf the web and see if there are any smaller fairs in your area—Campus Pride is a good place to start—especially in regions with strong ties to queer communities. By attending these fairs, you'll find a variety of resources relevant to LGBTQ life on college campuses across the country. Participating schools disseminate information on LGBTQ resource centers or groups on campus, campus buildings with gender-neutral bathrooms, queer housing options, as well as instructions on how to join their LGBTQ electronic message boards, and more.

QUEER-TIP: CAMPUS PRIDE

Founded in the Fall of 2001 by M. Chad Wilson, Sarah E. Holmes, and Shane L. Windmeyer, Campus Pride started as an online community and resource clearinghouse under the name Campus PrideNet. In 2006, the founders broadened their outreach efforts and restructured as Campus Pride. As the only national nonprofit organization serving LGBTQ and ally student leaders at colleges and universities, Campus Pride provides students access to resources that demonstrate support, education, and visibility on college and university campuses. For more information, log onto CampusPride.net.

Consortium Tips on Visiting College Campuses

by Jeremy Hayes, Assistant Director, Office of Diversity Services, Suffolk University

After you've thought about the type of school you'd like to attend, decided on the type of environment that might be best for you, and done all your research to figure out whether the queer climate at your schools of interest might be a good fit, you should plan to visit all the schools on your short list. A campus visit won't tell you everything you need to know about life at your prospective college, but it will give you a richer, more detailed view than you can get from surfing websites, browsing brochures, watching videos, or reading college guides. Every school has its own culture, its own unique way of doing things. You can't divine it from a brochure, though. Truth be told, you won't learn all there is to know from a brief visit; you will, however, get a sense of the "big picture" issues that define life on a campus. You'll probably get enough of a sense of those issues to determine whether the school is the sort of place where *you* will feel at home for four years. Here are some things you can do while you're on campus, to get a feel for whether a particular school is right for you:

- **Take the Official Campus Tour.** Campus tours vary from school to school, but you can count on your official guided tour hitting the major hotspots—from residence halls and health and student services centers to the sports center, dining halls, the library, and recreational centers. Bulletin boards in dormitories and student centers will provide a glimpse into on-campus activities, student concerns, and campus groups. Read the posters and flyers to get a feel for the general campus vibe. One word of warning however: Don't be unduly influenced by the tour guide. Your tour guide may seem really cool, or she may seem like a total dork. Either way, the guide is just one of many students who attend the school; don't judge the school based on this one person.

- **Wander the Campus.** This is one of the most important aspects of the campus visit. Leave time after the tour/information session to walk around campus on your own. Although the promotional material, the tour, and the information session will all be helpful, they all represent an image of the school packaged by public relations professionals. You want to spend some time seeing the school without that filter. Scout various places on the campus. There might be areas that are more frequented by queer students than others. Trust your instincts and turn on the gaydar! If your parents don't know you're queer, tell them you need a little alone time to feel the campus out and see it on your own.

- **Keep an Eye Out for Queer Event Signage or Banners.** There are all sorts of events and extracurricular activities happening on every college campus. Make sure to look around and see if there are any "rainbow flags" flying or banners hung up that proudly promote queer activities. If a college has an active LGBTQ student body, then you are likely to find some visible signs of what they are doing to be seen, heard, acknowledged, and valued.

- **Meet with the LGBTQ Center or Group on Campus.** The best way to evaluate the school's policies, services, and overall tolerance toward LGBTQ students is to visit the LGBTQ center and/or group on campus. These are the people most actively involved in queer activities at the college you are visiting. Try to get the real dish on the school straight from the horse's mouth. Ask if there are lots of queer events on campus, and whether these events are supported by non-queer students. Inquire as to how the faculty and administration works with the LGBTQ center or groups on educational and/or activist initiatives. Are relations tense between the LGBTQ student group and the administration? Do other groups respect gays on campus? Are other marginalized groups supportive of queer students and activities?

- **Check Out the Campus Newspaper.** The school's newspaper reflects the major attitudes and interests of the student body. A paper that deals only with seemingly safe topics might indicate a more conservative environment. Look for listings or ads for LGBTQ-friendly campus events. Ads from local stores, restaurants, and businesses are a good sign of locals welcoming students in the area.

- **Ask the Administrators.** Don't be afraid to ask admissions staff and college administrators hard questions about the school's LGBTQ policies and services. They want you to attend their school, so it's their job and responsibility to tell you whatever it is you want to know about the things you need from your school of choice. Their perspective may be different from the students you speak with and may prove quite valuable in assessing the pros and cons of each campus.

- **Locate and Meet with Queer Faculty.** If you're focused enough to know what field of study you might be interested in pursuing as an undergraduate, try finding a queer professor or faculty member to chat with on your visit to the campus. Knowing that there are openly LGBTQ members of the academic departments of the university you are looking to attend, helps alleviate the fear of feeling like the odd person out. Ask them how LGBTQ issues or topics are addressed or integrated into their class discussion. Find out if the university or the department supports queer students who wish to pursue gender studies or LGBTQ studies as a double-major or minor. As queer college faculty, they are themselves sexual minorities amongst their colleagues. They will most likely be thrilled to speak with an intrepid prospective queer student who has sought their opinion. Just make sure to set up and confirm an appointment ahead of time.

- **Feel Free to Flee.** If the campus you are visiting is full of red flags—no LGBTQ Center, support groups, resources, or queer studies classes, for example—it will more than likely be a school in which a vibrant, active queer scene is not tolerated or is unwelcome. You might want to consider whether the institution (no matter how prestigious, reputable, or academically superior it may seem) has the right environment and services for you. Ask yourself, "Do I want to spend the next four years at a school that might not really want me there?"

After the official tour is over, and you've walked around the campus, talked to students, and met with faculty, you may want to do your own reconnaissance of life in the local community to find out whether the off-campus attractions are as cool and compelling as the on-campus ones. Try to save time to tour the town or city in which the school is located. If you can't, at least take a walk around the surrounding neighborhood to see what sort of off-campus housing, restaurants, clubs, and retail shops are easily accessible. Here's what you should be looking for:

- **Check Out the Local Queer Scene.** Going to college is not just about staying on campus. You might find that there is an active and supportive gay community off campus. Look to see if there is a vibrant social scene replete with bookstores, restaurants, cafes, retail spaces, and bars catering to queers. If you end up deciding on a school that is a perfect fit but not super queer-friendly, then simply being near a thriving queer environment might be just the balance you're looking for.

- **Stop by the Local LGBTQ Center.** If the college you are considering attending is located in, or near, a major urban area, chances are high that there is an LGBTQ community center in the vicinity. Call ahead and arrange to speak with someone who might be able to provide you with some insight into the services that their center provides which your campus might not.

- **Chat with Queer Youth Off-Campus.** If you happen to be visiting the local queer neighborhood or community center, find people your own age and ask them about the gay scene. More often than not, they will give you candid opinions about the school, tips on the best hangouts, and information on cool things to do off-campus. Who knows . . . you might even strike up a friendship before your first day at school!

Choosing a college is a daunting task. Take the time to consider the myriad choices available to you, and think about how comfortable you will be as a queer student. With some careful planning, you can have a great college experience wherever you decide to go!

CHAPTER 3
GETTING IN AND PAYING FOR IT

Coming Out on the Application: How Out Should I Be?

So, you've decided where to apply. The next decision you might be facing is whether or not to come out in your college essay. While some administrators will claim that sexual orientation and gender identity/expression is irrelevant when it comes to the criteria considered when choosing applicants to admit, others might view it as a brave step and respond very positively. You never know, and it is always a risk to be open.

> "My college application to Brown was all about my sexuality. I talked about how it is a major component of my life and how comfortable I am with my lifestyle. Society is the one who has the problem."
>
> Damian, Junior, Brown University

Now more than ever, students are coming out on their college applications and finding that it helps, not hurts, their chances of admission. Admissions officers at many colleges and universities agree that students applying to their institutions would not be discriminated against for revealing their orientation.[1] In fact, many colleges are now aware that openly LGBTQ students add diversity to college campuses. So does this mean you should come out on the application? It depends.

"Certainly at conservative and religious-based schools, coming out [on the application] is probably not a wise choice," says Brett-Genny Janiczek Beemyn, Director of the Stonewall Center, University of Massachusetts—Amherst. "But at most other schools, it probably isn't an issue. I know many students who came out on college applications and were accepted, but you never know if you'll happen to get an admissions person who is homo/bi/transphobic. However, if most of the activities a student has been involved in during high school are LGBT-related, it would be in the student's interest to include them, or else the admissions committee will think the student has no extracurricular experiences."

---

1 Jaschik, Scott. "Affirmative Action for Gay Students." *Inside Higher Ed*. Oct. 9, 2006. www.insidehighered.com/news/2006/10/09/gay.

Coming out for its own sake may not help tip the scale in your favor at a competitive school. Still, to up your chances of admission at most colleges, it will help if you can write an essay showing how your sexual orientation and/or gender identity/expression strengthens your candidacy for admission. For example, have you used your summer breaks to work for social justice, after having been discriminated against personally? Or perhaps you have volunteered for—or even founded—an LGBTQ advocacy group, because you were driven by the growing realization you might be LGBTQ. Other students can demonstrate their leadership skills by describing their service in high school groups like the Gay-Straight Alliance. Admissions officers may also take special note of straight students whose activities demonstrate that they are LGBTQ allies and consider them excellent role models for diversity and tolerance on their campus.

Trans students have some special needs during this process, advises Lis Maurer, Coordinator of the Center for LGBT Education, Outreach and Services at Ithaca College. "This is a complicated issue, to be sure," says Maurer. Maurer recommends that trans students ask themselves if there are ways their identity impacts their application process, or if there are activities they have been involved in that they wish to describe in more detail. "How comfortable do students feel with self-disclosure?" Mauer asks. "With self-advocacy?"

Greg Sensing, a student who transitioned from female to male while attending all-women's school Simmons College says, "At the time I applied to school, I was still a dyke—I hadn't transitioned yet—so I didn't 'come out' (as trans) on my application. But I made no secret of my queer identity, whenever it came up. I felt totally comfortable being out on campus. I don't envy the administrators the responsibility of looking at the school's admission policies regarding applications of male-born transgender women, or of female-born students who choose to transition while attending. It's very complex. It would be easy to want to say 'everyone should be allowed to attend' but then that compromises the single-sex classification of the college—how can you allow male (FTM) students to attend a women's college and have it remain a 'women's college?' How could you bar a female (MTF) student from applying to a women's college? It isn't fair. Then again, there is no real precedent yet. And this is all assuming everyone shares the definition of what it means to be 'male' or 'female'—it's a multi-layered and complex issue."

Mauer says trans students might also need to ask themselves "Once on campus, would I like to be very out about being trans, or more 'stealth'? Who will I need to tell about my identity? And are there services or supplies I want or need access to regarding my transgender status at my campus of choice?" In other words, like other queer students applying for college, trans students need to think about where they will feel most comfortable once they get in, not just in the application process.

> I'm generally open with my sexuality, but I didn't refer to it in my college application because at the time I was still trying to figure myself out."
>
> Peggy, Senior, Wheaton College

Of course, no one can predict or promise you'll gain admission to any particular college just because you're gay, lesbian, bisexual, transgender, intersex, or even an ally. However, it's good to know that being an LGBTQ-identified student is now seen by many schools as a positive attribute. Bottom line: If you do decide to come out on your application, it is probably best to provide some context for any discussion of your sexual orientation/gender identity. If your sexual orientation and/or gender identity/expression can help illuminate some unique aspect of your background, it might be worth noting. The decision is, of course, very personal and one that should be considered carefully and left to your own best judgment.

QUEER & CANDID
STUDENTS SPEAK OUT ABOUT COMING OUT ON
THE APPLICATION

"I did come out on my college application. I made the decision to do so because I had been a leader in the LGBTQ student group at my previous school and wanted to use the opportunity to discuss my leadership abilities and what I'd learned from running the group. I think that coming out in a college application can't hurt—most major colleges these days are sincere in their anti-discrimination policies—but I think it's important to use an expression of your sexuality to say something greater about yourself. It can't just be 'Hi, I'm gay, you should let me in to your school.' If you can say that your coming out experience has taught you something about yourself, or made you a stronger person, or taught you leadership skills, that's the part that colleges are looking for."

Charles, Yale University

"I did indeed come out in my college application, in my essay specifically. I wrote an essay on challenging my high school administration's censorship of an article about gays on our campus, and in that same essay described my [experiences of] being gay in a Vietnamese family and coming out to friends in high school. My homosexuality is, undoubtedly, something I am very passionate about and I would be lying if I said I did not strategically plant my differentiating characteristics in [the application]. I knew my essay would introduce to the admissions committee facets of myself that would surely distinguish me from any ordinary applicant."

William, Yale University

"My entire admissions essay described the adversities I had faced growing up being gay (and having to stay closeted) in such a strictly conservative area of southeast Texas. I further stated that this is the very reason why I wanted to pursue higher education—to become a professor and reach out to college students, dispelling the many of the same tragic myths that consumed my adolescence."

Jacob, Junior, Columbia University

"On some of my college applications that required me to write more than one personal essay, I chose to include a short essay on my experience of coming out in a private boarding school. For other schools that did not have so many essays required, I chose to highlight other parts of my experiences. I think it is a very personal decision and you should weigh the relative importance of your experiences in deciding what to write about for your personal statement. I will say though that the schools for which I did come out on my application were very receptive of my essays on sexuality. When I spoke to admission officers, they were overwhelmingly supportive, and they were able to provide me with more information on LGBTQ specific resources at their campus as a result of my decision to identify my sexuality. This information was very important in helping me decide which school was right for me."

Justin, Senior, Yale University

WILL COMING OUT AFFECT ME FINANCIALLY?

Many LGBTQ students are afraid that coming out to their parents before or during college will result in them being financially cut off. Many wait until they graduate to tell their parents about their sexual orientation/gender identity so this does not become an issue. Indeed, some parents, deeply shocked by their child's coming out as LGBTQ, will hold tuition as a ransom. As Linda, mother of a gay son explains: "My son came out to me in his freshman year of high school. It did not change anything at all with me. However, my son receive[d] financial support from his grandfather, who he has yet to come out to, partially because he may not have helped had he known [he was gay]." Trans students who begin to transition while in college may also face this threat. Some parents feel that if their child feels financial pressure, they will "give up" being LGBTQ or quickly finish with "this phase" of being trans. Unfortunately, that's not how it works. Most parents eventually come around and continue to support their child once they realize their child is not trying to hurt them, and that withholding financial support may result in their student dropping out from school. Georgina, Oregon mother of an LGBTQ child echoes the sentiments of many when she says: "No way should this happen! No college student should experience financial consequences for coming out."

Some students do tell their parents before they head off to college, and hope for the best. As Yale student William Nguyen, who participates in a work-study program to help finance his education, explains: "I came out right before I headed off to college because I figured my parents should know before I left the nest. My mom took it rather well and would never do such a thing as cut me off. My dad took it rather hard, and coincidentally has yet to pay any part of the college bill. I can't say he would've helped pay if I didn't come out, but I think knowing that I'm something he didn't quite expect, certainly factors into alleviating his guilt for not helping me with the bills."

But what if you are a student who *does* gets cut off from parental financial support? Luckily, losing your parents' financial support does not necessarily mean that college is no longer an option for you. Colleges have financial aid officers who will assist students with securing alternative means of financing their education, including loans, work-study programs, and grants. If financial aid is of great import, consider starting at a community college and then transferring to a four-year school after initial credits are earned to keep costs down. However, even if partial funding help is found, it does not mean all tuition and living expenses are likely to be covered. If you are a student who is dealing with this issue, or feel that you may have to, take immediate proactive measures by talking to your college dean and/or a sympathetic administrator in your school's financial aid office, and contacting organizations like the Point Foundation to inquire about outside sources of funding.

Several supportive parents weighed in on this topic:

"Our [trans] daughter (MTF) came out to us during college. It did not change our financial support, nor change how we love her. My husband fared the best, he never skipped a beat. I knew I needed to get over it and I did. We have never stopped supporting our child."

"Bev," New Hampshire

"Our daughter is going to school with student loans, but her coming out has not affected how we would treat her financially."

"Scott," North Carolina

"We were lucky enough to start saving early to pay for our kids' college and we even paid for our MTF child's SRS surgery. When she first came out I said she'd have to pay for the surgery herself but in the end you want your child to be safe and happy so we paid for that too."

"Arlene," Washington

THE RISING COST OF LEARNING

Whether you are going to a local college or you're off to one of the hallowed Ivies, one thing is always the same: Attending college costs money—and lots of it. According to the Point Foundation, a college education today costs between $8,000 and $40,000 per year. And these numbers are growing higher and higher each and every academic year. So, how can you as an LGBTQ student afford to pay for school if your parents can't foot the entire bill? What can you do if you don't receive any financial support from your parents?

Fortunately, you're not alone. Most people cannot afford to pay the full cost of four years of college. Financial aid is designed to bridge the gap between what you can afford to pay for school and what the school actually costs. Whether or not you qualify for financial aid, education loans are available to supplement the difference between what schools say you have to pay and what you and your family can really afford. While there are no loans, educational tuition payment plans, or government grants specifically designed for queer students, many LGBTQ students may qualify for these programs based on other criteria including ethnicity and economic need.

Applying for Financial Aid [2]

Figuring out how to pay for college can feel like running blind inside a maze. Students and parents who understand the process for applying for financial aid and education loans put themselves in a position to get more money and better repayment arrangements. It doesn't mean you beat the system, but by understanding the system students and parents are able to take advantage of available options and get the best deals.

---

2   Excerpted and adapted from *Paying for College Without Going Broke* by Kal Chany. New York: The Princeton Review, 2007.

Every student seeking aid (including student loans) will need to fill out a standardized need-analysis form called the Free Application for Federal Student Aid (FAFSA). This form is available online at FAFSA.ed.gov, but also can be completed using a paper version that is readily available (usually in early December) from high school guidance offices, public libraries, and college financial aid offices. Make sure that you complete the proper version of the form for the academic year you are seeking aid and keep in mind that the FAFSA can be filed no earlier than January 1 of the year in which you are hoping to receive assistance. For example, a student seeking aid for the fall 2008 and spring 2009 terms would use the 2008–2009 version of the FAFSA and file it no earlier than January 1 of the application year.

Many private colleges and some state-supported institutions may also require you to fill out the CSS / Financial Aid PROFILE. This form is developed and processed by the College Board. A processing fee will be charged based on the number of schools to which you want the form sent. The PROFILE can only be filed online. Registration information will be available in the high school guidance offices or online at CollegeBoard.com. At some schools, the PROFILE will need to be filed with the College Board by late-December for regular decision applicants, so you may well need to file the PROFILE before you can even file the FAFSA.

Some schools require still other forms, all with their own deadlines; for example, many selective private colleges often have their own financial aid forms. To find out which forms are required by a particular college, consult the admissions/financial aid area of each school's web site. At most schools, the deadlines for financial aid will coincide closely with the admissions deadlines. Don't make the mistake of assuming you should wait to hear if you are accepted before you apply for financial aid. Since the demand for aid exceeds the supply, missing the financial aid deadlines can result in a significantly reduced aid package. If you cannot get the tax returns prepared in time to meet your earliest school's deadline for the FAFSA and/or the PROFILE, it is perfectly acceptable to estimate your income figures on the forms so that you meet all the deadlines.

All of the aid forms ask the same types of questions: How much did you earn last year? How much money do you have in the bank? A hundred or so questions later, a very clear picture emerges of the income and assets available to contribute to the costs of the student's education. Don't skip sections and prepare to be verified. You don't want any surprises later. You need to be as accurate as possible to get an award that is as accurate as possible. The processor of the FAFSA form uses a federal formula to decide what portion of your income and assets you can afford to give toward college tuition this year. This amount is called the Expected Family Contribution (EFC). However, some schools do not feel that the EFC generated by the FAFSA form gives an accurate enough picture of what the student and/or family can contribute to college costs. Using the supplemental information on the PROFILE form and/or their own individual forms, they perform a separate need analysis (using a formula called the institutional methodology) to determine eligibility for aid programs that those schools control directly.

Queer-TIP: FAFSA 101

- FAFSA = Free Application for Federal Student Aid.
- Deadlines: Don't wait to fill out the FAFSA until you have been admitted. Try to have everything turned in by February 14. Be sure to file in the correct year that you are applying for aid.
- Application Fee: Never pay to fill out a FAFSA. There are lots of companies that offer to file it for you for a fee. Just take your time, and you can do it for free.
- Complete It Online: File the FAFSA online. The information is processed faster, student gets results faster, and schools get results faster. Visit www.fafsa.ed.gov and create an account and pin number ASAP.

Check out FAFSA.ed.gov to get the FAFSA on the web.

Evaluating Your Financial Aid Package[3]

Once schools have made their admissions decisions, the financial aid officers get to work. Their job is to put together a financial aid package of grants, work-study, and loans that will make up the difference between what they feel you can afford to pay and what the school actually costs. The total cost of attendance for a year at college includes tuition and fees, room and board, as well as allowances for personal expenses, books and supplies, and transportation. The difference

3 Ibid.

between what you can afford to pay and the total cost of attendance is called your "need."

In theory, the Expected Family Contribution will be approximately the same for all the schools to which you apply. If your EFC is calculated to be $10,300 and you are accepted at a state school that costs $13,300, you will pay about $10,300 and the school will make up the difference—in this case $3,000—with an aid package. If you apply to a prestigious Ivy League school that costs $38,000, you will still pay about $10,300 and the school will make up the difference with an aid package of approximately $27,700. In theory, the only difference between an expensive school and a cheaper school (putting aside subjective matters like the quality of education) is the amount of your need. In some cases, depending on how badly schools want a student, there is not a penny difference between the costs of an exclusive private institution and a state school. This is why families should not initially rule out any school as being too expensive. The "sticker price" doesn't necessarily matter; it's the portion of the sticker price that you have to pay that counts.

Each offer of admission from a particular college is followed by an award letter. This letter will tell you what combination of aid the financial aid officers have put together for you in order to meet your need. The package will consist of three different types of aid:

- **Grants and Scholarships:** These are the best kinds of aid, because they don't have to be paid back. Essentially a grant is free money. Some grant money comes from the federal government, some comes from the state, and some comes from the coffers of the college itself. Best of all, grant money is almost always tax-free. Scholarships are also free money, although there may be some conditions attached.

- **Federal Work-Study (FWS):** The federal government subsidizes this program, which provides part-time jobs to students. The money earned is put toward either tuition or living expenses. Be careful when reviewing the award offers from colleges to discern how much of your award is based on work-study. Since this figure is based on anticipated earnings but does not guarantee them, the additional money may be misleading.

- **Student Loans:** These loans, usually taken out by the student rather than the parents, are often subsidized (and guaranteed) by state or federal governments. The rates are usually much lower than regular unsecured loans. In most cases, no interest is charged while the student is in school, and no repayment is required until after a 6-month grace period when the student has graduated or left college.

When you get a financial aid award, ask about renewability criteria and satisfactory academic progress criteria. You want to have a reasonable expectation that your aid award is going to be consistent throughout your four years (or however long it takes to get your degree). Learn about payment plans your school might have as option. In some cases, you may find that the college tells you that you have "unmet need." In other words, they were unable to supply the full difference between the cost of their school and the amount they feel you can afford. This is bad news. What the college is telling you is that if you really want to attend this college, you will have to come up with even more money than the college's need analysis decided that you could pay. Usually this means that you will have to take on additional debt. Sometimes the colleges themselves will be willing to lend you the money. Sometimes you will be able to take advantage of other private loan programs.

An increasing number of financial institutions are reaching out to students and their families to help them design effective tuition loan and payment plans. Many of these lenders are also actively looking to help their LGBTQ customers find the right lending options. Check their websites or call their customer service numbers to find out more. Before signing on the dotted line, know the consequences of borrowing loans. Make sure you understand the terms and conditions. Be aware of the debt, but also know that you are investing in yourself. The Human Rights Campaigns lists top-rated LGBTQ friendly-banks and lending institutions, as evaluated by company policies and practices toward LGBTQ employees and their partners. Visit HRC.org/cei for more information. If you have an unusual situation like independent status or complications with your parents/guardians that bear on your financial status, by all means bring it to the attention of your school. Or, if you get an award and the scholarship amount is not sufficient enough for you to attend the school, call and see if you can appeal. Schools may review your financial aid award if you have experienced a change in your situation since you filed your FAFSA. Sometimes showing offers from other schools helps you make your case.

The point is this: There are tons of ways to get money to go to school and there are countless books and websites dedicated to helping you find out how. For a comprehensive look at ways of paying for college, log onto PrincetonReview.com/college/finance and check out these Princeton Review publications: *America's Best Value Colleges* and *Paying for College without Going Broke*.

QUEER-TIP: CONSORTIUM LGBTQ SCHOLARSHIP RESOURCES

The National Consortium of Directors of LGBT Resources in Higher Education offers an extensive online list of LGBT scholarship resources. This helpful webpage includes information on scholarships:

- Given to self-identified gays/lesbians
- Given for community service to LGBTQ service organizations
- Given for the study of LGBTQ culture
- Given to the children of LGBTQ parents

Log on to LGBTccampus.org/resources/financial_aid.html for more information.

BEING QUEER CAN HELP YOU PAY FOR COLLEGE

In addition to the standard financial aid packages for which all students can (and should) apply, there are queer-specific opportunities you may want to take a look at to see if they may be the missing link to covering some of your college costs. With the increasing visibility of the LGBTQ movement over the past 25 years, more and more organizations are looking to empower queer youth by providing scholarships and awards to help alleviate the financial pressures of paying for higher education. There are also an increasing number of banks and lending institutions actively reaching out to queer students and their parents to help finance higher education. The following sections provide information on a variety of opportunities that you may want to investigate further.

QUEER-TIP: DEAF QUEER YOUTH SCHOLARSHIP

The Deaf Queer Resource Center sponsors a scholarship for deaf lesbian, gay, bisexual, transgender, intersex, or queer students who are out about their sexual orientation/identity. Candidates must be currently enrolled in high school or college, be under the age of 25, and have a minimum 2.5 GPA. U.S. citizenship is required. Deaf queer youth of color are especially encouraged to apply. Selection is based on a written or video essay. For more information, log onto DeafQueer.org/communities/youth/scholarships/index.html.

Scholarships for LGBTQ Students

Did you know there are scholarships for people who are taller than 6'2", who speak Klingon, who are left-handed, or who are out and proud teetotalers? Yes, there are scholarships for just about everything and everyone you can imagine. Oddities aside, what some of you may not know is just how many programs across the country are looking to give queer students money for education. What's even better is that you don't necessarily have to have a 4.0 GPA or have been the founder or president of a dozen queer youth initiatives to qualify for some of these awards. Of course it doesn't hurt your odds if your academic performance is exemplary and your extracurricular activities demonstrate a dedication to community affairs and outreach. But the truth is that many of you will simply fit the bill because you are "openly" gay. So, make a serious effort to dig up as many queer scholarship programs that you can find and fill out the applications. If you meet the criteria, and you make a solid case for your need and your unique queer experience—chances are you will likely strike gold with one or more of them. Just remember, these scholarships vary in value, and the awards may not cover everything you might need. But every little bit helps, and receiving one may even make you stand out among freshmen at schools with supportive queer policies. Following is a description of some of the most notable scholarships available to queer students. Scholarship criteria and/or dollar amounts are subject to change, so make sure to check out the websites listed below to find out the very latest on how you can apply for some cash that will help you pay your way through school:

- **Audre Lorde Scholarship Fund**

  www.zami.org/application.htm

  Established in 1995, the Audre Lorde Scholarship Fund is administered by ZAMI, an organization whose primary mission is to empower and affirm the lives of lesbians of African descent through scholarships, leadership development, support/discussion groups, social activities, drum performances, outreach and education. The first two Audre Lorde Scholarships were awarded in 1997 and since that time, the fund has awarded 83 scholarships to those women and men enrolled in accredited technical, undergraduate, and graduate programs. The scholarships are specifically designed to recognize out lesbians and gay men of color who are making significant contributions to their communities.

- **GLAF/TPF Athlete's Scholarship Program**

  http://glaf.org/scholarship.html

  The GLAF/TPF Athlete's Scholarship Program is designed to champion and financially support LGBTQ high school athletes, collegiate athletes and Olympic hopefuls in their pursuit of sport excellence. Five awards of $1,000 each are awarded to qualifying recipients named GLAF Athlete Point Scholars. These scholars and select applicants become members of the GLAF Fast Track program and also receive nonmonetary awards and mentorship from GLAF Advisory Board members.

- **LEAGUE Foundation**

  www.league-att.org/foundation

  Established in 1996, the LEAGUE Foundation scholarship fund has awarded 50 college scholarships totaling more than $80,000 to self-identified lesbian, gay, bisexual, or transgender high school students. These scholarships are available only to graduating U.S. high school seniors, based on the following: a cumulative grade point average of 3.0 on a 4.0 scale; significant involvement in community service; and acceptance to an accredited U.S. college or university.

- **The LIVE OUT LOUD Educational Scholarship**

  www.liveoutloud.info/what_we_do.html#scholarship

  LIVE OUT LOUD seeks to empower, energize and enable LGBTQ youth to celebrate the richness and diversity of their shared experience. As part of their ongoing services, LIVE OUT LOUD provides LGBTQ youth opportunities to speak with accomplished LGBTQ people who are making a difference in the community. The LIVE OUT LOUD Educational Scholarship was created to help provide LGBTQ youth with the opportunity to pursue higher education. Queer students who have been accepted into postsecondary educational and career training programs are encouraged to apply.

- **PFLAG Scholarships Program**

  www.pflag.org/Scholarship_Programs.scholarships.0.html

  PFLAG's mission is to celebrate diversity and envision a society that embraces everyone, regardless of sexual orientation or gender identity and expression. As part of this vision, in 2003, PFLAG created the PFLAG National Scholarships to help queer students find the funding they need to attend college. The program is made possible by several generous donations including The Palmer B. Carson Trust, the Gays, Lesbians, and Allies employees at Dow Chemical Company employee group, and countless individual donors. PFLAG Scholarships are available at the national level and are awarded by many of the local chapters. If you qualify, you can receive both awards.

- **The Point Foundation: The National LGBT Scholarship Fund**

  www.thepointfoundation.org/scholarships/scholarship.html

  Since its inception in 2001, The Point Foundation has invested more than $1 million in outstanding lesbian, gay, bisexual, and transgender students. The Point Foundation believes that LGBTQ students should not be further disadvantaged as they prepare for the future if they are unable to pay for higher education. A Point Scholarship covers tuition, books, supplies, room and board, transportation, and living expenses, and is set up with the individual college to meet the needs of the Point Scholar. Individual scholarship amounts range from $2,000–$12,000.

- **Pride Foundation Scholarship Funds**

  www.pridefoundation.org/our_programs/scholarships/funds

  Since 1990, the Pride Foundation, in conjunction with the Greater Seattle Business Association, has awarded more than $1.2 million to over 500 openly lesbian, gay, bisexual, and transgender students—making it one of the largest queer scholarship programs in the country. Pride Foundation and GSBA have over 40 different types of scholarships available, but students only need to fill out one application to apply for all of them. Scholarships run the gamut, and there are quite a number dedicated to assisting queer youth of color and youth from Pacific Northwest. Pride Foundation also recognizes students who may not be lesbian, gay, bisexual or transgender, but who have contributed to the LGBTQ community as allies.

- **Third Wave Foundation Scholarship Program**

  www.thirdwavefoundation.org/programs/scholarships.html

  The Third Wave Foundation helps support the leadership of young women and transgender youth ages 15 to 30 by providing resources, public education, and relationship-building opportunities. The scholarship is available to all full-time or part-time young women and transgender activists age 30 and under who are enrolled in, or have been accepted to, an accredited university, college, vocational/technical school, or community college. The primary criteria to qualify for a Third Wave Scholarship are vigorous engagement in activist work and financial need. The Scholarship Committee prioritizes applicants who have limited access to financial resources and whose civic, community, or cultural work shows a commitment to social justice.

See Appendix A for information on additional scholarship programs for LGBTQ students. Remember that being LGBTQ is only a part of your identity. There are plenty of other scholarship programs out there for which you may qualify that are not necessarily LGBTQ specific. Be sure to investigate all your options before ruling anything out.

A Word from the Point Foundation on Why LGBTQ Scholarships Matter

The Point Foundation is devoted to creating and nurturing a vibrant and diverse group of leaders who will be prepared to guide the LGBTQ community forward in the decades to come. Each spring, the Foundation reviews applications for the scholarships for the upcoming school year. This process underscores the reality that we are making decisions that quite literally change the lives of many LGBTQ people. We are always impressed by the quality of our applicants, as well as by the magnitude of the responsibility we face. In 2006, we received more than 1,300 completed applications from hopeful students—all very deserving and all competing for only a handful of scholarships.

We place a great deal of importance on the diversity of our scholars. The Point scholars represent a variety of educational fields, genders and gender identities, sexual orientations, racial backgrounds, economic circumstances, and geography. They are chosen for their demonstrated leadership, scholastic achievement, and commitment to the LGBTQ community—as well as for their financial need. The scholars are all looking to achieve their goals through higher education and look to the Point Foundation for the financial and emotional support to realize their dreams.

Queer-TIP: PFLAG Local Scholarships

In addition to the National Scholarships Program, many PFLAG chapters have substantial local scholarship programs in 24 cities across the country including New York, Louisville, Atlanta, San Diego, and Dallas. For a full list of scholarships (which is updated regularly) check out PFLAG.org/Local_PFLAG_scholarships.344.0.html. Also see Appendix A for more info on PFLAG local scholarships.

Point scholars also represent a wide range of life experience. Due to the impact of homophobia, not all scholars have had the same opportunities and degrees of cultural exposure. At this year's Point Foundation retreat, one of the scholars who grew up in an isolated area thanked a Point staff member for the gift bag that contained a number of books by LGBTQ authors, noting that the contents were her "first gay books." Interestingly, the gathering was also attended by other scholars who themselves are published authors.

As our community continues to gain visibility, so does our organization. Point scholars' stories were featured in a *Time* magazine cover story in late 2005, and in 2006, Oprah interviewed a Point scholar and her mother on her television show. The more exposure we continue to receive, the greater the potential that LGBTQ people and their families will find us—and reach out to us for help.

For more information about The Point Foundation or to find out how to apply for a Point Foundation scholarship, visit ThePointFoundation.org.

QUEER & CANDID
POINT SCHOLARS PERSPECTIVES

"Before I became a Point Scholar I had very few out homosexual friends and I had never met a transgender person before. Receiving the scholarship has not only enriched my understanding of the LGBTQ community, but it has also allowed me to make wonderful, life-long friends. The relationship I have with other Point Scholars is not only one of a kind, but it allows me to become more comfortable with my sexuality. Through the Point Foundation I have witnessed the power LGBTQ youths hold and how one's sexual orientation is not a limiting factor in the accomplishments one attains.

Also, becoming a Point Scholar has shown my family (specifically my mom, who thought my homosexuality would keep me from being a powerful and influential person) that [queer people] can be as influential, or more, than heterosexuals. And that even though I am a lesbian, I can still accomplish great things in my life.

I would definitely encourage students to apply for the Point Foundation Scholarship. This scholarship has had an immense impact on my life. Not only does the Point Foundation provide financial means to complete college, it also organizes conferences, arranges for each scholar to have a mentor and provides a great network of friends. In a time of strong emotional and physical stress (during college), the Point Foundation provides each scholar with the relief and support they need to succeed."

Rachel, First-year, University of Rochester

"The Point Foundation was exactly what I had been looking for. Not only do they offer financial assistance; but they provide a family: a community of supporters who love and encourage each one of us—through constant contact with a number of mentors—all throughout our collegiate career and even after graduation. Not to sound cliché, but The Point Foundation has given me hope. Their love and support is unconditional, which is vital for those of us who cannot find that in our families. Because of TPF, I can see my dreams materializing, and I am more confident than ever to achieve my goals.

TPF shows LGBT students that we are not alone—we become part of a tremendous family whose love, support, and guidance is invaluable."

Jacob, Junior, Columbia University

"I applied for a Point Foundation Scholarship because I knew that winning the scholarship would not only allow me to attend college financially, but would give me a chance to raise awareness about the experiences of bisexually identified college students. When I looked through TPF's scholar profiles before I applied, I noticed that there were not that many bisexually identified students who were out on the website. I felt because of my excellent academic background and experience in student government and progressive queer student leadership that I would be an excellent TPF candidate who would also help TPF's scholar pool be more inclusive. I was, of course, still floored when I received the scholarship; I never expected to be chosen from among the over 1,400 well-deserving students who completed the application.

TPF has enriched my life in so many different ways. TPF provided me not only with financial help and guidance, but with an instant set of new friends and family, too. TPF has opened many doors for me by increasing my network of contacts and opportunities; without winning my Point Scholarship, for example, I doubt I would have ever known to apply to be in this publication, or have written an article about bisexuality to be submitted to the online version of *The Advocate*. Additionally, my TPF mentor helped guide me through the law schools admissions process, and continuously tells me that I can contact him if I am having a hard day. To me, TPF is not just about money, it is about a commitment to helping support emotionally, financially, and professionally the next generation of talented queer youth. I fully intend on donating to TPF in the future, when I am in a financial position to do so. I am both honored and proud to be affiliated with such an excellent foundation. I would encourage all queer and ally student leaders to apply. The Point Foundation is an excellent organization, but without applications from talented students, TPF is nothing."

Lauren, Senior, Michigan State University

DIGGING INTO SCHOLARSHIP DATABASES

There are literally thousands of scholarships out there—and several scholarship search engines on the web. Beware. Some search engines are filled with outdated or non-existent scholarships. Some of these scholarship search engines lure you in with false promises of billions of dollars in aid, collect information about you, and then auction this information off to marketing companies (wondering how the credit card offers just start rolling in as soon as you turn 18?). Don't get sucked in! The Princeton Review is pleased to introduce a new scholarship search provider, BrokeScholar. By signing up for this free service, you will have access to a vast, searchable database of over 650,000 scholarships and be able to find the awards that best match your interests, backgrounds and qualifications. Just visit PrincetonReview.com for more information. If you want to see what additional scholarships and financial aid opportunities are out there for queer students, check out these two fine information portals:

- **HRC's Scholarship Database:** To better aid college-bound queer youth, the Human Rights Campaign has also put together a comprehensive list of scholarships and assistance programs that address the needs of LGBTQ and allied students. To access HRC's well-stocked database of LGBTQ scholarship programs, log on to HRC.org.

- **FinAid:** FinAid was established in 1994 as a free public service for those looking to locate information about scholarships, loans and other financial aid available to LGBTQ college students. The award-winning site has grown exponentially over the past few years and serves as the *most* comprehensive online source of information, tools and advice. They have an extensive section devoted entirely to LGBT scholarships broken down into the following categories: General Scholarships, Regional Scholarships and Campus-Specific Scholarships. For more information about FinAid, log onto FinAid.org.

The earlier you become acquainted with the world of scholarships, the better. Starting early will allow you to enhance your application by getting involved in new extracurricular activities, gaining more work experience, and improving your grades. Finally, a head start lets you get a jump on the time-consuming tasks of sending away for applications, filling them out, and writing the essays. As a result, you won't overburden yourself when you are knee-deep in the school admissions and application process.

When you find a scholarship that is of interest to you, there are several things you can do to improve your overall package. First, send a personalized letter or e-mail to the scholarship provider explaining why you believe you'd be a good candidate for their scholarship. Send this before you actually submit your application. When completing the application, make sure you follow directions! The biggest mistake you can make when applying for scholarships is to ignore the fine print. Winning scholarships is highly competitive, so even overlooking one small point can take you out of the running. Make sure your recommenders take the time to personalize their letters to help you stand out from the crowd. Finally, proofread your applications carefully and try to submit them early if possible. Take the time to make copies of everything for your records, just in case something gets lost in transit.

QUEER-TIP: CALLING ALL SCHOOLS

Call all of the colleges on your short list and ask to speak with the LGBTQ resource center or queer studies program. They should have information about local, regional, and even national scholarships for queer students. You may find that there are great opportunities—at a school you didn't give much thought to—or you might find that you get negative feedback from your top choice. It's a good way to test the campus climate early on in your search.

CHAPTER 4
YOU'RE IN! WHAT'S NEXT?

What to Expect as an Out and Queer College Student

So you want to know what your four years of college are going to be like? We can give you an idea of what lies down the road for you, but predicting what somebody will do in college is like predicting what somebody will buy in a well-stocked candy store. The person may emerge with a beguiling variety of interesting goodies, or may emerge clutching the same tasty treat that has pleased her palate in years past. So while we can't tell you what you'll buy from the store, we can give you an idea of what you'll find in the aisles.

As Daniel Coleman, the Program Coordinator for Gay, Lesbian, Bisexual, and Transgender Student Support Services at Indiana University explains, "For LGBTQ students the first year can be as varied as the colors in the rainbow. Most anything can and will happen during your first-year experience. Some students will experience freedom from the views and rules of their parents and possibly begin to come out. Others have already identified and come out, and are now beginning to share their voices and experiences in order to create change. There are an infinite number of scenarios that can occur just in the first semester or quarter of your college experience. The reality is that you will have positive and negative experiences with roommates, friends, professors, and other people that enter your life. You should view these experiences—whether positive or negative—as valuable tools to help you move forward in achieving your goals."

Preparing For The Big Day

When all those colorful "Back to School Sale!" fliers come to the house, it's easy to be convinced that in order to have a fulfilling college experience you need to run out and fill a shopping cart with a mountain of college-appropriate gear. For starters, that might include a storage trunk, a new comforter, stacking closet organizers, a more portable stereo, and oodles of those "just-add-hot water" noodles—a staple in college diets for generations over.

Before you make a decadent college shopping list, poke around the house and take stock of what you already have. Once your parents give you the go-ahead, do an internal shopping spree and collect anything that might be handy. (You can always put some things back once you sort through everything.) You might be more prepared than you think. If you can get creative and improvise with a few things you find under your own roof, your parents may be more likely to finish off the rest of your list at the store. A word to the wise: Remember how you're getting to school. If you're flying, what you can't carry on the plane will have to be shipped—and that gets expensive! Pack as light as you can. (For instance, leave the winter clothing at home until winter break when you can bring home the light stuff and take the warm stuff back with you.) Even if you're driving down to school, keep in mind how much your vehicle will hold and how many passengers you'll need to save room for.

Aside from items you'd never leave behind—computer, iPod, television—you'll want to pack your alarm clock and that extra-puffy pillow you can't sleep without. Decorative elements, like your posters, family photos, throw rugs, bedspread, etc., can also make your dorm room feel more like home. As for Mr. Cuddles the bear—we'll leave that up to you.

Checklist: What to Bring

1. **Clothing:** While it may be tempting to pack up your entire closet, try to be conservative. Remember to pack warm coats (and gloves, hats, and boots) if you're off to a colder climate, bathing suits (and shorts and sandals) if you're headed for warmer shores. In either case, leave off-season outfits at home, and plan to switch up during a break if necessary. Space is scarce in any residence hall room.

2. **Supplies:** When you've exhausted the resources around the house, then you're ready to go shopping. Include whatever you can't find on your list!

   - Backpack for schlepping your stuff around campus (some things never change)
   - Clothes hangers
   - Dry-erase board for the front of your door—for messages from all the new friends you're about to make!
   - Drying rack for clothes you can't throw in the dryer (again, only if you'll actually use it)

- Extra-long twin sheets (dorm beds are often extra-long)
- First-aid kit (pain relievers, Band-Aids, etc.)
- Flip flops for the shower
- Foam, egg-crate mattress (to use between your sheets and the mattress they provide—you'll appreciate the added comfort)
- Full-length mirror you can attach to the back of your door
- Good can opener
- Hand towels, washcloths, bath towels (or beach towels), and blankets
- Laundry bag (a laundry basket makes a good hamper, but a bag is easier to tote)
- Plastic basket or bucket for carrying toiletries to and from the hall bathroom
- Removable tacky stuff, so you can hang posters without making holes in walls
- Small sewing kit (even college students need to sew on a button once in a while)
- Toiletries (that's everything you use—even occasionally—in the medicine cabinet at home: shampoo, soap, toothpaste, etc.)

3. **Furniture and Appliances:** It's always a good idea to coordinate purchases with your new roommate (or roommates) before shopping so you don't end up with two (or more) irons! And don't forget to pick up some sturdy boxes to pack everything in. Here are some things you'll want to make sure you (or your roommate) has on your dorm furniture list—be sure to check your dorm policy to get a list of the appliances which meet your school's dorm safety regulations:

- Fan
- Iron and mini-ironing board (but only if you know you're going to use them)
- Microwave
- Mini-fridge (these can often be rented)
- Over-the-desk or over-the bed reading light

- Small safe or lock box for important papers
- Stackable crates
- Surge protectors (for plugging in your computer, fridge, microwave, etc.)

4. **Computers, Phones, and Electronics:** Today's college students should either own or have ready access to a computer. Many of your class assignments will be available online, and some schools even post lectures and exams online. If you're planning to bring your own computer to campus, check with campus IT services to make sure it is compatible with any Ethernet and/or wireless services available. In addition, make sure your virus software has been fully updated! If you don't already have a cell phone, consider getting one. While your school will provide you with a land-line for a monthly fee, you can probably get a better deal on long-distance calling—not to mention fun stuff like text messaging, picture sharing, and video streaming—through your cell phone service. Finally, it may be a good idea to bring a television and CD/DVD player for those rare occasions when you don't have any assignments due and you want to just want to kick back and chill out with your homies from down the hall.

Checklist: Things to Take Care of Before You Go

1. **Medical and Health Insurance:** Many schools assess students with a student health fee to cover the cost of basic university health services including doctor's visits, X rays, lab visits, and medicine. This should not be confused with health insurance, which most schools will offer as optional coverage. Many parents choose to continue to insure their college-bound child under their own health plans. Whatever option you ultimately choose, make sure it has services in place to meet your needs. See Chapter 10 for more information on the services your health center should provide, and additional services that might be of interest to you as a LGBTQ student. For a list of gay-friendly healthcare clinics by location, visit Gay Health.com.

2. **Setting Up a Budget:** Before you head off to school, it is important to sit down with your parents or your guardian and come

up with a realistic, easy-to-follow budget that will get you through the semester. Factor in personal expenses for things such as travel costs, laundry and dry cleaning, the occasional dinner or movie, etc. In addition, try to keep track of your educational expenses for books, tuition, and student fees. This will allow you to get an early start on intelligently managing your finances. The Federal Student Aid office offers loads of information on effective ways to set up monthly and yearly school budgets through interactive calculators and software that make it super easy to keep abreast of your financial situation. Check them out at: ED.gov/offices/OSFAP/DirectLoan/student.html.

3. **Bolstering Your Plastic Power:** Another source of income for new college students will be of the plastic variety. Credit card companies see college students as potential lifelong customers—and being queer doesn't make you an exception. However, it's important to be responsible when it comes to your credit card spending. Your credit history is something that will follow you for the rest of your life. So many college students dig themselves into mounds of credit card debt before they ever graduate from college; it can take years to pay off balances at the high interest rates offered to most college students. Don't fall into this trap. Use your credit card responsibly: for emergencies, school books, travel, and maybe the occasional dinner with friends. If you feel that you can handle the responsibilities that come with credit cards, you'll be delighted to know that, there are credit card companies out there that specifically target the LGBTQ marketplace—some of which even donate a portion of your spending to community causes. Here are some options for keeping your spending within "the family."

   • **Human Rights Campaign Visa Platinum Card** (www.providiancard.com/bap/hrcwa/jumpApp.jsp): The HRC has partnered with Washington Mutual to provide a credit card that offers discounts and special offers on everything from clothing and travel to groceries and electronics. Every dollar that you charge to the HRC Visa Platinum Card generates a contribution to the fight for lesbian, gay, bisexual, and transgender equality through a variety of initiatives led by one of the most important queer nonprofit outfits in the world.

- **Olivia Card** (www.olivia.com/creditcard/index.cfm):
  Want to put your lesbian dollar to work for you and support a lesbian company? Then consider an Olivia Card, a credit offered by MBNA America Bank in conjunction with Olivia, the world's largest lesbian lifestyle company. Customers earn points for their purchases, which can be used to buy down the value of Olivia trips, get upgrades, or even purchase entire vacations.

- **Rainbow Card** (www.rainbowcard.com):

  Every year since its inception in 1996, the Rainbow Visa Card has provided financial support for the Rainbow Endowment which has awarded over two million dollars in grants and financial support to organizations in the LGBTQ community that provide social and health services, advocacy, and educational information to the community including: The AIDS Information Network, Gay and Lesbian Advocates and Defenders, National Lesbian and Gay Health Association, National Youth Advocacy Coalition, and Women's Educational Media. Every time you use the Rainbow Card to purchase an item, travel, dine out or pay for your school books, a portion of the transaction goes directly back into the queer community.

QUEER-TIP: "NINE STEPS TOWARD MORE FRUGAL COLLEGE STUDENTS"

In her popular book, *The Parents' Guide to College Life,* author Robin Raskin offers the following tips for creating more frugal college students[1]:

1. Parents and students should go on a shopping trip to the supermarket together. Do a little real world math review to see if the student can figure out whether 16 ounces at $1.50 is better or worse than 8 ounces at 95 cents. Have the student create a budget for several meals and then do the shopping for them. When they're strolling the grocery aisles at school, they'll have some newfound confidence.

1   Robin Raskin. *Parents' Guide to College Life.* New York: The Princeton Review, 2006. 222—223.

2. Ask for student discounts and frequent stores that offer them. College towns appreciate students' business and many offer student discounts. Students should always carry their school ID and not be afraid to ask about student discounts.

3. Plan ahead: The supermarket or warehouse store is typically cheaper than the local deli for snack foods. Try to buy in bulk, and then ration. Shop with friends when stores are offering two-for-one sales or discounts on bulk purchases.

4. Figure out how you'll deal with service items like haircuts and whether you or your parent is going to pay. Most students wait until they come home on break, but maybe they'll find a budding stylist on campus.

5. Consider using Craigslist.com to buy items and services. Whether you need a pair of skis, a chemistry tutor, or someone to help haul your sofa home from the Salvation Army, this is the place to look. eBay works for good deals on certain items as well.

6. Watch those photocopying, laser printing, and late charges at the library.

7. If you like late-night snacks, it's cheaper to keep bread and cold cuts in the dorm room than to run out to a fast food joint or buy a ready-made deli sandwich.

8. If you get textbook lists early enough, check out the prices online at sites such as Half.com. You'll pay a fraction of what you'd pay in the campus bookstore.

9. Find friends who also need to be frugal. It's more fun to see how little you can spend on a Friday night and still have a good time when you have a few pals who are on the same mission.

On Your Own: Separating From Your Parents

For most teenagers, leaving home for their first year of college is the first time in their lives when they will be away from their parents for an extended period of time. For some of you, the experience of going to college will be liberating and a great opportunity to engage in new activities, pursue diverse academic interests, meet new friends, as well as explore your sexuality and gender identity/expression. If you come from a conservative home, this may be an unbelievably empowering time in your life. Others may have very supportive parents who have been instrumental in helping you come out as a queer individual. In this case, making the transition to being on your own can leave you feeling lonely and without a "tried and true" support system, and it may take some time for you to be comfortable being on your own.

Even if you don't come down with a classic case of homesickness, you'll quickly realize that suddenly there's no one there to look out for you. This has its pros and cons. If you sprain your ankle trying to organize your closet the first week of school, there's no mom or dad in the other room to pick you up, put you in the car, drive you to the hospital, and get you a milkshake on the way home. Yes, you will make friends, but college students are busy, and you might be hard-pressed to find someone you've just met to drop everything to come to your rescue the way your parents would have. Just remember to take it slow. How you adjust to campus life is an individual experience, and no two students take to it the same way. Give yourself time, and understand that the opportunities that await you will soon overshadow any sense of displacement and homesickness you may be feeling now. Before you know it, you'll settle in, be assigned more homework than you ever thought humanly possible, and be involved in too many activities to keep up with. Eventually, you'll probably forget you were ever homesick. If you do continue to feel out of sorts, stop by your LGBTQ Center or check out some of the tips for managing feelings of isolation and depression provided in Chapter 10.

PFLAG Parent Tip: Supporting Your Queer College-Bound Child

Many parents have found a striking similarity between how they felt when their toddler took his or her first shaky steps and how it felt sending a child off to college. The resulting pangs of pride coupled with a new fear for the child's well-being strike most parents right on cue. After all, your child will be coping with college selection, course decisions, living on his or her own, financial planning and time management, and more serious opportunities for socializing and dating on their own. Even just the purchase of items for his or her dorm room or apartment is a big step towards independence. So what role should you play as your child prepares to make this transition? How can you best support your college-bound child?

As one mother of both lesbian and heterosexual college-age daughters said, "LGBTQ students need not be prepared differently than any other college-bound child." In other words, the process of preparing your LGBTQ child for college will be very similar to any other parent's experience in most basic ways. "Make sure your child knows without a doubt that you care about their safety, the quality of their education, and support services/groups available to them at their university of choice," says the mom of one gay college-aged son. And remember, this is your child's college experience, not your own. Whatever hopes you may have about the "best" college for your child to attend must be considered secondary to finding the "best fit" school for your own child, and this decision must ultimately be made by him or her—not you.

However, there is indeed an important difference for parents sending their LGBTQ students off to live in new environments far from the protections of home. For probably the first time, your LGBTQ child will need to cope with his or her sexual identity/gender identity in a place that will either be more welcoming, or more hostile, than his or her own home, and they will have to navigate these differences mostly alone. For this reason, some pointed advance preparation is a good thing.

Most supportive parents of out LGBTQ college students will tell you that the most important way to keep your child safe, and indeed thriving, is to select a college which is not only known to be tolerant, but that is actually truly welcoming of its LGBTQ students. As Brett-Genny Janiczek Beemyn, Director of the Stonewall Center at University of Massachusetts—Amherst and a board member of the Trans Law and Policy Institute, explains: "Beyond strongly standing behind their students' sexual orientation and gender identity and expression, parents can support their students by helping them decide on a college or university that has LGBTQ-inclusive policies and a welcoming climate for LGBTQ students."

To find out what kind of environment a school fosters, examine each school's course offerings in lesbian and gay studies, the number of active LGBTQ student groups on campus, whether LGBTQ students are actively recruited by the college, and even whether a school has a policy about transgender housing and gender neutral restrooms. In fact, if you have a child who is transgender or transitioning, this will be an issue of huge importance over the next four years. You might also consider checking the website of each college's LGBTQ studies program or queer student center, and contacting a director or other staff person who might be available to provide an inside perspective on the college's policies and resources.

One very accepting mother of a lesbian student says, "We think it is critical to find a school with an abundance of diversity. Student diversity colors everything on campus: classroom discussions, social life, and more." By having a supportive attitude about both your child's universal needs as a college-bound freshman and his or her unique need for support as a LGBTQ young person, you will go far in ensuring that they are ready for college.

Settling In

So you've taken that road trip, flight, train or bus ride to campus, and unpacked the duffel bag crammed with your most prized possessions. You've introduced yourself to your roommate, and waved goodbye to your parents. You are officially a first-year college student. Now what? Maybe you planned to party like a rock star from the second you set foot on campus until the moment you're due at your first class, but chances are, partying will be the last thing on your mind. You hardly know anyone, you don't exactly know your way around, and the money in your bank account needs to last all semester. It's totally natural to feel overwhelmed at this point, even a little scared. After all, you've arrived at the ultimate first day of school. The good news is that most colleges offer orientation activities, and if your campus has an LGBTQ Resource Center you'll want to make sure you stop by their "Welcome Freshman" mixer. The ice-breaker games at these events may seem a bit cheesy, but they're an easy way to develop that we're-in-the-same-boat bond with other students, and you'll probably pick up information and advice at orientation that'll come in handy later.

> "It's interesting how the dynamics of coming out in college are different today than the past. For example, when I arrived at orientation, many people already knew my [sexual] orientation from my Facebook profile and nobody asked me if I had a girlfriend, which was my planned way of addressing the topic."
>
> Scott, Sophomore,
> Brandeis University

Fresh Starts: Reinventing Yourself on Campus

Some people try to create the same comfort zone they had for themselves in high school as soon as they get to college. They'll take the same classes, join the same kind of organizations and activities, and seek out the same types of people they were friends with at home. But hey, why not just go back to high school and redo your senior year? The point of college is to branch out, try new things, meet new folks with different backgrounds and ideas, and risk something in the process.

The opportunity to reinvent oneself at college is especially appealing for queer college students. Some students choose to reinvent themselves by "coming out" at college while other choose to explore their sexual identity or gender identity expression through a variety of ways unique to their individual needs and interests. College is a time ripe with possibilities, and being in college brings about a sense of maturation. Sure, there are parties and papers and roommate drama galore, but more importantly, there is a lot of time for introspection and self-exploration. You already know that not everyone fits into the neat little boxes that our culture often prescribes for us, and your college years will give you the space and time to detonate those confining spaces for good. Enjoy the journey. Learn what makes you tick and about the issues and beliefs that feel right for you. Hold this time near and dear, as an opportunity not to just explore statistics, literature, and other academic subjects, but also to discover what makes you unique. Remember: It's okay to change your mind, and it's even ok to make mistakes. This learning experience, like the thesis you may be required to write during your senior year, is much more about the *process* than it is the *outcome*.

SPOTLIGHT ON: JACOB, JUNIOR, COLUMBIA UNIVERSITY STUDENT AND POINT FOUNDATION SCHOLAR

"Being out on campus is my way of telling others that I am not afraid of who I am and they shouldn't be either. By speaking openly about my sexuality, people are often more likely to ask questions—rather than jump to generalizations—about what it means to be in the LGBTQ community."

QUEER & CANDID
REAL STORIES ABOUT COMING OUT AND BEING OUT ON CAMPUS

"I am an athlete, and my cross country team at University of Rochester has an e-mail list so everyone can get to know each others before the season starts in August. Knowing that I would be running with these 30 girls for the next three seasons (fall, winter, and spring), and possibly the next four years, I told them that I was gay and asked them for help with my roommate—who was having trouble accepting the fact that she was a devout, heterosexual Christian who would be rooming with a [queer] Jew for a year. Everyone on the team was extremely supportive and accepting. Once I arrived on campus and pre-season started for cross-country, I assumed the whole team knew that I was gay. During one of my runs, a fellow teammate asked me if I really was gay, because someone else told her I was, and she had never met a lesbian before (she obviously didn't check her e-mails during the summer). I told her I was gay, and we talked about [being queer]. I have now become the go-to girl whenever anyone has questions about being a lesbian and what it is like to be gay. I believe you must be comfortable with your sexuality on campus. College is stressful enough as it is—hiding a big secret like one's sexual identity makes college even more stressful than it has to be. "

Rachel, First-year, University of Rochester

"I've come out as several identities over the years, first coming out as bisexual to my mother at 16, then gay to both of my parents a short time later, and have recently come out as trans (at 21). I had a professor in a queer studies class who encouraged me to confront my questioning of my identity and make the step to change the name I used in class from my legal name to the name that I preferred to use in my personal life. He gave me the support I needed to be able to see the possibility that I could be out in the classroom and elsewhere on my campus. From then on I have gradually been convinced to feel safe to first explore and then implement changing the name and pronouns I want to use. I am currently the only out trans undergraduate student that I know of on this campus."

Marcus, Senior, Brandeis University

"I had several talks with my roommate my junior year about how we agreed that gender was a fluid thing and not something that could be one side or the other. I also took a class called "Sexuality and Gender" in which we learned about the gender continuum and discussed how it was possible to be in the middle of that continuum. That was when I first heard the term "genderqueer," and I identified with it immediately. I didn't think it was something that I needed to "come out" about, so as it came up in conversation I told my friends. One of them a few weeks ago was especially surprised and excited, which I thought was funny. He wanted to know all about it, as if it were something to discuss. I told him I had always been that way, and that it was just normal. He said he thought he was genderqueer, too."

Mallery, Senior, Susquehanna University

SPOTLIGHT ON: KAYLA LUBBERS,
FRESHMAN, ST. CLOUD STATE UNIVERSITY

"Being out on campus is very important to me because being a lesbian is a huge part of who I am."

PFLAG PARENT TIP: DEALING WITH YOUR CHILD'S COLLEGE ADMINISTRATION

Despite how well your child is prepared for college, problems will arise. Most parents we surveyed encouraged their children to handle basic issues themselves, primarily by dealing with the appropriate campus staff (residential advisor, dean, peer counselor, etc) or by simply waiting out minor annoyances. Though a mother or father's most basic urge is to protect her offspring, many parents interviewed for this book advised simply not interfering at all in a student's life at college.

As "Maryellen," a mother from Pennsylvania said, "Kids are so flexible, the things that can loom so large before they leave for college or in the beginning of the term seem to work themselves out within weeks." Another mother of three from Delaware, "Edie," stressed the no-nonsense approach: "We encouraged our daughter to deal with her college problems herself, and therefore had no dealings with the administration."

A number of parents stressed that they were impressed by how well their LGBTQ students were treated at college and the amount of effort that went into overseeing all aspects of student life. "We were always ready to run interference for our (FTM) kid, but he dealt with the administration on his own and never needed us," said one mother. "Darlene," a California mother of a MTF student said, "We contacted the administration the very first day at orientation and explained our son was transitioning and they printed a new ID with her new female name on it." "Audrey," another parent of a MTF child stated that "We wanted her to keep us informed in case she needed help. So far, everything has worked out for her. Her needs with the university first came up with housing. They were very accommodating to her. Next came filing the name change papers with the university. Again, they were fine with it. She met with her faculty; they are fine with it. Most faculty who did not know her before just assume she is a female." "Brian," a father from New Jersey, summed it up by saying, "I would suggest that the parents of LGBTQ kids relax and just be there if their children need them. Most colleges today are fine with LGBTQ kids."

With many systems in place to oversee students, particularly first-years, many small crises, including anxiety and minor depression, can be resolved with early intervention. As "Phillip," a father of a gay son from Texas, noted, "Schools are so much better at getting students help than when we were in college."

Other parents did have the experience of needing to deal with the administration. As "Elaine," a mother from Connecticut noted, "We contacted our daughter's advisor once right in the beginning of freshman year when a professor of hers made an insensitive comment regarding gays. Our daughter was so upset, but reluctant to step out on a limb. But the teacher was called on it and apologized to the entire class, acknowledging his insensitivity next time the class met."

Since the nondiscrimination clause at most colleges and universities allows them to pursue disciplinary action for language or acts against LGBTQ people, professors, administrators, teaching assistants, librarians, dining hall and custodial workers, and everyone else at a school must comply or face repercussions. Since most schools don't want internal strife, negative publicity, or even lawsuits on their hands, compliance is obligatory. This is a clear benefit for today's generation of LGBTQ college students, and has contributed greatly to an improved atmosphere of tolerance and respect on many college campuses. As "Dawn," mother of an FTM child noted, "We never once had to interfere even during the early part of our son's transition. Oberlin is totally respectful of gender-variant students and our son dealt with faculty and administration on his own from day one."

In this age of instant communication, some parents also found that e-mail was a good way to reach administrators with minor concerns. As "Judy," a mom in Connecticut with a lesbian daughter stated, "We never had any big issues with her school, but we used e-mail when we wanted to let the college know that we didn't agree with their stand on something, and we always got a prompt response."

This is not to say that bigger issues and real emergencies don't come up. In such cases, parents need to advocate for their child if called upon to do so. But sometimes even a parent's advocacy may not be enough to salvage a truly bad situation. In such unfortunate situations, a parent may find that although they could not deal successfully with a school's administration, they were still needed afterwards to help pick up the pieces for their child.

DEALING WITH ANXIETY AND THE FIRST-YEAR EXPERIENCE

It's okay to be nervous about college. In high school, you were the big fish in a little pond, but now you're headed into an ocean. It's a big change, and the level of competition will indeed be higher than that to which you might be accustomed. Still, in your new setting you'll have more resources to tap into, more intelligent people with whom to discuss your problems and theories, and (hopefully) great professors to help you achieve your academic goals. For some students it's the first time away from home for any extended period of time. Unless high school and home were slow agony, you're bound to get homesick to some degree. It's natural to miss your family and friends, but it's easy to combat the blues. For the first time in your life you will have total freedom in choosing your direction; the number of paths you can take and activities you can get involved in are staggering. For LGBTQ students, it will also be an opportunity to decide how "out" you want to be on campus and also a time to begin exploring your sexual orientation and/or gender identity in a less restrictive space than living at home. So wander around, explore your new world and make it yours. Stop by the LGBTQ Center to see what is happening for queer students on campus. Have lunch on the quad, attend parties in your residence hall, stroll across campus asking random people where the duck pond is (even if you know there isn't one), find a coffee shop and share a cup of coffee with a stranger—whatever it takes. The more you leave the solace and rock-hard comfort of your bunk bed, the more confident you will be in all your decisions. Here are some common anxieties that all first-years face followed by advice on how to handle them.

WILL I BE ABLE TO HAVE A SOCIAL LIFE AND STILL MAKE GOOD GRADES?

Some students worry that they won't be able to have any sort of social life because they fear that they won't be able to handle the academic workload. If you're one of those students, relax—if you didn't show that you were capable of doing the work, you wouldn't have been admitted. You just need to be aware that some students have a terrible first year academically—they party too hard, drink too much, get involved with other drugs, or lose themselves in new relationships. But you can avoid that fate with a few easy tips.

- Talk to your advisor about selecting a reasonable schedule for your first year since it's going to be the hardest as far as distractions are concerned.

- Schedule times for homework and study. Treat them as if they were important classes you can't miss.

- Find a place away from phones, TVs, friends, and other interruptions to study. Try the library, or a coffee shop near campus.

- Ignore your friends when they tell you, "You can't miss this tonight! It's a once-in-a-lifetime opportunity and it's your moral imperative to attend this [raging party, insane concert, etc.]."

- Study with friends. Make work social by quizzing each other, reading to each other, and reviewing notes together.

WHAT IF I CAN'T HANDLE THE WORK?

In high school you were in class 25-plus hours a week, whereas in college you'll probably be in class for half of that time. The amount of work needed to keep your grades up might surprise you, though. The keys to handling your workload are organization and prioritization. You will quickly learn which types of assignments require the most attention and which types can be put off. Last minute papers and cram sessions aren't uncommon for first-years (and even some college veterans), but while they might have worked in high school, they're a dangerous gamble in college. Use your time wisely and you won't have trouble keeping up.

If you do run into problems, use the support system available to you. That exorbitant tuition you're paying buys you access to a number of resources. Don't hesitate to talk to your professors, teaching assistants, and/or your academic advisor if you feel that you're unable to handle the workload. It's their job to help you succeed. Take advantage of study groups and peer tutoring—they're another great way to meet people!

How will I choose which classes to take?

And worse, what if I can't decide on a major? It's not easy to decide which courses to take and which major to choose. If you don't know what you want to do after college, select courses that interest you and will expose you to different fields. The average college student changes his or her major at least once, so don't think you're alone in your confusion. Even if you are unsure or later decide that your choice wasn't the best one, you can always discuss a switch in majors with your advisor. Don't forget, your major doesn't have to determine what you do for the rest of your life—it's simply a stepping-stone to help you on your way. Often the key to doing well academically in college is to choose a major in a subject area that you enjoy. Picking a "practical" major isn't always the best choice. If what you're doing is boring you to tears, then most likely you aren't going to try particularly hard to do well. But if your classes interest and excite you it's going to be much easier to excel and stand out in the crowd.

Remember: Most college fears are wiped out during the first week of school. Don't be afraid to try new academic and extracurricular activities—especially ones that you can put on your resume. College may be a challenging and time-consuming endeavor, but it should also be richly rewarding and, ultimately, fun.

CHAPTER 5
BEING QUEER IN THE RESIDENCE HALLS

LIFE IN THE RESIDENCE HALLS

Everyone has to sleep sometime, even college students. And where you choose to sleep (and eat and study) plays a substantial role in the happiness and success of your college experience. These days, schools are investing a lot of dollars into providing some pretty cushy residence hall living (if you don't believe us, just check out the profiles for the schools on our "Dorms Like Palaces" ranking list in the *Best 366 Colleges*!). Some universities also offer residential colleges where cross-sections of like-minded students and faculty function as intimate communities. This is an especially popular option for LGBTQ students interested in living and inter-acting with other LGBTQ students and allies on campus.

In fact, part of the experience of going away to college is the oppor-tunity to establish your independence from your family and from your childhood friends at home by exploring new friendships, interests, and activities. Self-sufficiency is a beautiful thing; it's also a challenge. Fortunately, living on campus makes it easier for you to meet other college students and participate in on-campus activities. Here are some tips to help make your transition to residence hall life as stress free as possible:

- **Tip 1: Keep it real.**

  The summer before your first-year, the housing office will send you a questionnaire about your living and studying habits in order to help match you with compatible roommates. Fill these out honestly! If you're a messy person who likes listening to music at all hours, don't be ashamed to admit it. More impor-tantly, you may want to give some serious thought to disclos-ing your sexual orientation and/or gender identity on the questionnaire, as doing so can help you avoid being paired with someone who will not be accepting of you. Many univer-sities do not ask about sexual orientation in their surveys, so if you feel like rooming with a heterosexual will be problematic for you, contact the Residence Office and explain your situa-tion. While they may not out and out inquire about student's sexual orientation and/or gender identity/expression, they may be very helpful and willing to find you the perfect room-mate. It doesn't hurt to ask! On the other hand, many LGBTQ students never decide to come out on their residence hall floor, although they might be highly visible members of the LGBTQ campus community elsewhere. Whatever you decide to do is okay, as long as you are comfortable.

- **Tip 2: Speak your mind.**

  Get to know your roommate. Even if you're not great friends, you'll be able to get along better if you understand each other. Discuss what you expect from each other. Don't be afraid to tell your roommate if his/her actions bother you. Let each other know when important events (tests, papers, competitions, etc.) are coming up.

- **Tip 3: Know when to shut-up.**

  Yeah, we just told you that you shouldn't be afraid to discuss things with your roommate, but you'll probably be better off if you don't tell your roommate about all of her little annoying habits. Think long term. You're going to have to live with your roommate for an entire school year, so don't nit-pick or judge her on how she acts the first week of school. It takes people awhile to adjust to college life and living with a stranger, so give roommates the benefit of the doubt before criticizing their actions.

- **Tip 4: Look to the future.**

  Decide how you're going to handle financial obligations (e.g. phone bill, groceries) ahead of time so there won't be any misunderstandings when it's time to pay. You should also discuss whether borrowing or using each other's property (food, clothes, etc.) is okay. Establishing boundaries is fine as long as both roommates are aware of them. Many roommates write "roommate contracts" together in order to hold each other accountable for certain respectful behaviors/responsibilities. This is an important and useful way for new roommates to communicate their interests and habits.

- **Tip 5: Establish company policy.**

  Decide whether it's acceptable to bring a boyfriend/girlfriend back to the room. Some roommates may be perfectly fine with the "idea" of your queerness...that is, until the day you begin entertaining a guest and things heat up on the common room couch. Just set up some parameters, open up an honest dialogue, and let him or her know about company ahead of time.

- **Tip 6: Do unto others . . .**

  Whether you like your roommate or not, treat him or her with the consideration that you'd like to be treated with. Set an example and with any luck, your roommate will catch on. Respect their sexual orientation as much as you would like them to respect yours.

- **Tip 7: Give a little.**

  You don't have to subvert your personality to get along with another person, but be prepared to compromise. If you're naturally a slob, you should learn to be neat to the extent that you don't encroach on your roommate's space. If you're a neat freak, remember that your roommate may not be as offended by messiness as you are.

- **Tip 8: Relax!**

  Most roommates naturally figure out how to get along even if they don't become best friends. In the unlikely event that you find yourself in a living situation that's unbearable, you'll probably be able to switch to another room. Talk to your Resident Advisor about your options, should any conflicts arise.

- **Tip 9: Don't tolerate homophobia.**

  It is your right to be yourself and express your feelings, desires, and identity. If you find that your roommate is harassing you, take it to the RA and discuss a plan of action to get yourself into a safe situation.

- **Tip 10: Give yourself, and your roommate, room to grow.**

  Most of you will find that college is a time for exploring a variety of new interests. People change. Just because you may no longer share "everything" in common with your former "best friend" and roommate doesn't mean you can't maintain a civil and mutually supportive relationship. Learn from each other, let go of the little hurts, and keep it moving.

The Role of The Resident Advisor

Say hello to the person who may need to act as your older sibling, your therapist, your guidance counselor, and your confidante. The Residence Advisor, most often known as the "RA," is someone you connect with and feel safe talking to about any concerns you have regarding your housing situation. Other times, he or she may act more like an officer of the law, judge, or jury and call you out on all sorts of behavior inappropriate for the residence halls. In either case, these folks (and fellow students) are there to help guide and support you. Some schools have gone the extra mile to train their RAs on effective ways to support LGBTQ students living in the residence halls. While many RAs will be open-minded and sensitive to your needs, others may not be. If you find that your RA is turning a blind eye or deaf ear to your requests, needs, or questions, go talk to his or her boss—the Dean of Residence Life.

Queer students can also maximize their relationships with their RAs by asking them to identify and publicize the names of individuals within residence life who are knowledgeable about queer or trans concerns and can provide support to these students. If your residence hall has not had a training session on trans or queer issues, try to work with the LGBTQ Center or Student Life office to develop and implement some much-needed training. For more information, educational materials, and tips on ways Residence Advisors can better serve queer students, log onto CampusPride.org/resources.asp.

What Are Gender Neutral Housing and Restrooms?

Most universities assign first-year housing based on a student's birth sex. This can create huge anxieties and problems for transgender and transitioning students. Many colleges are taking the lead on this issue by creating and promoting inclusive housing policies that require all students to be housed in accordance with their gender identity and expression. What does this mean for an incoming transgender student? Primarily, these policies include the possibility of having a single room on a general dorm floor or being housed in special "gender-neutral housing." This might mean turning one floor of an existing dormitory into housing where students of different genders and sexual orientations live openly and safely together. Besides transgender and transitioning students, these floors attract students who may have stated on admissions documents that they have "no preference" for their roommate's gender. Often these accommodations include mixed-gender dorm suites and gender-neutral bathrooms.

Of all the needs of transgender people, finding a safe public restroom ranks as a top concern. "Butch" lesbians and other women with short hair or otherwise "masculine" looks are often stopped from entering or harassed in women's restrooms. As Tony, an FTM living in Connecticut says, "I could never use a public restroom anywhere, ever. If I went into the ladies room, I'd get told to go find the men's room. And I felt apprehensive about using a men's room in case I was identified as biologically female." Women transitioning to male may even get arrested using a women's restroom. Similarly, effeminate men may be unsafe in men's restrooms, and unwelcome in women's rooms. For college students living on campus (or spending large amounts of time there), this is an equally pressing concern. Student and activist groups like "Restroom Revolution" are trying to promote change around this issue. It seems to be having an effect. On college campuses across the country, schools are either switching over previous restroom designations, or creating an increasing number of lockable, single-stall, unisex or "family-style" restrooms. These "gender-neutral" bathrooms are safe, comfortable places for a person of any gender.

It is becoming much more common for campuses to have at least one of these restrooms in each dormitory, and at least one or two in larger classroom buildings. Some schools are even creating gender-neutral changing rooms in athletic facilities. Universities are now publicizing the location of these restrooms on their websites. If you are transgender, it is worth finding out the availability of such facilities at schools you are considering attending. For current information on colleges and universities that offer gender-neutral housing and restrooms, check the website of the Transgender Law and Policy Institute at TransenderLaw.org.

Queer-Tip: Don't Fall in Love with a Roommate!

Whether you're gay or straight, hooking up with someone from your residence hall can be a sticky matter, but we'd be lying if we said it didn't happen all the time. Despite your "can't be contained" attraction to that lacrosse stud across the hall from you who keeps telling you he is "bi-curious," or to the sexy Resident Advisor who always seems to be around when you need to talk to someone, dating in the dorms can sometimes lead to stressful situations if your feelings are not reciprocated. Just ask yourself this question: "If I wouldn't date my neighbor at home, or my teaching assistant, or the cute guy who works the same shift with me at the campus library, why risk dating my roommate or residence hall pal?" Our advice for you: Avoid the drama!

Consortium Tips for Being Queer and Living on Campus

by Camaron Migamota, Coordinator, LGBT and Intersex Student Services at University of Hawaii—Manoa

Residence Life departments should recognize the need to provide a safe and comfortable living environment for all students who live in the residence halls—this includes LGBTQ students. Remember that as you decide which college or university you would like to attend, you have every right to expect that your campus housing will live up to your expectations. Some things that you might look for include:

- **LGBTQ Housing Options:** Many campuses provide themed housing (either a residence hall floor, section of a building, or even entire housing complex) specifically for those interested in having LGBTQ roommates and neighbors. Even if there is not a specific "Rainbow Floor" or "LGBTQ and Ally Building" on your campus, you might look for other types of learning communities that support diversity. Often times, housing that supports diversity might allow for greater opportunities to interact with allies.

- **Gender-Neutral Housing:** Some campuses will make housing assignments without looking at the gender of the student, allowing people of any gender to live together as roommates and share common facilities, such as lounges and restrooms. A few campuses might have an entire wing or floor dedicated to housing that isn't segregated by "sex," while other campuses might allow a student of any gender to live as roommates in "traditional," or sex-segregated housing.

- **Diversity Statements:** Many Residence Life Programs have codes of conduct for their residents that specifically state that acts of violence against or harassment of LGBTQ community members are not acceptable or will not be tolerated. Some might have statements that affirm that every student, regardless of their gender identity or sexual orientation, is an integral part of campus life and the residence hall. Still other will state that they are supportive of transgender students and will work to meet their needs and/or requests in housing.

- **Look at Housing Applications:** Some campuses might have a question on their housing application that lets you indicate that you require an "LGBTQ friendly" roommate. Some applications can indicate how supportive they might be for transgender students or have a section for "Sex or Gender" that allows you to mark, for example, "M", "F", or "TG". Still others will have a line that says "Please indicate your gender" and allows you to fill in the blank.

- **Accommodations for Transgender students:** No matter where you fall on the gender spectrum, you can expect various kinds of support from your campus housing assignment. Many campuses now host unisex restrooms across campus and in the residence halls, and have different practices or policies that are designed to meet transgender student needs. Some campuses have statements of support to work to meet the specific requests of transgender students. Examples of support can include: providing a single room with an adjoining restroom for students who are transitioning/on hormone therapy and feel that privacy is necessary for their safety; assigning a roommate of any gender on a floor designated for either "male" or "female" students; assigning a student a roommate of any gender on a gender neutral floor with an adjoining unisex restroom; making arrangements in a sex-segregated living environment for a student to have access to a unisex or private restroom/shower.

If you are thinking about which college you would like to attend, but unsure about the climate in housing, why not call their department of residence life and ask if they have any of the above housing accommodations? If there are LGBTQ student clubs or a LGBTQ Resource Center on campus, you might consider contacting them as well. Finding supportive living arrangements is an important part of your college experience. You should expect that your campus will act on its commitment to provide a safe and comfortable living environment for all students.

QUEER & CANDID: QUEER STUDENT SHARE
THEIR EXPERIENCES WITH HOUSING

"I think it's good that there is not special housing or ceremonies for LGBTQ students. We don't need to be segregated. We have community through our club and activities and staff who support us, and many LGBTQ and ally students choose to live in the Alternative Philosophy theme house."

Corinne, Sophomore, Knox College

"We have a theme house called the "Pink Triangle"—an LGBTQ resource center within a living/learning community. The house has only been around for 3 years. Once the founders of the house graduated, things have really slowed down. Now there aren't any LGBTQ students living in the house. This is a problem because no one at that resource center has first hand experience with coming out and other LGBTQ issues."

Laura, Junior, St. Lawrence University

"The last time I lived in campus housing I was on an 'all-girls' hall. It didn't go well. I moved off campus junior year and couldn't go back if I wanted to, as there is no housing for transstudents on campus. The closest thing is suite-style living, where 'males' and 'females' can room together, which Res Life insists is adequate for transstudents, even though I would be listed as 'female' and considered only on that basis. There is currently no other option, but Brandeis is working on this."

Marcus, Senior, Brandeis University

Consortium Tips for Dealing with Discrimination and Harassment in the Residence Halls

by Adrea Jaehnig, Founding Director of the Syracuse University LGBT Resource Center

Homophobia is the fear and hatred of lesbian women, gay men, or bisexual individuals. Transphobia is the fear and hatred of transgender individuals or other people who do not conform to societal norms related to gender. Heteronormativity is the pervasive assumption that everyone is heterosexual and that heterosexuality is superior to homosexuality or bisexuality. These fears produce intolerance, discrimination, harassment, and in extreme cases violence, leading LGBTQ students to feel excluded and marginalized on campus. Given the oppression of LGBTQ people in the larger society, there are likely to be students on every campus who live in the residence halls who may act in homophobic, transphobic, and heteronormative ways. What can you do if you experience harassment, discrimination, or don't feel welcomed based on your sexual orientation and gender identity?

If something happens to you, it is always your right to report what happened and you should be supported. The first thing is to make sure you are in/or get to a safe place. Call campus security, and/or someone you trust to let them know what happened or reach out for support. It is good to figure out beforehand what resources are available to you. Likely places where you could find support include your campus LGBTQ Resource Center (if your campus has one), your Resident Advisor and/or Residence Hall Director, and/or the Dean of Students Office. If none of these seem like safe options for you, you may want to confide in a friend or seek support from the Counseling Center. Talking to a counselor would be a safe and confidential way to figure out what you need and what resources are available to you.

While a high percentage of students who experience bias-related behavior do not report these incidents to campus authorities due to fear of further victimization and the possibility of being "outed," reporting homophobic behavior can provide needed support, holding other students responsible for their actions, and leading to the creation of a safer campus climate for others. Some campuses may provide the ability to report bias-related incidents anonymously. Contact the Dean of Students' office or search your college's website to find out how to report such incidents.

Save any evidence of the discrimination or harassment, even if you are unsure if you want to report it. Take pictures of graffiti, save e-mail messages or notes, keep a journal of what was said, when it occurred, and as much information about the person so that they can be identified. Having this information documented will be important if you decide to report the incident at some point in the future.

SPOTLIGHT ON:
JOSH, JUNIOR, GEORGIA STATE UNIVERSITY

"My first year on campus, I didn't know who I was going to be living with and I was extremely nervous. While ready to leave home, I didn't know if I was ready to live with three straight guys. I walked into my apartment-style dorm room shy and intimated; I thought for sure that once I told these guys I was gay they would never talk to me. I couldn't have thought further from the truth. My new roommates accepted me and befriended me for the most part just like they would have any other guy. Of course, they were very macho about the whole thing and one said, as long as I didn't hit on him, he was cool with me, and the other said, he just didn't want to come home and see me making out with another guy on the living room couch. After the initial awkwardness of coming out to them wore off, we all got along very well, and often hung out together watching TV, playing video games, or playing sports. I think the important lesson I learned from living with three straight guys is that being gay is only part of who I am. It doesn't make up everything about me, and it certainly shouldn't isolate me from mainstream society."

LIVING OFF CAMPUS

At many colleges, first-years and sophomores must room on campus, and some schools even require you to live on campus for all four years. However, many students consider living off campus at some point during their undergraduate career. Here is a breakdown of the things you should take into account when trying to decide whether off-campus living is right for you.

- **Considering Costs:** If you rent your own place, you'll have bills for electricity, water, gas, and phone in addition to rent and groceries. Many federal programs let you roll the cost of living into your student aid, so you don't have to front all that cash yourself. (At least, not until you start paying off the loans in four years, but that's another story.) Alternately, many students choose to commute from home, and there's no doubt that staying with your parents is a huge money-saver. Of course, there's a chance that living with your parents is not an option. In this case, the cost considerations you must take into account are compounded with tuition costs. If you are facing such a situation, don't panic. Many universities make allowances for students who find themselves without their family's support. Others do not. Take the bull by the horns and ask your administrators what you can do to help subsidize costs. Be resourceful and look at all your options. If you want to go to college there is always a way.

- **Thinking about Transportation:** This is another major consideration. Do you have your own wheels, or will public transportation get you where you need to go on campus? Will your need for frequent access to facilities like a computer lab or art studio make commuting a drag? Skates and bikes may rule in neighborhoods close to campus, but before you move farther off, remember: It's hard to get a degree if you can't get to class.

- **Assessing Safety:** Safety is another thing to think about when it comes to deciding whether to live off campus. Campus facilities usually have on-site security guards and Resident Advisors whose respective jobs are to watch your back and steer you toward helpful activities and resources. (In fact, by applying to become an RA in your junior or senior year, you can save on your own room and board. Chalk that up under "Costs"!) But safety is an especially important issue for queer college students. The security systems in place for on-campus housing may or may not be available off campus. Ask your administrators or LGBTQ or Student Affairs offices, what type of safety measures are in place for women, minorities, and LGBTQ students, both on campus and off.

There is no escaping the fact that living alone is hard, often lonely, and can be very expensive. Getting the cable and internet bill paid on time, reminding the landlord about a leaking toilet, and figuring out what to cook when you're out of pizza money can be a lot to deal with as you're cramming for that women's studies midterm. Not to mention that when you live alone or even with a few roommates off campus, you will not engage with as diverse a group of people as you will when you live in a traditional residence hall.

On the other hand, if you feel that your campus is unsupportive of LGBTQ students, or that the housing options are not welcoming to your personal growth, transition, or sense of safety, then living alone or with roommates off campus may provide you with the safe space you need to maximize your time and energy during your undergraduate studies. The best way to figure out if living alone is the right option for you is to discuss your concerns with a residence advisor or with someone in the LGBTQ or Student Affairs Offices. They may even be able to tell you about off-campus housing options that will be supportive of your needs.

Choosing between on- and off-campus living can feel like a prize-fight between your inner social butterfly and your introverted hermit. As discussed earlier, campus life entails a ready-made community, and can go a long way toward easing homesickness and boosting your energy and motivation. On the other hand, having your own place, while undoubtedly distancing you from some campus activities, can free you from disruptions and force you to cultivate a social life based more on common interests than convenience. Ultimately, deciding whether to live on or off campus means defining for yourself the kind of atmosphere in which you, as a queer individual, can thrive. While it's important to weigh the pros and cons, you can always try it both ways, too. Unlike your major, you can change residence halls or apartments every year if you want to and still graduate on time.

CHAPTER 6
OUT OF THE CLOSET, INTO THE CLASSROOM

WHAT SHOULD I STUDY?

Today's college students feel a lot of pressure when it comes to choosing a major. The stakes—not to mention tuition expenses—are high. As you deliberate on your major, take a minute or two and think about why you're going to college in the first place. Do you want your college education to prepare you for a specific job? If this sounds like you, then consider a career-focused major like engineering, business, education, or nursing. Your education will be geared toward a specific vocation, and you'll likely take a job in that field when you graduate.

Many students who would be happier in a liberal arts degree program, choose a pre-professional or technical track because of the career assurance those programs are purported to bring. Don't forget that attending college in order to expand your general knowledge is just as valid a reason for enrolling as is attending with a specific career in mind. Generally, in this case you should consider the liberal arts, since these majors emphasize critical thinking, creativity and integration of information, and a variety of other valuable skills that you will use in many, if not most, job settings. Majoring in a field such as history often won't lead you to a specific type of job (how many historians do you know?), but you'll graduate with a slew of marketable and legitimate job skills, and you'll ideally be ready to test the waters in a variety of positions and industries.

As a LGBTQ student, you have the opportunity to approach your studies with an added dimension . . . queerness. Students are now (for the most part) no longer stuck in the academic closet. Over the past 3 decades, changes in academic discourse, shifts in theoretical thinking and scholarship, and progress in the gay liberation movement have created opportunities for LGBTQ students to

"I am an English major with a concentration in creative writing. The best way for me to express myself, and my view on the world, is through my fiction. I'm also attempting a certificate in LGBTQ Studies. Unfortunately, University of Maryland does not have an LGBTQ major. I hope that what I learn from LGBTQ Studies will help in my interpretation and my fiction."

Leisha, Senior,
University of Maryland—
College Park

explore their personal queer experience at college, and figure out how it impacts, informs, or even reconstructs their thinking and research. Being queer doesn't mean that you have to look at everything through a "gay" lens, but it does mean that you will find ample opportunities to at least address your perspective in the classroom and on the campus.

Tips for Choosing a Major

Although everyone ultimately finds their major in their own way, here are some ideas on how to start your search.

First, remember that you're not in high school anymore. College is a whole new ball game, and the subjects you hated in high school might come alive in a college classroom. In other words, don't automatically rule anything out, even if you don't think it's for you. You never know. Take advantage of some of the general education courses you're required to take—don't just pick whatever's easiest. If your college offers several courses that will fit the requirements, try to choose ones that strike an inner chord, even if they also sound more challenging. Once you're in your classes, be aware of what really compels you. Did the lecture in history on Enlightenment philosophers have you on the edge of your seat? Did your ears perk up when your bio professor mentioned the debated origins of life? Set your radar for picking up clues that might be pointing you in new directions.

Bear in mind that "testing" a major by taking a course in that field sometimes isn't the best way of investigating a major. Courses within a major often focus on a specific topic, and if you happen to find that one topic uninspiring, you might rule out the entire field prematurely. Look for introductory courses that are broad enough to paint a clear picture of what the major is like—some colleges offer survey courses for just this reason—or talk to your advisor or the head of the department for reasonable options.

Here are some other tips to get you on the right track:

- Use your college bulletin. Highlight any class that even remotely interests you. Notice any patterns? If you've marked two engineering classes and twenty English classes, well . . . your interests might be clearer than you think.

- Talk to your advisor about possibilities and doubts. That's why they're there.

- Look online to find class syllabi. Do the requirements for the courses in one major seem more palatable than another? If you're drawn to math problem sets over essay assignments, that's another clue to where you might be headed.

- Discuss majors with upperclassmen, like your Resident Advisor. Find out if they're happy with what they're studying and why or why not.

- Talk to professionals in fields you find interesting. Ask them exactly what their jobs entail, how the jobs do (or don't) relate to their college majors, and what those college majors were. Learning about the paths others took to get where they are is often valuable and enlightening, and even more often, surprising.

- Pay attention to your passions! If you love watching independent films, that might mean you'd love making them.

- Investigate courses on gender studies and sexuality offered across numerous academic departments. While not solely focused on queer experiences, these courses may open up a variety of dialogues that you can use to help figure out what major or course of study is most exciting to you.

Your queer identity is something that can be a valuable asset in helping you create dimension and depth to your studies, no matter what they may be. Take a proactive role in exploring possible majors. Remember that no one major is objectively better than any other, and different people are cut out for very different things. Most importantly, your major does not determine your life. You may not know what career you want right now, but give some thought to the general post-college life you want to build for yourself, and that will help guide your decision on choosing a major.

Consortium Tips on Finding Queer or Queer-Friendly Undergraduate Advisors and Administrators

by Jamie Grosser, Assistant Director of LGBT Resource Center, University of California—Riverside

The opportunity to connect with queer or queer-friendly administrators and advisors is one that many lesbian, gay, bisexual, transgender, and queer students search for at some point in their undergraduate career. Though scary and at times difficult, there are ways to be successful in this venture. The key is to take these suggestions and see what will truly work on your specific university or college campus. Factors including campus size, location, type of institution, student population, and queer-supportive policies can greatly affect the climate for queer students and visibility of queer and queer-friendly staff. The process for finding support can vary widely from campus to campus.

Generally speaking it is easier to find queer-*friendly* staff and administrators than queer ones. For reasons encompassing discrimination and lack of institutional support, being out as a LGBTQ staff person is not always safe to do. Two policies that can attract more out queer staff and administrators are:

- Nondiscrimination policies that include sexual orientation and/or gender identity and expression.
- Domestic partner benefits, including health insurance, for same-sex partners of employees of the university.

With policies in place to ensure that out staff can't not be fired on the basis of their identity, and that extend the same benefits opposite-sex partners of employees are offered, the likelihood of finding more LGBTQ-identified staff on campus is greater than on campuses without these protections.

The reality for many students is the need for support at institutions *without* these policies. Regardless of whether your school has these protections or not, there are still many ways to discover and access supportive advisors and administrators. The Consortium recommends looking for these six indicators that a staff person might be queer-friendly:

1. **Participation in Safe Zone and Allies programs.** Many schools have created opportunities for campus members to be visible supports for LGBTQ people through a sign or placard on their office door or cubicle. The placard is an indication of the person's commitment to providing support and resources free from homophobia.

2. **Inclusion on a campus wide "Out List."** Some institutions, whether they have Safe Zone or not, will include a list of either out or friendly staff in school newspapers and newsletters.

3. **Attendance at queer-focused or queer-inclusive programs, speakers, and other events.** An individual's presence at LGBTQ events on campus can speak to that person's commitment to supporting queer students.

4. **Statements of inclusion or diversity in campus offices and departments.** Some campus departments have started to be more proactive in their support of students' multiple identities. Such statements might be online or displayed in a reception area or lounge indicating that the space is meant to include and value all.

5. **The presence of queer posters, images, or other diversity symbols.** Many advisors and administrators will make sure their office spaces include decorations that depict a wide array of diverse people, ideas, and quotations.

6. **Recommendations from other queer students and straight allies.** Often, the best advice can come from a peer. Pay attention to what other students are saying about whom on your campus is supportive of LGBTQ students.

The process of finding queer and queer-friendly advisors and administrators may seem daunting, but these tips can help you find and navigate support from advisors all the way up to the top administrators on campus.

SPOTLIGHT ON:
CARMELLE CASE (LEFT), GRADUATE ASSISTANT FOR THE DEPARTMENT OF GLBT SERVICES, FIRST-YEAR GRADUATE STUDENT, ST. CLOUD STATE UNIVERSITY AND TIMOTHY GARDNER (RIGHT) DIRECTOR FOR THE DEPARTMENT OF GLBT SERVICES AT ST. CLOUD STATE UNIVERSITY

"Being the Director for the Department of GLBT Services and an out professional queer on campus is important to me because it allows students, staff, faculty, and community to know that the GLBTPIQA community has a voice and a place at St. Cloud State University."

GETTING CREDIT FOR THIS! (OR HOW DO I TAKE LGBTQ STUDIES?)

Now that you're off to college you can finally take a variety of classes that were definitely not offered in high school! As a LGBTQ student, you may be interested in taking some courses with lesbian and gay content. Perhaps you want an overview in the history, culture, and politics of the LGBTQ movement in the United States. Or maybe you want to specialize even further, and take classes on AIDS literature, lesbian spirituality, queer cinema, or international gay politics. Where can you find such classes, and how can you officially study gay and lesbian topics at college?

The good news is that there are more than 150 colleges and universities in the United States (and more internationally) offering lesbian and gay studies courses. Some schools offer undergraduate majors and minors in the subject. Schools where LGBTQ studies majors and minors may not be available offer programs in which students can take a concentration of courses in the subject area and receive a "certificate" upon their completion of the course work. Students who take such courses are typically a mixture of queer students, questioning students, and straight students, with the majority being openly gay or lesbian. Often queer students have an advantage in such courses if they have read, thought about, or lived the topics that will be studied. But don't expect that just because there are other LGBTQ students in a class that everyone will have the same opinion on the readings. Potentially controversial topics such as S/M, polyamory, queer theory, lesbian separatism, "outing," religion, and AIDS will likely come up in any introductory class, and will stimulate intellectual debates that can be heated. Overall, these classes are usually a safe space on campus for queer students and a chance to interact with a self-selected group of other students interested in gay, lesbian, bi, and transgender topics.

The bad news is that only a small number of schools actually offer a degree in LGBTQ studies. Chances are, the school you attend or are considering attending won't be one of them. However, there are thousands of LGBTQ-related courses offered across the country at all types of colleges and universities, with plenty of openly queer professors teaching them (and some homo-smart straight professors too). Most of these courses will not be coded specifically as "LGBTQ" in course guidebooks. This is because lesbian and gay studies has developed as an interdisciplinary field of study, incorporating knowledge from a broad range of subject areas including psychology, political science, and literature. Thus, classes of partial or full LGBTQ interest tend to be "cross-listed" between two different departments in a school's course catalogue, especially departments of history, American studies, English, art, anthropology, and African American studies. The other program with which these courses may be cross-listed is Women's Studies, and at most colleges you can get a major in that.

In fact, Women's Studies, or, as it is sometimes called, "Gender Studies," "Sexuality Studies," or even "Women's, Gender, and Sexuality Studies," often acts as the academic umbrella for LGBTQ-focused classes. So if you don't see a concentration listed specifically as Lesbian and Gay Studies in a college brochure or website, search by a keyword such as "gay" or "lesbian" or "queer" in the course catalogue, or look at the program information listed under Women's Studies. Typically, here's where you'll find listings of classes, information on completing an undergraduate major or minor track in LGBTQ studies (within Women's Studies programs), and even tips on how to get a certificate or graduate degree in the subject area.

Some classes may have obvious titles, others are more subtle, but you'll find them if you look. Whether they jump out at you or not depends on the institution, department, or program, and whether the particular professor teaching the course has been asked to "tone down" the title so it won't "out" a student on his or her transcript. As Emory University Professor of American and Women's Studies Saralyn Chesnut explains: "The first time I taught an American Studies course on lesbian history, students asked that I give it a title that did not contain the word 'lesbian,' since their grade reports and transcripts would then include the "L word" and potentially anger their parents or affect future employment opportunities." Therefore, Studies in the History of Human Sexuality could actually be called Queer Sexualities; Introduction to Gender and Sexualities could also be called Introduction to Lesbian and Gay Studies. These are examples of the same course—one title is just more euphemistic than the other.

You don't have to officially be majoring in LGBTQ or even Women's Studies to take some lesbian and gay-themed courses. You can always take a few as electives. It is up to the individual student to understand how such classes fit into their own program of academic study. Check your school's literature on courses of study that may be available in this subject area, and talk to your advisor or the chair of various departments listing such classes. Even if you can't officially major in Queer Studies, with a little luck and good planning there should be room for at least a few LGBTQ classes in your schedule. Most colleges have an introductory class, often now called "Introduction to Lesbian, Gay, Bisexual, and Transgender Studies." Beyond that, a whole world of interesting courses is offered, with every school's selection differing depending on student interest, professorial resources, and administrative support.

So what courses are really out there? Here are some actual recent classes offered at a variety of colleges. Remember, this is just a small sampling, and what you may find will be completely different, and equally as interesting.

- **African American Literature and Queer Theory** University of Colorado—Boulder
- **Art, Sex, and the 1960s** Yale University
- **Black and Queer: Reading the Harlem Renaissance** Yale University
- **Critical Geography: Introduction to Radical Ideas on Space, Society, and Culture** University of Toronto
- **Cultural Representations of Sexualities: Queer Visual Culture** University of California—Berkeley
- **Eros and Education: How Desire Works in School Narratives** Cornell University
- **Gay Histories/Queer Cultures** Indiana University at Bloomington
- **Gender and Sexuality in Chinese Literature** McGill University
- **Gender and Sexuality in Latin America** Duke University
- **Homophobia and Coming Out** San Francisco State University
- **Interpreting Gender in Culture: Women in Sport** American University
- **Introduction to Fashion Theory and Methodology** Yale University
- **Introduction to Transgender Studies** San Francisco State University
- **The Literature of AIDS** Mercer County Community College
- **Masculine Anxiety in Drama and Film** Duke University
- **Psychology of Lesbian Experience** University of California—Los Angeles
- **Queer Knights: The Romance of Lancelot and Galehaut** Wesleyan University
- **Queer Musicology** University of California—Los Angeles
- **Queer Women in Hollywood** University of California—Los Angeles

- **Sex Crimes** City University of New York Graduate Center
- **Sex and Gender in Cross-Cultural Perspective** Indiana University at Bloomington
- **Sexualities: Social, Organizational, and Legal Contexts** University of Toronto
- **Transgender Theory** Princeton University
- **Sexuality in the Classical World** University of Chicago
- **Women and Spirit** University of Kentucky
- **Youth, Gender, and Sexuality** University of Chicago

See Appendix B for a list of the colleges and universities which currently offer undergraduate majors, minors, certificates, and/or concentrations in queer studies.

QUEER-TIP: ONLINE RESOURCES FOR FINDING QUEER-STUDIES COURSES

The following organizations offer countless resources for students and professors looking for information, links and databases on queer-studies courses, seminars, conferences and queer scholarship:

Center for Gay and Lesbian Studies (http://web.gc.cuny.edu/clags/index.html)

National Consortium of Directors of LGBT Resources in Higher Education (www.lgbtcampus.org)

Queer Theory.com (www.queertheory.com/academics/index.cfm)

QUEER & CANDID: LGBTQ Students Share
Stories about their Studies

"I am double majoring in Urban Studies and History. I chose Urban Studies because of its flexibility and interdisciplinary [nature]. I chose History because it is perhaps the most important force in constructing humanity's past and contemporary worldviews. Historiography—the study of writing history—has been enormously influential in vanquishing dominant myths, notably, the inferiority of people of color and women and the danger of the homosexual. I want to be part of that fine tradition of writing a more just history of the world."

Robert, Sophomore, Brown University

"I don't have a major yet, but I want to do something with Journalism, Photography, and Women's/Gender Studies/Sociology. I chose these because Journalism is a practical application for my love of writing, I love photos, and I am very interested in Gender/Queer/Women's Studies and feminism."

Caylena, First-year, Ithaca College

"I have chosen English as my major because I want to teach, and I feel that no other academic subject challenges the intellectual and the thought process as much as English. English pushes students to look at different perspectives in life through reading many different works from an eclectic array of authors. If I can push my students to look at their world in a whole different way, then I can teach them to step into someone else's shoes and understand what that person's life might be like."

Damian, Junior, Brown University

"I have found that the University of Chicago has great resources and a very healthy atmosphere for LGBTQ students. Many faculty members are out and even incorporate gender theory into their classes. Also, the University of Chicago was the first institution in the country to have a Gender Studies Department, as opposed to a 'Women's Studies' Department. I am currently in a Biology of Gender class which became so popular since it was first added to the course list that a second section was added, and enrollment more than tripled. People here are very socially and politically aware and gendered issues are certainly no exception."

"John," Junior, University of Chicago

When Being Queer Is Not On the Syllabus

Increasingly, some students are finding that the climate on college campus is allowing for them to engage in LGBTQ-specific studies and also explore and utilize their unique perspective as queer individuals when it comes to their academic studies. With the rise of sexuality and gender and identity studies and scholarship, an openness about queerness has proliferated at many schools throughout the country. Some schools, like Yale, Columbia, Berkeley, University of California—Santa Cruz and NYU are leaders in fostering progressive thinking and queer-inclusiveness in the classroom, welcoming LGBTQ perspectives and encouraging students to engage in rigorous academic explorations. At more conservative schools, this may not be the case and students may find that academic departments and professors are not too keen on letting LGBTQ students explore their identity in their research. After all, you have to read *Death in Venice* as a work of great German literature or study the basics of psychology before you begin to deconstruct it and apply queer theory (and a more personal) lens.

Even if a more conservative school is not necessarily queer-sensitive or supportive, that doesn't mean enlightening academic discourse about sexuality and gender identity can't happen in the classroom. It is up to you to gauge how "out" you want or need to be in the classroom and in your work. If you feel uncomfortable with your professor, you might want to check in with the advising center, a counselor, or a fellow student who has taken the class before to find out more about the professor's reputation and academic leanings. Unfortunately, being queer will not always be accepted, or even a factor, in your academic situation. If you feel the need to be aggressively queer in the classroom, remember that not everyone will agree with you or understand where you are coming from—even some professors won't get it. But if you engage in class participation and conversations that explore queerness in relevant ways to the course materials, you may find yourself helping fellow students open up to a different perspective, and that is a great thing!

PFLAG PARENT TIP: NOTES FROM THE CLASSROOM: PROFESSORS SPEAK OUT ABOUT THEIR QUEER STUDENTS

Parents may worry how their LGBTQ child will be perceived in the classroom. Will their child find professors who can appreciate their unique perspective and sensibilities? Will he or she feel comfortable being out in the classroom? The answer at most institutions is yes. At some colleges, your child may even be lucky enough to meet a variety of openly gay teachers and teaching assistants as professors and/or advisors.

But how do these professors really feel about their LGBTQ students? Do these teachers think openly LGBTQ students stand out in the classroom? How so? And do they feel a special bond with their LGBTQ students? We asked a mixture of LGBTQ and queer-friendly straight professors at noted universities exactly this question. Their answers should reassure concerned parents.

The good news is that these professors feel a special empathy and appreciation for their LGBTQ students, and welcome the diverse perspectives they bring to the classroom. They can even be allies if they see students grappling with their sexual and gender identity issues at school. After all, in some capacity, they've been there themselves. As award-winning novelist and Professor of Comparative Literature at Yale University, Barry McCrea says, "The classroom environment, with its difficult mixture of private and public personas, its mix of young fears and desires, reminds me again and again how difficult the step of coming out is. Watching and interacting with students in the classroom reminds me that, even though times have changed and my campus is liberal, coming out requires an extraordinary level of bravery and conviction."

Tirza True Latimer, an art historian who has taught at several colleges including Mills, Stanford, and Yale, admits she too watches over her LGBTQ students. "I always feel a special bond with queer students. I admire them for being out, and for continually performing their 'outness' in the successive academic, pre-professional, and social contexts they traverse during their college years. Part of my job, I feel, is to create opportunities for these students to develop their critical thinking skills, because I believe that these skills are absolutely essential for survival, let alone fulfillment."

Other professors find inspiration in the intellectual maturity LGBTQ students may display compared with other students their age. Kenji Yoshino, who has recently taught at New York University School of Law and is the Guido Calabresi Professor of Law at Yale University Law School notes, "I'm always moved by my LGBTQ students. I'm inspired by their engagement with the civil-rights issues of our time." Yoshino says he sees aspects of his own younger self in the students he teaches, and appreciates their passion and perspectives. LGBTQ students, he says, "(H)ave an inspiring independence of thought and action that is a precious resource for any teacher."

Students may feel especially welcome by professors in Women's Studies programs. Whether a student majors in this department or not, classes offered within its parameters can be safe havens for LGBTQ students and their allies. This is because the feminist context of these programs, taught by straight feminist and/or lesbian and gay professors, emphasizes course material and structures of learning comfortable for LGBTQ students. Geetanjali Singh Chanda, a senior lecturer in Women's, Gender, and Sexuality Studies at Yale University, says she finds that "LGBTQ students are academically well informed about contemporary social issues and willing to push the boundaries, constantly questioning the accepted notions of what the majority considers 'normal.' Their ability to frame the personal within the context of an overall theoretical discipline and their sensitive perception of the close interface between the personal and the political self is noteworthy."

Margaret Homans, Professor of English and Women's, Gender, and Sexuality Studies at Yale, agrees. She cites a course she teaches on feminist and queer approaches to literature, in which students study both traditional and revisionist fairy tales. She finds that LGBTQ students are particularly able to identify with alternative visions in such stories like *The Paper Bag Princess*, a book, Homans says, "Where the princess has better things to do than marry the prince." Such students, she says, grow into adults who are "strong, and smart...with the critical tools to take on the institutions of heteronormative sexuality."

Finally, LGBTQ students may find that of all the classes offered on campus, queer studies courses are taught by professors with a vested interest in their welfare. Seth Silberman, an independent scholar who recently taught at Emory University, says "Lesbian, gay, bi, trans, and queer students come to the class with agile anticipation. They remind me of the responsibility queer studies classes carry. More important than any opportunity to reflect sexual identity, these courses generate a safe intellectual space."

It is certainly possible that your child will go through college without ever having a LGBTQ or allied professor. This will depend on the coursework he or she chooses, and the school which they attend. It may or may not even be an issue that feels important to them. However, as a parent, it can be reassuring to know that supportive professors do exist at most schools, and that they indeed have a vested interest in both your child's safety and intellectual growth.

QUEER STUDY GROUPS

There's no easy, fool-proof way to receive straight A's in college. Classes are tough, professors expect to consistently see you put your best foot forward, and the temptation to hang out with your friends in the community instead of hole up in the library has never been stronger, but a healthy balance can be achieved. Because professors know that college coursework is so demanding, you'll find plenty of opportunities to get extra help if you need it—or even if you don't. Take advantage of one-on-one tutoring, review sessions, and extra credit assignments. If you're having trouble, some of your classmates probably are too. And if your professor hasn't already taken the liberty and done so, you should think about forming your own study group.

Queer study groups could be a terrific way for you to explore your identity among other LGBTQ students within a "safe space." Some classrooms will lend themselves to open dialogues about how you engage with the material through your unique experience as an LGBTQ-identified person. Others will not. Participating in a study group comprised of other LGBTQ students may afford you the opportunity to talk about things you can't in the classroom. It may also provide you with a variety of queer perspectives different from your own that can help you get a stronger and more complex grasp on the material you are studying. Check with your LGBTQ Resource Center to find out about queer study groups available on your campus. If you can't find one, start one.

NOTABLE QUEER THEORISTS AND SCHOLARS

"As a Biblical Studies major, I got to take a class in which I read "The New Testament and Homosexuality" which describes why the verses are incorrectly interpreted in light of the culture of the authors' period, and when the decision was made to include homosexuality as being against the school's moral stance, the Hebrew professor spoke up and said that if any student of his simply threw in a citation of certain verse references in a paper, without any argument of why the words should be interpreted that certain way, the student would not pass."

"Randi,"
Senior, Azusa Pacific University

Over the past several decades, the work of "queer scholars" has continued to grow and influence much of the thinking across a broad range of disciplines in higher education. While some of these scholars may or may not be LGBTQ themselves, their work is important in that they explore sexuality and gender in ways that have up until recently not allowed for a queer perspective. Whether or not you plan on pursuing Queer Studies as your major, you might be interested in learning more about these notable and influential thinkers:

- **John Boswell** was one of the most prominent scholars and philologists working in the field of "queer history." Many of his award-winning, yet often controversial, texts explore the roles that gay people and same-sex couples have played in Western tradition and Christianity. Suggested reading: *Christianity, Social Tolerance and Homosexuality* (1980); *Same-Sex Unions in Pre-Modern Europe* (1994).

- **Judith Butler** is the Maxine Elliot professor in the Departments of Rhetoric and Comparative Literature at the University of California—Berkeley. She is a noted post-structuralist philosopher whose work has focused on reexamining and challenging Western feminist thought and the roles that sex, gender, and sexuality play in the construction of identity. Her more recent work has looked at transgender and intersex issues. Suggested reading: *Gender Trouble: Feminism and the Subversion of Identity* (1990); *Bodies that Matter* (1993), *Undoing Gender* (2004).

- **Michel Foucault**, French critic and cultural historian also known as the "Father of Queer Theory," is widely acknowledged as one of the most influential philosophical minds of the twentieth century. His groundbreaking texts on the history of medicine and psychiatry, the socio-political structure of the law and the construction of sexuality are among the most oft-referenced and studied works in academia. Suggested Reading: *The Birth of the Clinic* (1963); *Discipline and Punish* (1975); *The History of Sexuality: An Introduction* (1976).

- **Judith Halberstam** is a Professor of English and the Director of The Center for Feminist Research at the University of Southern California. Among the most prolific and influential of current queer theorists, her work has challenged the notion of the naturalness of male masculinity. A proponent of drag kings and "gender queering," Halberstam's most recent work has focused on queer subcultures and the displacement and disruption of heteronormative constructs as defining factors in gender and sexuality. Suggested reading: *Skin Shows: Gothic Horror and the Technology of Monsters* (1995); *Female Masculinity* (1998); *The Drag King Book* (1999); *In a Queer Time and Place: Transgender Bodies, Subcultural Lives* (2005).

- **Audre Lorde,** African American activist, post-colonial critic and innovative poet, was one of the pioneering lesbian thinkers of the 1970s and 1980s. In both her essays and poetry, she encouraged black women of different sexualities to come together to fight for social and political change. Some of her most notable work examines the way black lesbians are stereotyped by the white community, as well as by the black community. Her groundbreaking 1982 memoir, *Zami: A New Spelling of My Name* is a seminal work of lesbian writing and considered the first "biomythography," a fusion of history, biography, and mythology. Suggested reading: *Man Child: A Black Lesbian Feminist's Response* (1978); *Zami: A New Spelling of My Name* (1982); *I Am Your Sister: Black Women Organizing Across Sexualities* (1985).

- **Eve Kosofsky Sedgwick,** a Distinguished Professor at the City University of New York's Graduate Center, is one of the leading "queer theorists" of the past 25 years. Though influenced by feminism, psychoanalysis, and other schools of thought, her academic writing uses a variety of literary and theoretical approaches to address how race, gender, and sexuality inform our culture. Suggested reading: *Between Men: English Literature and Male Homosocial Desire* (1985); *Epistemology of the Closet* (1991); *Touching Feeling: Affect, Pedagogy, Performativity* (2003).

Consortium Tips for Queering Your Work and Expressing Yourself

by Saralyn Chestnut, Director of the Office of LGBT Life, Emory University

Most lesbian, gay, bisexual, and transgender college students would agree that few things are more affirming than to have their identities—their *lives*—recognized in the classroom. After all, for many decades LGBTQ lives were rarely mentioned in public, even by those who lived them. In academic settings, if these lives were acknowledged at all, it was only as examples of social/sexual pathologies or mental disorders.

However, in the academy as in society as a whole, the silence has been broken definitively over the past 15–20 years. Like African American Studies and Women's Studies before it, LGBTQ Studies is a thriving academic field of study, generating new theories, bodies of knowledge, and perspectives. LGBTQ students now have the opportunity not only to take courses in LGBTQ/Queer Studies, but also to incorporate queer perspectives in the papers they write, the class presentations they give, or the research they conduct.

For LGBTQ students, courses in LGBTQ/Queer Studies offer the best opportunity to express themselves in the classroom and in their work, as well as to learn more about themselves as LGBTQ people. However, for a number of reasons it can sometimes be hard to identify LGBTQ/Queer Studies courses. For one thing, the field is inherently interdisciplinary, including work in the humanities, social sciences, physical sciences, law, medicine, theology, and public health. Therefore, depending on their focus and scope, Queer Studies courses may be taught in an English department, an interdisciplinary program like American Studies or Women's Studies, or any number of other academic departments or programs.

Another difficulty in identifying LGBTQ Studies courses is that their titles use such a variety of terms, due in part to the interdisciplinary nature of the field, and in part to the variety of ways in which the subject of a course may be described. A history-oriented course may be titled History of Sexuality, for example, or instead of LGBTQ Studies, a course could be called Studies in Gender and Sexuality. Finally, sometimes LGBTQ Studies course titles are intentionally vague and general.

For students who are not fortunate enough to have LGBTQ/Queer Studies courses offered on their campuses, all is not lost; since LGBTQ/Queer Studies encompasses so many disciplines, it is possible to do work in the field in virtually any academic discipline. This also means that upper-level students who have used up their elective courses and must now take only courses required for their major can still focus on LGBTQ/Queer issues.

QUEER-TIP: GET YOUR QUEER SCHOLARSHIP PUBLISHED!

Queer is the only intercollegiate undergraduate journal dedicated to critical discussion around what it means to be queer. An international online and print publication with editors at nearly 20 undergraduate institutions across the United States and Canada including University of California—Berkeley, Texas A&M, Dartmouth, Duke, Barnard, and Rutgers, it is designed and operated through Campuspride.net. *Queer* is distributed to over 100 schools nationwide and makes its entire content available online.

For more information on how to submit queer-themed papers or read up on what other young LGBTQ scholars are writing about, log on to Queer-Journal.com.

OUT AND ABOUT: SHOULD QUEER STUDENTS THINK ABOUT STUDY AROAD?

Study abroad is a process that takes you out of your comfort zone to challenge you at every turn. Nothing else in college life so totally affects your knowledge, values, notions of self, or your social awareness. Students who study abroad undergo rapid change in how they view things, but they don't just ditch everything they learned up to this point: They blend the old with the new, arriving at new understandings, new habits, and more sophisticated attitudes and beliefs. Frequently, they even return home with a better idea of the direction they want to take in life.

Depending on the study abroad program, your course load may resemble one similar to what you'd be taking back at school, or it may be very different. Instructors may teach in English, the national language, or both. A few programs may even encourage you to take a part-time job during the semester for an added dimension to your experience. Many study abroad programs present an opportunity for students to live with local families and face the challenges of a foreign-language environment while learning the language and culture of their destination country. Remember that not all families may understand, welcome, or tolerate a queer individual. It is important to find the right homestay to make your trip a fruitful and safe experience. Talk with the program coordinator about these issues and ask whether you will be comfortable being "out" in your study abroad situation.

Whatever the specifics of your particular program of interest, there are a few common factors that every student considering studying abroad should consider:

- **The cost factor:** The first question many students and parents want to know about study abroad is, "Can I afford it?" Schools differ in how they charge for study abroad. At most schools, the cost of the study abroad program is equivalent to tuition charges for that semester. Your room and board costs abroad may be included in the total program cost or left for you to pay on site. Either way, housing (not to mention books, local travel, and other personal costs) is a legitimate study expense, and therefore eligible for financial aid. But it is usually not the charges for tuition and room and board that can drive up the cost of study abroad: It is the very manageable cost of independent weekend entertainment and travel. Investigate the cost of living in your destination country beforehand. If it is significantly higher than back home, you will have to plan carefully to keep costs down. In the many countries where costs are lower, your money will go further.

- **Finding a program:** Find out what your school's study abroad recommendations are. The most trouble-free options (in the bureaucratic sense) will be those already approved by your school. If your school doesn't offer a program that you're interested in, you should start looking online for other options. The Institute of International Education (www.iie.org) is a good place to start. Once you know the options that will be acceptable to your school, decide how much independence you need. Some programs arrange virtually everything for you, from group flight to medical services to credit transfer. At others, especially the direct enrollment schools, much of the initiative (and work) is left to you. Some of the best programs are in places you may never have heard of. Paris, London, and Tokyo are common destinations, but do you know Strasbourg? Swansea? Chiang Mai? Lesser-known destinations can also be good study abroad sites. Don't make your final program selection until you have spoken with your parents, advisor, and fellow students about your options.

- **Safety concerns:** For the purpose of student safety, it's often wise to try to blend in with the local population. Lack of knowledge or respect for local traditions, customs, and practices can make you stand out in a negative way. Make an effort to respect local customs when it comes to dress and behavior, especially in locations where American visitors are less common. Openly LGBTQ students traveling abroad must take responsibility for their safety. A program advisor or professor can only shield you from so much. Some countries will be very anti-gay, while others will be very liberal and have thriving queer scenes and support systems. It is up to you to decide how "out" you can be within the environment you find yourself. One of the best preventative measures you can take is to read travel guides or websites about the cultural climate of your destination country.

Though it's not all adventure, study abroad is "worth it" in every sense. You'll learn to manage linguistic confusion, homesickness, and the awkwardness of sticking out in a crowd. You'll mature into a competent world citizen ready to play an important role in today's global society. Employers eagerly recruit candidates who speak another language, have traveled extensively, or understand the unwritten rules of operating in another culture. Graduate schools are similarly global in their interests, and they favor students who have familiarity with other parts of the world. For the right student, study abroad can be an incredibly rewarding experience.

PFLAG Parent Tip: Studying Abroad: Parents' Concerns

Parents of LGBTQ students considering studying abroad have many of the same concerns that all parents do. They wonder what the experience will be like for their child, how they will stay in touch with their child, where their child will be living, and what their child will do when they're not taking classes. Yet, the biggest worry for parents is always whether their child will be safe, and this can be amplified when a child is LGBTQ identified.

Students who are LGBTQ may also worry about how they will adjust to their host country, and whether they can be out and find other openly gay people to hang out with. Lis Maurer, Coordinator of the Center for LGBT Education Outreach and Services at Ithaca College, says that students and parents need to consider several basic questions about studying abroad.

The first is how open their child can be about their sexual orientation and gender identity with teachers, peers, friends, and host family in the destination country. This can vary widely, even in gay-friendly countries and cities. As Yale student Charlie Cardinaux explains, "I had no problems being gay in Paris, but I had not anticipated feeling awkward about coming out to my host family. I decided not to, mostly because I felt I couldn't gauge how they would react. But most people's host families that I knew of tried not to pry too much into their students' lives and mine definitely respected my privacy."

On the other hand, Yale student Andrew Dowe, who also studied in Paris, said: "I was completely 'out' to my host—I explicitly requested that my program place me with a host that was not only tolerant but queer-positive. Being comfortable at 'home' while abroad is really an essential part of enjoying the study abroad experience."

Other questions parents should ask themselves include how important it is for their child to find other sexual minority students and friends while abroad? In addition, they should ask how their child will make connections with others regardless of sexual orientation or gender identity in their host country, and do research beforehand to find out what the local attitudes and laws regarding LGBTQ people are. Says Maurer, "Every place in the world has different policies and cultural attitudes towards LGBTQ people, and the people who are perceived to be [LGBTQ]." Yale senior Arianna Davalos, who also studied in Paris, agrees and advises, "Pick your destination wisely. Blending into a culture that is not tolerant of homosexuality can be oppressive and dangerous."

Besides being safe as a gay person, women will also need to know if there are special considerations or safety factors that they need to consider. Even in the most queer-friendly cities, women may still get harassed or intimidated, and should be prepared to deal with this. As Dowe pointed out, "Although safety in Paris hasn't been an issue for me as a gay man, the concept of 'sexual harassment' is quite different here, and I would advise women that they will probably be harassed if they walk alone at night."

Even when safety itself is not an issue, being out as a lesbian might be an issue. As Jennifer Lewis, a current Yale graduate student who spent time studying abroad in Costa Rica while an undergraduate at Bryn Mawr, remembers: "The transition from the small progressive liberal arts college to the world of Latino culture and machismo appeared daunting." In order to be comfortable there, she says, it was necessary for her "to live a dual life, one in which my host family and program professors considered me a straight student of tropical ecology and another in which I had access to dance clubs, cafes, and LGBTQ nonprofit outreach organizations in the capital city." However, said Lewis, since she "quickly learned that the assumption within this culture is that women are always straight, there was limited explaining that I had to undertake with Costa Ricans when identified as a student of biology."

Indeed, study abroad peer counselor Amy Curran of Mills College says that queer students researching study abroad programs tend to consider not only location, but "how their identity will be impacted in that location." She says that students do "choose specific locations, such as London or Amsterdam, in order to go where they believe the community will be thriving and they will have an opportunity to get involved." She says, the number one concern of LGBTQ students studying abroad, "is how the student will fit in socially. They want to know if other queer students have gone to that destination before, if they will have a community once abroad, if the university has clubs abroad of groups for queer students, and how they will be treated by their host country in general."

As Yale student Justin Ross reports, "I chose to study abroad in Copenhagen, Denmark. I enjoyed being in a very liberal place. Denmark was the first country to offer civil union benefits to same-sex couples. Many of my friends studied abroad in other big cities in Europe and had similarly rewarding experiences, academically, personally, and socially." Another popular destination for gay students is Paris, which Dowe remembers fondly: "Exploring the difference in thought at my university here, exploring the city, meeting French people, and learning about French culture have all made my experience in Paris one of the most amazing of my life."

Besides Europe, study abroad programs can take students into areas not necessarily known for their gay-friendly environs. For example, China only officially de-criminalized homosexuality a few years ago, and an awareness of gay rights is still forming amongst its people. "Even so," says Yale's Ross, who also studied abroad in China, "I enjoyed my experiences in China immensely. I was able to make friends with my fellow study abroad students as well as some of the local students. While I was initially a little bit more guarded than in Denmark, I found that homosexuality in the Chinese context was viewed with a sense of curiosity and novelty that was almost refreshing. I explored some of the gay bars in Beijing, and went to the sixth anniversary of the first gay bar in that city! I feel that because of my sexuality I had a unique opportunity to gain insights at a very pivotal moment for the acceptance of gay people in China. Furthermore, I made a host of friends that I still keep in touch with and I am hoping to go back to do some research in China on the importance of peer education by homosexual organizing groups in China on HIV/AIDS."

Curran says that safety is indeed a concern among students and parents, but assures worried parents that study abroad offices and their affiliated programs "will do everything in their power to ensure that students are informed and prepared for their host country's particular safety issues." Curran also says that she would "never advise a queer student to avoid any location. I think it's important queer students do not feel their options are limited because of their sexuality." Lis Maurer concurs: "Many LGBTQ students let a lot of concerns keep them from even considering going abroad. If I could suggest one thing, it would be that students spend some time getting answers to their questions instead of assuming it just wouldn't work for them."

Trans students should also be aware of a few extra considerations, says Maurer. They should be prepared for the reality of potentially needing medical supplies and/or services, and the potential hassles of obtaining them. "A big issue was hormones and how to get them to her," said Alice, mother to a transitioning MTF student. "Legally she could take in one month's worth but she was there for four so after the first month I sent them by mail." Transgender students presenting differently than the gender on their birth certificate or passport should be aware that this might cause hassles or interrogation when crossing borders or with police. Such students should carry extra documentation with them as a backup, and the number of someone to call locally if they are detained.

Maurer hopes this doesn't discourage transgender students from considering studying abroad. "I'd encourage students and parents to see these not as barriers, but as important themes for exploration and discussion during the decision-making process." "Joan," Florida mother of MTF Tracy, agrees: "She spent two summers in Spain as an exchange student with no problems. She also went to Australia and said it was the best time of her life. I would highly recommend that being trans not stop any student from studying abroad. Just make the program aware of your status before you leave the country so if there is a problem they know how to deal with it."

Here is what some other parents had to say about their LGBTQ child's study abroad experience:

"My daughter studied abroad in New Zealand—it was a good experience for her, and I would let her do it again."

"Molly," New Hampshire

"My son studied abroad in Portugal. His experience was wonderful, except that he couldn't come out because he felt his host family wouldn't be supportive. It was hard on him to hide that for a whole school term."

"Denise," Oregon

"One of my daughter's dear friends, who also happens to be a lesbian, had a fabulous study abroad experience in Fiji, where she happened to meet her current girlfriend."

"Patricia," New Hampshire

PFLAG PARENT TIP

CHAPTER 7

QUEERING THE CAMPUS: LGBTQ SUPPORT NETWORKS AND ACTIVISM

What is a LGBTQ Campus Resource Center?

Tom Bourdon, the Assistant Director of UCLA's Lesbian, Gay, Bisexual, Transgender Campus Resource Center notes that "For many students, an LGBTQ center feels like home away from home. These centers are meant to provide a space where no one is judged. We don't check for 'gay cards' at the door. An LGBTQ center is a place to feel comfortable just being yourself, where you can respectfully ask and answer questions to which there are no 'wrong' answers. People come to make new friends or catch up with old ones. Some stop by to eat lunch, do homework, talk to a staff member, report a problem, use a computer, grab free condoms, or just get a hug. The more a center is able to provide, the more reasons people have to come in for a visit!"

> "There are tons of resources for GLBTQA students at Carleton! Whether someone wants an outlet for coming out, to participate in activism, or read up on queer/identity issues, the resource exists. If something does not yet exist the school makes it easy to develop new programs and events or offer other resources."
>
> Robin, Senior, Carleton College

Today, many schools provide LGBTQ Resource Centers on campus. Obviously the presence of these centers can be an important factor in gauging how supportive your school is of queer campus life. However, just because a school does not have an LGBTQ Resource Center on campus does not mean you should automatically assume that the campus environment is unwelcoming to queer students. Whether or not your school has designated resources for LGBTQ students, there are things you can do on campus to create and improve support networks for LGBTQ students. In the process of pursuing these initiatives and helping to lend visibility to the LGBTQ campus community, many college students find their queer identity. This chapter will hopefully provide you with tips and suggestions on how you can get involved, and features some candid words of support from queer student leaders.

QUEER & CANDID: STUDENTS RECALL FIRST CONTACT WITH THE LGBTQ CAMPUS GROUP

"The LGBTQ resource center is well-run at Carnegie Mellon. Students work with the office of Student Affairs to ensure that LGBTQ programming is offered. We have 'OUTSpoken' talks (which have topics ranging from being gay and in a fraternity to addressing transgender issues). The resource center has office hours held by the LGBTQ Issues Intern and anyone who is SafeZone trained who wants to hold office hours. It is stocked with relevant books and movies as well as safer-sex supplies and information. The LGBTQ Issues Intern also coordinates our recognition of the National Day of Silence, National Coming Out Day, and Pride Month. Two student groups, Out and Allies, run events like the National Coming Out Day Dance, movie nights, and trips to the local popular LGBTQ club."

Stu, Senior, Carnegie Mellon University

"While initially the transition to college was kind of hard, I've gotten a lot more comfortable on campus now. I had always imagined college as some sort of 'lesbian utopia' and while I knew that Olin wouldn't be that way, I hadn't quite let go of that dream. Since Olin is a very small school, the gay population is obviously not that large either. Fortunately, after getting over that initial disappointment, I've been able to appreciate all of the positive support that exists on campus for the queer community."

Casey, First-year, Frankin W. Olin College of Engineering

"While there is no LGBTQ Resource Center at Columbia, there is an amazing LGBTQ support structure in place through the Office of Multicultural Affairs. There is an LGBTQ advisor that works within the Office of Multicultural Affairs who attends to the needs of the LGBT students and student groups on campus and is our greatest administrative ally. Columbia was actually the first university in the world to officially recognize an LGBTQ student organization in 1967. The organization was called the "Student Homophile League" and it was so scandalous that the *New York Times* printed an article on its front page about it. The LGBTQ student rights movement really began here at Columbia."

Peter, Sophomore, Columbia University

Consortium Tips on Creating Campus Support Groups

by Daniel Coleman, Program Coordinator, LGBT Student Support Services, Indiana University—Bloomington

The existence of a campus LGBTQ support group is more powerful than you can imagine. By providing a medium for resources, connections, and help it is valuable to everyone in the community. Your support group will be seen as a safe haven for people who are closeted and as a symbol of pride for others. As you are creating your campus support group, consider the potential impact and positive outcomes of the work you will be doing. Most importantly, understand that all of your decisions and actions will affect your new group, so be certain before taking action.

Beginning a campus LGBTQ support group requires momentum and one or more dedicated student leaders. Student-led initiatives are the most powerful and effective movements at a university. This is because students know exactly what support and opportunities they need, which can often be overlooked by their institutions. But remember that universities are businesses whose goal is to provide students with an education and diverse experience that will ensure their personal growth and future success. Most importantly, students offer fresh perspectives and intimate understanding of their demographic's concerns. In most cases students will need help with direction and focus, have a faculty or staff advisor by your side as you move forward in this exciting new endeavor. The advisor will provide support, mentoring, direction, and a valuable link to the administration and other faculty.

What will be the benefit of this support group for your campus? Have this answer in the front of your mind as you move forward. The benefit may be too difficult to measure at first, but knowing where you can anticipate results is very important. By understanding the benefit of your support group and establishing a clear set of goals, you'll be able to keep track of the big picture.

Goals will help you track your progress and growth. Start simple, and let them evolve into more complex aims. Remember: It is more important to accomplish milestones than it is to be the best in the world. Your milestones will be your group's very first meeting, the first social event, obtaining an office, reaching anniversaries (i.e. Year One, Five, etc.). As your group develops, you need to allow for change and growth. You should always think forward and only look back for guidance.

Determining simple concepts like the organizational structure of your group will help provide a solid reference for future initiatives. The importance of defining who runs the group, how and when it meets, and other such organizational matters will help ensure a smooth operation. Creating and using a constitution that states the group's mission will allow you to structure your organization, define its membership, and set goals for meetings and other events that will create a clear identity and purpose for the group.

After developing these "blueprints" for your group and holding your first meeting, it is time to let go and enjoy the ride. Your focus should always be in front of you, as you look ahead to accomplishing your next predetermined goal. There is no one way to create your LGBTQ support group. Focus on coming up with the blueprint, think positively and proactively, and remember to keep track of the goals and benefits.

QUEER CAMPUS LEADERS SPEAK OUT

The new generation of out campus leaders is here. With such intelligent, diverse, and impassioned student leaders at the helm, the future of LGBTQ activism is in good hands. While on campus, queer students may be responsible for a variety of positions and responsibilities, most often as unpaid volunteers. These include running hotlines, staffing queer resource centers and info tables, holding activities for Coming Out Day and World AIDS Day, organizing protests, events, and social activities, welcoming LGBTQ first-years to campus, and becoming "queer peers" to their fellow students. Student activists also are an important link between the student body and the administration. They know what the concerns of their fellow students are, and quite frequently can spur change on campus. At many colleges this has included working towards obtaining more services for transgender students like gender neutral restrooms and housing. Luckily, the full range of what students can become involved in is as limitless as their imagination.

As University of California—Irvine graduate student Emma Heaney says, "My advice to LGBTQ students who are entering college is this: It's your responsibility to contribute to an environment in which everyone is fully safe and heard. If your college or university doesn't have the course offerings you need, agitate for them. Make sure that queer professors, university administrators, and staff get the same partner benefits that their hetero-colleagues do. If there are buildings without bathrooms that are safe and accessible to trans students, it is all of our responsibilities to do something about it. Participate in all groups that represent those whose needs are not being met in the same way that those of their white, straight, male, able-bodied counterparts are. If there is an event addressing issues of sexual assault on campus, gay men better be there. If there is a forum to address concerns of students and faculty of color, it is not just the responsibility of queers of color to show up."

Many students find a home on campus for their activism through their school's Lesbian and Gay Resource Center or LGBTQ Student Co-op. Arianna Davalos, a senior at Yale University says, "I think it's safe to say that about half of what I learned in college I learned running the LGBTQ Co-op. If I hadn't thrown the parties, organized the meetings, talked to the administration, asked the alumni for money, or trained peer counselors and all the other crazy stuff I did, I wouldn't have learned all of the skills I needed to do all of those things. When you think it's important and you want to make it happen, you learn fast. This, I think, is one of the biggest rewards I got out of it." Justin Ross, a senior who was her fellow Co-op co-chair agrees, "When I got to Yale, I very quickly became involved with the LGBTQ Co-op. Over five semesters of running the Co-op I learned more and more about social organizing, the diversity within the queer community and also the difficulties of appealing to such a broad audience. Through academics, extracurricular activities, participation in the Co-op and just discussions with the diverse group of friends I made, I was able to learn a lot more about the personal and public roles of sexuality. In other words, even though I was already 'out' when I came to campus, I still learned a lot about my own sexuality and developed and refined my personal understanding of sexuality."

Columbia University sophomore Peter Gallotta has also found that his student activism played a rewarding part of his college career. "I help run most of the LGBTQ events on campus because I'm the Vice President of the Columbia Queer Alliance and also the President of the Queer Awareness Month Committee. I am very much involved and am very much exhausted from being so, but I love it. I think I have helped change the LGBTQ experience at Columbia because I have strived to make our events more celebratory and more visible to the greater community. Queer Awareness Month, which takes place each October, is really the greatest time when we do this. We're really changing minds and getting ourselves out there. What I always used to say is that the LGBTQ community at Columbia was present, but did not have enough presence. We're definitely changing that! It's really exciting."

Other students find that their motivation to become activists comes from a lack of current resources at their school. As "LE," a junior at St. Lawrence University, says, "I identify as queer/lesbian. Everyone who knows me, or everyone I am friends with, is cool with this. If we want to start up a long-lasting LGBTQ Resource Center, we're going to need some motivated LGBTQ student leaders. I'm sick of a repressed LGBTQ student population and heteronormativity. I can't be silent anymore." Zachary Morrison, a junior at Loyola University in Chicago concurs, "I am a member of the GLBTQA organization on campus, and I am helping to plan a conference this summer for 28 Jesuit colleges and universities' GLBTQA leaders. It is very important in this day and age to get involved, to fight for your rights, and to show that we, as GLBTQ people, are no different from anyone else. We fight for the right to marry, the right to love, and the right to be people, equal in the 'Land of the Free and Home of the Brave.' I get involved because the issues facing our community are too important for one to sit on the sidelines. We must stand up and be heard."

Student activists are indeed finding that college administrators are hearing them, and are welcoming a broader spectrum of diversity onto campus. As William Nguyen, a Yale University junior observes, "You don't hear too much about gay Asians at university now do you? Asians in the Ivy League—sure, there are plenty. But gay ones? As of high school, I had yet to meet anyone quite like myself, and I intended to take full advantage of my 'unusual' gay and Asian combo. I believe that not only did this give me a leg up in the admission process, it provided me with many leadership opportunities on campus." Transgender students, too, are increasingly making their voices heard. A growing number of schools now have organized transgender groups, and many students are willing to take leadership positions in them. Greg Sensing of Simmons College says, "As a transman, I was asked by a student group to sit on a panel discussion on the subject of transgender students at our small women's college. I think it was really good for the administrators to hear first-hand from those closest to the issue, those most directly affected."

Whether it means working towards social change or bathroom equity, increasing the number of queer studies courses or protesting homophobia, sexism, and racism on campus, staffing information tables or assisting fellow students in the coming out process, LGBTQ students make a difference with what they do, everyday. Many students find that working as campus activists may even be as rewarding as their classes, and they can take the skills and experiences they gain out into the wider world after graduation.

SPOTLIGHT ON:

LAUREN, SENIOR, MICHIGAN STATE UNIVERSITY, POINT FOUNDATION SCHOLAR

"For the last four years, I have been very active in LBGTAQ issues on campus. My freshman through junior years, I was on the executive board of my dorm's queer caucus, PRISM. PRISM was mostly an emotional and social support network for students who were newly out on campus. After being elected to the executive board, I helped to plan and facilitate meetings, making sure to include meetings about bi and trans identities, as well as on safe sex. My second through fourth years, I also worked with the political arm of the queer movement on campus, the Alliance of LBGT Students. My third year, I was elected Chair of the Alliance, and I brought ally relations and queer visibility to the top of the group's agenda. I also made sure that leadership skill building, racial/ethnic integration of the e-board, and consensus-style decision making was emphasized.

During my fourth year, I raised awareness about an upcoming ballot initiative in Michigan to ban affirmative action and helped to make sure that the Alliance was duly represented in the fight to block the initiative. Through my involvement with MSU's Student Government and the Alliance, I was also elected to chair Michigan state's Second Ad Hoc Committee on Gender Identity, the university task force that was compiled to outline the impact that the addition of gender identity to MSU's anti-discrimination policy will have on campus. It is important to mention, though, that I could not have helped to accomplish any of this without the time and effort exerted by my fellow MSU queer activists. Michigan State University has a very out, active, talented queer population. Without MSU's supportive atmosphere and proud queer students, I never would have become the queer campus leader I am today.

Still, I feel that my contributions to the queer and progressive causes on campus are specifically needed, because I am a face of the typically non-represented bisexual community within MSU's queer community. Although LGBTQ students all have a strong presence at MSU, it is often the "B" that is underemphasized. My efforts, along with those of several other bi activists on campus and advice from staff in MSU's Office of LBGT Concerns, are working to change that. Our goal is to 'mainstream' bi identities in both the queer and straight communities by coming up with innovative ways to increase bi visibility."

QUEER & CANDID: Students Share Their Thoughts about Creating Campus Support Groups

"Our LGBTQ/queer campus club, Open, is one of the most active and well-respected clubs on the Olin campus. We find that targeting our events towards everyone on campus—people of all sexualities and gender identities—is very helpful in uniting our campus together in acceptance and tolerance."

Casey, First-year, Franklin W. Olin College of Engineering

"As a very small, Methodist school in the Midwest, it's no surprise that there aren't LGBTQ resources. On the other hand, I don't feel that we should get special treatment (as far as a separate graduation or something) as long as people in the school and community are accepting. For me, I am surrounded by accepting people which makes my experience a lot easier."

Rebeka, Junior, University of Evansville

"There is not an abundance of resources [at Calvin College]. There is, however, a confidential group that meets to support LGBTQ people, and offers a safe environment for discussion. This is led by one of Calvin College's counselors, who has pointed others and me in the direction of pertinent literature and information (because our college does not carry any information like that). Calvin College also just started an organization (B.E.T. Broene Educational Team) whose focus is to raise awareness about sexual orientation in a community-focused, respectful way."

"Roger," Junior, Calvin College

"We have a strong enough support system among the students that we really don't have a need for school-sponsored resources. However, the administration knows that we have a large LGBTQ population and doesn't do anything to discourage that."

Wayne, Senior, Cornell University

Consortium Tips on Creating LGBTQ Resources on Campus When Your School Is Unsupportive

by David Kessler, Coordinator of the Allies Program, The University of Texas at San Antonio

Students may choose a college or university for numerous reasons, but they don't always consider what it means to be lesbian, gay, bisexual, transgender or queer on campus when it comes to making this choice. Factors such as culture, locale, or religious affiliation can lead the campus to have a challenging atmosphere. First, LGBTQ students must realize that they are not alone. Even when a campus seems unwelcoming, remember that there are other students out there just like you who are also seeking resources that will help them discover and find comfort in their sexual and gender diversity. In addition to these peers, there are LGBTQ staff and faculty, as well as other student, staff, and faculty allies, who believe that resources including student groups, a Safe Zone or Allies program, and a sexual orientation and gender identity center should exist on campus.

The process of establishing these resources at this type of institution requires energy and passion for a journey that takes time and effort. Some things you should consider doing are:

- Form a network with individuals who represent the many facets of campus. Students can have a strong voice as they compose the majority on a campus, yet a critical mass that includes faculty and staff amplifies the power of this voice. The strength in numbers will also allow for a greater number of strategies to advocate effectively for change.

- Find a mentor who can guide you through the process of establishing resources and making change. Members of the faculty and staff, like a Dean of Students or faculty council representative, can help queer students and their allies understand the process of decision-making on campus.

- Connect the ideas to the mission of the college or university. Communicating a message that ensures resources will match the academic goals and institutional values serves to increase the acceptance of LGBTQ initiatives. Also, it is necessary to consider the long range needs to make these resources possible, including funds and space, and to be knowledge-able about sources for this support.

- Use campus media (newspapers, radio, television) and other outlets to bring attention to the lack of resources to a wider audience that can also help advocate for change.

Most importantly, you'll need perseverance, as this process may take months or years with progress coming in incremental steps. Advocacy and activism by queer students and their allies have proven successful at many institutions. A collaborative, informed, and continuous movement makes change possible so that resources are created to ensure that future LGBTQ students enjoy the same academic and campus life as others. For this journey, keep in mind that many campuses continue to make positive advances in enhancing lesbian, gay, bisexual, transgen-der and queer student life, and this can happen anywhere.

QUEER & CANDID: STUDENTS DISCUSS CAMPUSES WITH FEW LGBTQ RESOURCES

"We do not currently have a student health center, but one will be opening in fall of 2007, and student groups such as the Student Health Advocacy Group are pushing to make sure this center addresses the needs of LGBTQ students."

Ellen, Junior, Knox College

"Our school has a Gay Straight Alliance group, but other than that there isn't much for the LGBTQ community at our school because we are a Catholic college and it is against their principles."

"Paul," Junior, Mercyhurst College

"Religious school = no LGBTQ resources, unfortunately."

"Lisa," Junior, Manhattan College

"With DePauw being so conservative and an 'old boy's club,' finding ways to express your sexuality can be hard. Also, the number of students here that are out is very small, probably less than 2 percent of the campus. That makes it extremely difficult to find friends within the LGBTQ community, let alone someone for a romantic interest."

"Aaron," Senior, DePauw University

WHAT ARE SAFE ZONES?

According to Kerry John Poynter, the former Assistant Director at the Duke University Center for Lesbian, Gay, Bisexual and Transgender Life and the Coordinator of the SAFE on Campus program, a Safe Zone or Allies program consists of publicly identified students, faculty, and staff who are affirming toward lesbian, gay, bisexual, and transgender people. Members of these programs hang a sign or sticker featuring a pink triangle, a rainbow flag, or some clearly visible queer visual symbol signifying their membership. Safe Zones are places free of homophobia and/or heterosexism, in which members are open to discussions around homosexuality, bisexuality, or gender identity, and empowering to students who wish to "come out," explore, or reveal their sexual orientation or gender identity.

Consortium Tips for Setting Up Safe Zones on Campus

Kerry John Poynter offers the following 10 Tips for creating and managing a Safe Zone on your campus:[1]

- **Training is for Everyone**

  Always require attendance at a training or orientation session. Required attendance insures that self-selected members are dedicated to the affirming mission of the program. Similarly, these new members will already possess a higher level of awareness, knowledge, and contact with LGBTQ people than those who choose not to attend. Training should thus emphasize skills-building and "how to" conversation practice with potential anti-gay role playing and coming out scenarios.

- **Advisory Board: Movers and Shakers**

  When initially creating your safe space program, make sure to recruit faculty, staff, and student leaders who know the campus and have political power. Recruit the faculty member that everyone knows and loves. Invite the Dean of Students and president of the faculty union. Include officers and elected leaders of the student government, fraternities, sororities, and residence hall association. These campus leaders will provide legitimacy and potential avenues for funding.

- **Logo Design: Be Public!**

  A hallmark of these programs is publicly identifying members that hang a "safe" symbol that incorporates a pink triangle, rainbow and/or the word "ally" or other such identifiable LGBTQ symbols. Designs should be recognizable and visible when hung. Do not begin a safe space program that is not able to be "out" about its existence.

---

1   Kerry Poynter and Nancy Tubbs. "Safe Zones: Creating Safe Space Ally Programs." *Journal of Gay & Lesbian Issues in Education.* In press. http://lgbt.studentaffairs.duke.edu/programs_services/programs/safe/dvd downloads.html.

- **Be Inclusive**

  Consider who you are inviting to participate. Always reach out to other marginalized groups, people of color and religious leaders. Make sure that advisory board members are diverse and that training topics include multiple minority LGBTQ role plays, scenarios, and panelists.

- **Create a Membership Contract**

  New members should sign a contract at the end of the training. This contract should emphasize that they are providing a safe zone for anyone dealing with sexual orientation or gender identity issues, that they are not a counselor but can provide support and referral, and that they will provide affirmative support that upholds the mission of the program.

- **Recruit Help from Professionally Staffed LGBTQ Services Offices**

  Regardless of who coordinates your program it is inappropriate for the college or university to rely solely on students to provide this service and education to the campus community. Always ask for help from a professionally staffed LGBTQ services office on campus or at a nearby campus. Include faculty and staff from campus whom you can develop and mold as future allies.

- **Membership is Voluntary**

  Noone should feel pressured to join your safe space program. You want people who are genuinely motivated to join. It is inappropriate for department chairs or organization presidents to require attendance or tie performance reviews to membership. Always make sure that people can opt to not join when your training ends.

- **Will Every LGBTQ Person Come Out to You Now?**

  Just because you hang your safe sign does not mean that all LGBTQ people will come out to you. However, LGBTQ people will feel an increased comfort level with you that can lead to conversations about coming out and basic indirect interactions such as changing a perceived negative campus image.

- **Provide Ongoing Activities**

  Some members will want to be more involved and meet members beyond posting their sign or sticker. Ongoing educational activities will help build a diverse LGBTQ community. Activities can include socials, focused workshops, brown-bag lunch discussions, and invitations to LGBTQ events.

- **Assess, Assess, Assess**

  You are likely planning to spend a lot of time, energy, and funds on your safe space program. Therefore you will need to justify its continued existence as well as areas of success and needed improvement. Anecdotal evidence is not going to persuade critics, funding agencies, or administrators at the school. Employ various techniques that use evaluations, surveys, and focus groups. Make sure to keep records of your membership that include email addresses and campus mailing addresses for use in your assessment.

ADDITIONAL RESOURCES

Although there is no centralized resource for implementing a safe space program, the following resources contain more detailed information that should prove useful.

Poynter, Kerry and David Barnett. National Consortium of Directors of LGBT Resources in Higher Education. "How Do I Start or Implement a Safe Zone Program at My College or University?" Frequently asked question. www.lgbtcampus.org/faq/safe_zone.html

Poynter, Kerry (Producer) and Christina Wang (Director). *SAFE On Campus DVD: A Free Training and Development Resource for LGBT Safe Space Ally Programs.* Digital Video Case Studies. 2003. Available from Duke University Center for LGBT Life: Durham, NC. http://lgbt.studentaffairs.duke.edu/programs_services/programs/safe/index.html

QUEER & CANDID: STUDENTS SPEAK ABOUT SAFE ZONES

"Our campus has a Human Rights Center that is a designated 'safe space' for LGBTQ students and is also the home of the Commonground club, which works to provide social support and political activism around LGBTQ issues."

Ellen, Junior, Knox College

"Santa Clara University has very limited resources for LGBTQ affiliated students. A Safe Space program exists, but it's only an alliance claiming that the university accepts LGBTQ students."

"Ben," Senior, Santa Clara University

"Colorado School of Mines seems to avoid LGBTQ issues. Sigma Lambda (CSMs LGBTQA club) is working on this issue by holding educational seminars for students and faculty. Sigma Lambda hosts Safe Zone training, and urges faculty to display the Safe Zone sign in their offices to indicate that they are a LGBTQ resource."

Joelle, Sophomore, Colorado School of Mines

QUEER & CANDID

DO LESBIANS NEED SEPARATE SPACES?

An all-inclusive queer or LGBTQ community sounds like a politically correct dream, right? But the truth is that like any group of individuals clustered together there are bound to be situations and circumstances that do not always fully represent its constituents. Many of the queer women we spoke with while researching this book noted that the culture at large, as well as on college campuses, skews towards gay male visibility and presence. Many voiced the lack of support that they felt even within the "gay community" and the need for women to take leadership roles and more fully represent LGBTQ women. Others were adamant that there is a clear benefit to having queer-focused spaces for lesbians, trans, and queer women on college campuses. Amanda, a senior at Mount Holyoke College, thinks that on her all-women's campus "straight people sometimes feel left out of the social scene because it's so dominated by the lesbian community. There's also pretty good visibility within the faculty and staff of the LGBTQ community, and a lot of trans acceptance, especially for an all-women's college."

On the other hand, others voiced that there is an overwhelming dominance of queer women at certain schools and that sometimes builds a chasm between the "real world" and an idyllic "campus world." "Stephanie," a senior at Smith College, feels that "Being here is like being in a safety bubble, or an oblivion bubble. I can live my life without feeling like a marginalized social group; whereas off campus in the real world, I'm very conscious of other gay people and I feel like we are in a small, secret society. Off campus I have to fight to be heard as a person rather than as a dyke. On campus, it's taken for granted that I am a person first. It's a very low-stress environment in that regard."

In either case, women on the whole have had to fight for the rights often taken for granted by men, even gay men. On top of that, queer women have had to struggle against homophobia as well as sexism on and off the campus—but things are looking up. "Lesbian women are much more visible in the campus community now than several years ago," says Shane Windmeyer, Executive Director of Campus Pride. If you are a queer woman and feel that you need a safe network of strong activist women around you, you may want to consider attending a women's college or a school that has a history of female student empowerment. Students should also look for a Women's Center on campus. Most college and universities have one; in fact, many women's centers also host LGBTQ events. Of course, you can always work to make your campus safer and more supportive to queer women by taking up the good fight wherever you are.

TRANS GROUPS ON CAMPUS

Trans activism is going strong on many college campuses today. What was seen as a fringe movement just several years ago has now become a widely organized, articulate, and integral part of the student LGBTQ movement. To find out if there is a trans group on your campus, contact your school's LGBTQ student center. Many centers list myriad groups on their websites, along with contact information for these groups. Individual trans groups may be small, but they're probably vocal, working to change policies and provide a safer campus environment for trans students.

Trans student groups do this in a number of ways, including working for gender-neutral restrooms and housing on campus, pushing for schools to allow gender self-identification on forms, and providing a convenient space and policy on campus for students to legally change their name. Trans advocacy groups might also press for sensitivity training for professors and health care personnel, or for the student health center to provide hormones for transitioning students. If their health center will not do so, students might inform one another of where else hormones can be obtained, or how to find a good surgeon for sex-reassignment surgery (SRS), or even where supplies like binding wraps can be ordered. Most likely, these groups will also function as safe spaces for trans students to gather socially. As Marcus, a senior at Brandeis University explains: "I'm the director of the trans group on campus (we started TransBrandeis last year) and I'm the co-coordinator of the student-run Queer Resource Center on campus, which is the only source of LGBTQ education, support and advocacy on campus. Being involved with these two organizations both helps and hurts my transition process because while I nominally have a community here to back me up, I am also tokenized as 'the trans kid.'"

One of the most visible college trans groups is Phi Tau Mu, a support group for "Transmasculine identified students" at Michigan State University. Its founding member, T. J., was featured in the groundbreaking series TransGenerations, about transgender college students. The 15-member group, which is not a fraternity nor affiliated with any Greek organization, chose its name because the Greek letters Phi Tau Mu directly translate to "FTM." Their organization, according to its website, fosters "a sense of brotherhood" between its members and provides a safe space for them to meet. They also work on gender identity issues on campus, and hold popular events like a "bathroom crawl" to highlight the need for gender-neutral bathrooms. Other colleges have confidential support and discussion groups linked to their LGBTQ Resource Center facilitated by a staff member, and/or more activist-oriented groups like Cornell's TAG—Transgender Activism/Awareness Group.

If your campus does not have a specific trans student group (and most may not) and you would like to start one, seek guidance from similar groups on other campuses, your college's LGBTQ Co-op, or the Director of LGBTQ student affairs at your school. If you run into opposition or want professional advice, contact advocacy groups like the Transgender Law and Policy Institute (www.transgenderlaw.org).

Consortium Tips for LGBTQ Students of Color

by Amit Taneja, Assistant Director of the LGBT Resource Center at Syracuse University

The college environment can be an especially challenging place for LGBTQ students of color. These students might experience homophobia within their cultural/ethnic communities and racism within the white LGBTQ community. As a result of their intersecting identities of race, gender, and sexual orientation, some LGBTQ students of color may face significant barriers to full inclusion and participation within the campus community. Despite these challenges, many LGBTQ students of color lead full and vibrant lives on their campuses. Here are some tips to assist LGBTQ students of color in making the most of their college experience:

- **Find a Mentor**

  Most campuses have out LGBTQ faculty and staff, some of whom happen to be people of color. Ideally an out LGBTQ faculty or staff person of color would be great to find, but depending on your personality and needs, you might be able to find support from students and staff on your campus who can serve as a mentor for you who are not necessarily a part of your social group. Mentors can lend a helpful ear, provide advice, and also help you deal with any issues that arise. Most mentors are busy people, so they might not seek you out. Don't be afraid to initiate a conversation with them first.

- **Create a support network**

  It is important to surround yourself with people who understand you, and can relate to your experience. Often it is helpful to connect with others who share a similar identity, but it is also important to meet and befriend people from different backgrounds. Your residence hall, classes, and student groups are ideal places to make new friends.

- **Be active on campus**

  Join a student group, especially those that work with LGBTQ students or students of color. The level of support you may find within each group may differ from campus to campus, but you won't know what it will be like unless you join the group first.

- **Always report bias incidents**

  If you experience homophobia, racism, sexism, or any other form of discrimination, report it to the authorities! The administration will not know that there is a problem unless someone tells them. If you are uncomfortable personally reporting or talking about an incident, you may want to report the incident anonymously (several campuses offer this option). You may also want to engage other students and challenge them when they do or say things that are hurtful.

- **Form a LGBTQ People of Color Group**

  If your campus does not already have a LGBTQ People of Color group, then start one! The Dean of Students Office or the LGBTQ Resource Center (if there is one on your campus) might be able to offer support in the creation of such a group. If a group exists, then make it a priority to attend meetings.

- **Speak your truth**

  It is important to share your experience on campus with other students, faculty and staff with whom you feel comfortable. Campus climate change does not happen overnight, but every story can have a lasting impact. Share your experiences in every day conversations, in classes, in assignments, and even in the school newspaper.

QUEER-TIP: GAY BLUE JEANS DAY

In a statement to show support for gay rights and queer visibility on campuses, dozens of LGBTQ groups at colleges across the United States each year coordinate with national initiatives such as World AIDS Day, Gay Pride, and National Coming Out Day and encourage students to wear jeans and an item of clothing or a ribbon that reflects the colors of the Rainbow Flag. Want to take part? Check with your LGBTQ Center or queer organization on campus to see what they have planned. If nothing's scheduled, consider taking the necessary steps to plan the first one on your campus!

Consortium Tips for Students of Bisexual and Fluid Identities

by Dre Dominique, Assistant Director, Office of LGBT Student Services, New York University

As individuals begin to explore and interact with members of the LGBTQ community on a given campus, one may discover that there are several sexual and gender identities beyond that of the traditional concepts referred to within our larger society. Many individuals feel that their sexual orientation is not accurately represented by such labels as lesbian/gay or hetero-sexual. Many others feel that their gender identity does not necessarily align with the gender categories of male and female. Rather than identifying themselves within these prescribed and often limiting terms, some individuals may choose to select sexual identity terms that better reflect their sexual and/or romantic experiences and better align with the continuum of gender identity and expression.

The word bisexual typically describes the sexual identity of an individual who is romantically and/or sexually attracted to men and women. Some people feel that this term is limiting since it does not reflect the notion of attraction to those who identify as transgender, intersex, or genderqueer. Rather than using the word bisexual, some individuals will opt to use broader and more inclusive terms to express their identity. Examples of these terms are below. Please note that these terms in no way intend to serve as definitive explanation of these identities.

- **Fluid:** A term adopted by individuals who feel their sexual orientation is broad and not definable by any singular position on a continuum of sexual orientation. These individuals identify as neither heterosexual nor gay/lesbian, but somewhere in between. This identity is wider than bisexual, as it leaves open the possibility for the attraction to individuals who identify as transgender, genderqueer, and/or intersex.

- **Queer:** Originally a derogatory slur, it has recently been reclaimed by some as an umbrella term for all of those within the sexual minority community. Some individuals chose to identify with this term as a personal sexual identity if they feel terms such as lesbian, gay, and/or bisexual do not accurately represent their sexual orientation or may choose to use the term as a way of expressing their political views.

Keep in mind that the above terms are not used on all campuses and represent only a few of the numerous sexual identities beyond that of gay, lesbian, and straight. The following are some suggestions from current college students who identify as bisexual or fluid on how to find community and support once on campus:

- **"Be visible... you are not alone."**

  Be out and proud about your identity and know that there are other people on campus who share your experiences. Do not get discouraged if you do not find a community or establish a support network right away.

- **"Get involved with queer groups on campus."**

  Students continually expressed participation in general queer organizations on campus as the best way to meet other students on campus.

- **"Create a space for yourself."**

  As a way of creating visibility and building community, some students have established bisexual and fluid identity-specific organizations on various campuses. Students of these identities often describe these groups as "safe spaces" to express themselves without having to face biphobia, and homophobia that may be present in the queer and larger campus community respectively.

- **"Define yourself for yourself."**

  As you engage in the queer and larger campus community, you may find that others will want to place sexual identity labels on you. Remember that your identity is just that— *yours.* You can chose to take on (or not take on) any label that makes you most comfortable.

PFLAG Parent Tip: Dealing with Your Child's Activism

It is often very difficult for straight parents when their children come out to them as lesbian or gay, transgendered, bisexual, or questioning their sexuality. It can be a second shock when parents realize that their now openly LGBTQ children have also developed strong political or spiritual beliefs which clash with their own. Or, they may be accepting, but simply may not understand what being an LGBTQ activist involves. As Yale student Arianna Davalos says, "I think it's hard for my parents to imagine the scope of the work I have done in the LGBTQ community. They are just too far separated from this world."

So how do parents handle potential conflict over this, and learn to accept their child's activism? Many find it deeply challenging:

"My daughter's being an activist was hard for me to accept at first. I didn't understand why she was so defensive and supportive of the gay community."

"Bree," Wisconsin

"The important thing here is to be prepared to come out to friends and family before they see your child on the evening news and only then learn of their orientation."

"Sarah," Texas

"My daughter's activism is 'sexual activism' and I struggle with that. My sense is that sexual identity and behavior is 'private', and my daughter and her friends are politicizing their sexuality. But since I am an old school activist, I do try to find ways to 'bridge' to my daughter's activism."

"Jane," Vermont

On the other hand, some parents find it second nature to be supportive, often because their children already hold values fairly similar to their own:

"My husband and I find ourselves on the same page as our (transgender) daughter. She is not an activist but if she becomes one, we're fine with that. We are liberal thinking but probably fall in the middle somewhere. My husband is black and I am white, which probably also brings a unique view to a lot of these issues."

"Andrea," Florida

"I think my son is actually having to catch up with me in this regard as I immediately joined PFLAG and found my life's true calling!"

"Rochelle," Pennyslvania

"I do have very much of an activist transchild but since I grew up in the 1960s it's something I not only understand but embrace."

"Andy," Illinois

Still other parents may find that having a LGBTQ child an unexpected catalyst for changing their own beliefs, political perspectives, or those of their friends and family:

"Having a granddaughter who is lesbian has prompted her grandfather to more easily identify religious, social, or political hypocrisy, and to reconsider how he votes and to which organizations he donates."

"Henry," Georgia

You've raised your child the best you can, providing strong morals and role models along the way. Now it's their turn to explore the world they have come up—and out—in. You may find that you're in perfect harmony with your child's perspectives on most things, on some things, or in fact on nothing much at all. Your child is nearly an adult, with his or her own attitudes and experiences, and over time you'll probably accept your differences, or at least try to laugh a little at them. Your role as a parent at this point is to be supportive as your child now stretches his or her own wings—even if they ruffle some feathers along the way.

Consortium Tips on Knowing Your Rights and Educating Yourself about Campus Policies

by Heidi Stanton, Director of the Gender Identity/Expression and Sexual Orientation Resource Center, Washington State University

Once you get your bearings and learn your way around campus you start to take a closer look and decide that it is time to shake things up and make your mark. You decide that your campus is barely tolerant of LGBTQ issues and that the administration just doesn't understand or care about its students and you want them to make a commitment to creating a safer and more inclusive campus.

When it comes to activism, the point is to rock the boat, not capsize it. Most administrators really do care, but students and administrators sometimes speak very different languages and see things from very different perspectives. Here are some tips and resources to help you get started:

- Familiarize yourself with your campus' Strategic Plan, Mission Statement, and/or goals for equity and diversity.

- Ask, don't demand, to meet with the administration.

- Clearly articulate what you want from the administration in a way that enables them to hear what you're saying without putting them on the defensive.

- Be willing to point out some things that you think are positive about what your campus is doing in terms of equity and diversity.

- Be prepared to clearly identify some of the things that you feel need to change.

- Be ready to offer solutions or at least some constructive ideas for creating change.

- Work with your campus police to know what the laws are in terms of demonstrating on campus.

- Work with student affairs to understand your campus conduct code as it pertains to student activism.

- Last, but not least, seek out a trusted advisor, faculty, staff, or the Director of your LGBTQ Center to help you work with the administration.

Queer-Tip: The Origins of the Rainbow Flag

While multi-colored flags have been used by various organizations and political movements all over the world, the "Rainbow Flag" (also referred to as the "Freedom Flag") is now synonymous with Gay Pride and serves as an unmistakable reminder of the rich heritage of the LGBTQ community.

Created in 1978 by San Francisco artist Gilbert Baker, it currently consists of six colored stripes of red, orange, yellow, green, blue, and violet and has come to represent, on a global level, the need for increased visibility, growing acceptance, solidarity, and the acknowledgement of the countless accomplishments and struggles of queer individuals and organizations.

Ever wonder what the colors on a "Rainbow Flag" mean?

Red:	Life
Orange:	Healing
Yellow:	Sunlight
Green:	Nature
Blue:	Serenity
Violet:	Spirit

QUEER & CANDID: TAKING PRIDE IN ON-CAMPUS ACTIVISM

"We have a day where the LGBTQ community gives out free shirts that are bright orange and say 'Gay? OK by me' to show campus support."

Matt, Sophomore, University of Dayton

"I don't feel like I have to participate in LGBTQ events to be accepted, and plenty of straight people come to the LGBTQ events just because they're fun. Probably one of the coolest things I saw was a date auction run by Allies, the LGBTQ awareness/activist group. It was co-sponsored by a sorority. People who were auctioned were allowed to choose which gender(s) they'd be willing to date, and nobody felt excluded. We raised lots of money for a good cause, too!"

"Sam," Senior, Carnegie Mellon University

"The Rainbow Pride Union seems to facilitate the large majority of events and resources for LGBTQ students. That being said, a large variety of other organizations, mostly minority ethnic and religious organizations, are very involved with and supportive of the Rainbow Pride Union. You will also find a large following of heterosexual students on the front lines of LGBTQ initiatives."

Greg, Junior, Binghamton University

QUEER & CANDID

Consortium Tips on Creating Pride Events on Campus

by Matt Carcella, Assistant Director, LGBT Center, Princeton University

Pride events on campus don't have to take the form of a throng of people chanting "We're here! We're queer! Get used to it!" outside of the Dean's office. Events on campus have come a long way since the beginning of the LGBTQ movement. One of the most empowering experiences of college life is planning events knowing that you are truly making a change on campus.

You don't have to be a student group in order to organize a queer pride event. Oftentimes, the best events are those that are spearheaded by a single person that brings together your LGBTQ Resource Center, student groups, academic departments, and administrative office. Creating such an event is a good way to highlight the LGBTQ community to the entire campus community, as well as provide an outlet to bring the queer community together. Don't be afraid to pitch your idea to your administration or student government. They are both great places to find resources and support.

Many colleges and universities have Pride weeks or months that serve as a series of programming. Consider planning mostly small to medium-sized programs throughout the week/month with a large program to highlight your pride week/month such as a nationally known speaker, performer, comedian/enne, or by hosting a drag ball. Organizing such a series is a good way to celebrate diversity within the community.

In addition, there are many national events that you can organize around on campus. In early October, National Coming Out Day is a good time to celebrate with a very visible program such as a rally or public performance. October also serves as LGBTQ History Month, so consider collaborating with academic departments such as history, women's studies, English, etc. to plan programs that will speak to a cross-section of the campus community. In April, consider planning events around National Day of Silence, a day when members of the LGBTQ community and allies are encouraged to remain silent in recognition of those among us who feel silenced because of their sexual orientation or gender identity. But don't let all of these "days" stifle your creativity. Think outside the box. There are many powerful events that you can spearhead that do not require a lot of planning or money to orchestrate. These include:

- Use sidewalk chalk to call attention to the community on major pathways on campus.
- Create a small-scale film series or festival dedicated to films with LGBTQ themes or directors.
- Plan an open mic night at a local or on campus coffeehouse.
- Ask professors on campus to present their queer academic work.
- Sponsor a potluck dinner.
- Collaborate with other student organizations, administrative and academic offices, and your office of student affairs.
- Hold a gay jeans (flip-flops, t-shirt, shorts, etc.) day where you ask the campus to wear a certain common article of clothing in support of the LGBTQ community.
- March in your local community's Pride Parade, usually held in May or June.

The most important aspect of creating a Pride event or series is to be inclusive of all people on campus who identify as a member or ally of the LGBTQ community. Remember, don't be afraid to ask for what you need to create a great Pride event on campus and have fun!

SPOTLIGHT ON:

Ellen, First-year, Princeton University and Point Foundation Scholar

Ellen gave this speech during a Coming Out Day celebration rally:

"With all the talk, the posters, the slogans about coming out, what does it actually mean?

Coming out is the search for public authenticity. Coming out is a more accurate revision of one's perceived, given, or assumed identity. Coming out is an act of inclusion—it is the inclusion of others in a truth.

Public authenticity. Accuracy. Identity. Inclusion.

Okay, so let's put that on hold for a second and talk about t-shirts.

Today is a day of visibility, a visual statement of acceptance of the gay and lesbian people in our communities and in our world. Thank you for taking the time and the heart to be here. Thank you for making room in your wardrobe and in your life for the cause of today. Thank you for standing tall as a crucial—I repeat, crucial—pillar in our community and in our movement. You are a part of us.

Making ourselves visible is important as we move forward, growing into a society of respect, love, and acceptance.

Alright, so now that we've talked about visibility, let's talk about vision.

Vision is far more than the ability to see what has already been made visible for you. So says the dictionary, it is the image of what the future will or could be like. More importantly, it is the ability to think about or plan the future with imagination or wisdom.

The idea and execution of this project—these t-shirts—was conceived in 1989, 17 years ago, when I was only 2 years old. I imagine that this was a truly visionary step. And clearly it has affected what our future would or could be like. After all, we're wearing the t-shirts, aren't we?

So I ask you: What does today's vision say?

In a vision of visibility, I can't help but see what's not being made visible. Just like language, a slogan certainly has its limits. 'Gay? Fine by me.' Seems fine enough, right?

Gay? Fine by me. I recognize the power of a slogan to collectivize and I can see from where I'm standing now the power of a t-shirt to unify. This t-shirt is to be the stand-in as visibility for our community as a whole. 'Fine by me', says your shirt, I support gays, and the word 'gay' being a stand-in for the word lesbian too. But is that all of our community? We are supposed to see ourselves reflected in these t-shirts. After all, today is supposed to be the day of visibility for our community. Today is to be the day of coming out. So in the spirit of coming out, in the spirit of the search for public authenticity, let me take a second to do that. I am a bisexual, queer, woman-identified-woman. And I am not on your shirt. But I certainly consider myself a part of the LGBTQ community. It is as much a part of me as I am of it.

Let's return to the word vision. The ability to think about or plan the future with imagination or wisdom.

Where's our wisdom? All of the LGBTQ community has experienced the disservice of having one's identity assumed. So, that being said, what does it mean to have one's inclusion assumed? Shouldn't we know better? If gays and lesbians have felt the inaccuracy, the in-authenticity, the exclusion of having one's sexual orientation assumed to be straight, why are we continuing to assume about our own community? Worse yet, why are we imposing the expectation on the rest of the LGBTQ community that we will assume ourselves as included? Haven't we already been there? Shouldn't we know better?

The ability to think about or plan the future with imagination or wisdom.

Imagination. In a poem from the book *Revolutionary Voices*, a multicultural queer youth anthology, Maria Poblet asserts that, 'We must invent the words we cannot find.' We aren't even using half of the words we've already found. And what are we to do when those words are inherently flawed to begin with? The term bisexual reinforces the assumption that gender is a binary—that gender is either one or the other, with nothing in between. And the term transgender, speaking of in betweens, is a stand-in for an enormous spectrum of all things gender, ranging from gender expression to gender identity to transitioning and becoming a transsexual, to the genderqueer people in our community.

It is a spectrum, and we've seen the spectrum, we've seen the rainbow. We know the iconography. But if we're going to use the platform of an entire community to talk about colors, we need to talk about all of them. And a slogan can't catch a rainbow, can't capture a spectrum. It is too wide for four words. Our diversity is too deep.

So I ask you, do we have to wait for the slogan to find us before we truly take on the task of visibility? Coming out is the search for public authenticity. So when are we going to get real? Coming out is a more accurate revision of one's perceived, given, or assumed identity. When will we stop assuming and put our revisions into practice? Coming out is an act of inclusion—it is the inclusion of others in a truth. When will we truly come out as a community? I understand that steps are slow—but slow is not permission for delay, to turn process and progress into a leisurely pace, nor is it a permission not to take the next step. So let's take that next step, with vision. Let's turn a support for just some into a solidarity among all."

CHAPTER 8
BEYOND BOOKS: QUEER STUDENTS AND CAMPUS LIFE

LIFE OUTSIDE THE CLASSROOM

Believe it or not, the majority of your time at college will *not* be spent in a classroom. With classes averaging twenty hours per week, you are looking at 100 hours of non-classroom related time on your hands. Of course, a huge chunk of that time will be spent studying (and some of it might even be needed for a few hours of sleep). But, if you start adding in time for eating and hanging out with friends, you could end up having one seriously tight schedule. It's easy to get caught up in all the work, so make sure to flesh out your schedule with extracurricular activities you truly enjoy. Every college offers plenty of activities to choose from, from clubs, teams, parties, and volunteer activities to lectures, movies, concerts, performances, and late night dorm bull sessions. In fact, even if your social life is thriving, it's not a bad idea to make yourself check out at least one or two activities that you've never tried before. It couldn't hurt and it'll probably be free or cheap. The key to successfully engaging in extracurricular activities at college is balance. Students should be mindful of their course load and any part-time or full-time work obligations before joining groups on campus. Read on for tips on how you can maximize your time and still find ways to participate in non-academic activities that will make life outside of the classroom a truly fun and fulfilling experience.

QUEER-TIP:
CATCHING UP ON THE QUEER CLASSICS

College keeps you up to your eyeballs in homework, extracurricular activities, projects, and parties—you barely have time to eat. But if you're craving an escape from it all, why not carve out a few hours for yourself, find a quiet corner on campus, and curl up with a good book.

The Publishing Triangle, the Association of Lesbians and Gay Men in Publishing, recently put out its list of the *100 Best Lesbian and Gay Novels,* in order to "broaden the appreciation of lesbian and gay literature and to promote discussion between all readers gay and straight."[1] The list was selected by a panel of noted judges, including lesbian and gay writers and authors. Here's a partial list of their recommendations:

1   The Publishing Triangle. "100 Best Lesbian and Gay Novels." www.publishingtriangle.org/100best.asp.

- *Death in Venice* by Thomas Mann
- *Giovanni's Room* by James Baldwin
- *Our Lady of the Flowers* by Jean Genet
- *Remembrance of Things Past* by Marcel Proust
- *The Immoralist* by Andre Gide
- *Orlando* by Virginia Woolf
- *The Well of Loneliness* by Radclyffe Hall
- *Kiss of the Spider Woman* by Manuel Puig
- *The Memoirs of Hadrian* by Marguerite Yourcenar
- *Zami* by Audré Lorde
- *The Picture of Dorian Gray* by Oscar Wilde
- *Nightwood* by Djuna Barnes
- *Billy Budd* by Herman Melville
- *A Boy's Own Story* by Edmund White
- *Dancer from the Dance* by Andrew Holleran
- *Maurice* by E. M. Forster
- *The City and the Pillar* by Gore Vidal
- *Rubyfruit Jungle* by Rita Mae Brown
- *Brideshead Revisited* by Evelyn Waugh
- *Confessions of a Mask* by Yukio Mishima
- *The Member of the Wedding* by Carson McCullers
- *City of Night* by John Rechy
- *Myra Breckinridge* by Gore Vidal
- *Patience and Sarah* by Isabel Miller
- *The Autobiography of Alice B. Toklas* by Gertrude Stein

For the full list, additional recommended works and more information about Publishing Triangle, log onto PublishingTriangle.org.

MORE THAN QUEER: EXPANDING YOUR SOCIAL NETWORK

Okay—let's get one thing "straight." Being queer (or whatever you wish to call yourself) is not the only thing that will define you while you're attending college—or throughout your life. Sure, the LGBTQ community on your campus is an amazing and important resource that you should value, support, and interact with on a regular basis. But you also need to integrate your life fully into the fabric of the college community as a whole. It's all about taking advantage of what your particular college has to offer and realizing the value of building an "integrated" social life.

A great way to do this is by getting involved in extracurricular activities. These clubs and groups can provide you with ample opportunities to explore areas of interest as well as help the greater community both on and off campus. As Caylena, a first-year at Ithaca College explains, "I am a member of the IC Feminists, a feminist organization that sponsors all sorts of events and activities on campus and in the Ithaca area that are related to empowering women. I am also a member of the Peer Volunteer Corps, a group that is involved in volunteering in the Ithaca community. With my involvement in these activities I am learning the benefits of participating in volunteer work and activities, related to empowering my sense of self and my femininity. I am also learning about the current injustices faced by women all over the country, and am challenging myself to help in fixing them and extinguishing them for those in the transgender community."

Of course, being involved in a variety of organizations or groups also increases your chance of casting a wide-spanning net that can help you meet an eclectic mix of queer *and* non-queer friends and acquaintances. Participating in on-campus groups like student government and the school newspaper gives you the chance to gain some much sought-after skills that might prove useful in the real world once you graduate. Check out the Student Activities Board for information about what activities your campus has to offer. Below are some of the most common types of groups on campus—don't be shy about asking how you can start your own!

- **Cultural Organizations:** For many students, attending college may be the first time in your life that you get to interact with a wide range of people from different ethnic, cultural, and socioeconomic backgrounds. As a queer college student, it's important to remember that you are not the only one on the campus who feels marginalized. By participating in extracurricular activities that focus on cultural exchange such as Jewish, Pan-Asian, or African American heritage clubs, you can learn more about different groups of students and the unique experiences and perspectives they bring to the campus. You may even discover some surprising commonalities.

- **Sports Organizations:** For most of us, playing sports on an intercollegiate level is just not in the cards. But that doesn't mean that you can't participate in an intramural league or find some other athletic diversion while in college. Peggy, a Senior at Wheaton College and the leader of an intramural flag football team on her campus agrees: "It's just a motley crew of us having fun on Saturdays. I am doing this because it keeps me physically active, and is something non-academic to have fun with! I don't think I have the time to be involved in anything more committing than the intramural." Most campuses have a variety of sports groups and teams you can join. Feel a few of them out until you find the one that feels right for you. Some schools may be more "athletics-focused" than others, but there should be plenty of options available that will allow you to feel comfortable being openly queer and a jock!

- **Student Media:** Student media has come a long way from the days of quarterly magazines and weekly newspapers. These days, most colleges have a wide variety of media outlets and organizations to keep its student body informed, and many LGBTQ students find that their involvement in student media provides them with a great platform for getting LGBTQ issues heard and discussed. If you've got the journalism bug then run, don't walk, to one of the campus newspaper offices. Take your cues from Michael, a senior at Saint Anselm College: "I am the editor of the college's newspaper. I started as a news writer my freshman year, and then rose to news editor my junior year and finally to editor-in-chief. My position allows me to shape the editorial content of the paper and provide a voice for students as well as a positive resource for conveying ideas among the entire college community." On the other hand, if you love music or want to develop your verbal communication skills, check out your college radio station. If you dream of being a newscaster, march on over to the campus television station and see what they have to offer. If you are a budding poet or fiction writer, then the campus literary magazine could be a perfect fit and a great way to channel your creative energy.

- **Theatrical Arts and Performance Groups:** Deep down you may really want to be a singing, dancing, and acting "triple threat." If theater and/or performing arts isn't already your major and you can find the time, joining an on-campus amateur performance group is a great option for all you budding LGBTQ "divas!" Jennifer, a first-year student at Brown University says: "I've been playing the trumpet since the 4th grade, and I'm currently the trumpet section leader. Band is a great social outlet, and it definitely boosts school spirit, though the football team rarely wins." Most colleges have a variety of choral and dance groups, music ensembles, theater production groups, and film and video departments on campus that are always looking for students who want to get involved. Ellen, a first-year at Princeton University, takes full advantage of her school's arts resources: "I am a singer/songwriter and play concerts in coffee shops near campus. I also write and publish a 'zine' (a small-circulation, photocopied mini-magazine of my writing). As a poet, writer, musician, it's second nature, but also crucial for balancing out the academia."

Remember, it's your right, and, on some level your responsibility, to participate in any activity or organization that you want on campus. Do *not* let being queer deter you from engaging in any pursuits in which you are interested. Your "queerness" can be an empowering asset, whatever you decide to do. By simply being "out" and involved in on-campus activities, you can help a campus organization push its boundaries and gain a more diverse membership while benefiting from your unique experiences and point of view.

QUEER EMPOWERMENT THROUGH STUDENT GOVERNMENT

Think politicians just jump into office? Think again. Most leading queer political leaders took part in some form of student government activity while attending college. So, if you aspire to a career in politics, public advocacy, law, communications, or just want to get involved in the daily workings of your campus, make your unique voice heard and participate in student government. Most student government associations mimic the organizational structure of the United States government, and include executive, legislative, and judicial branches. The main goals of most SGAs are to:

- Represent the interests of the student body and act as liaisons to the school administration
- Design and implement student fees for activities
- Allocate funds for a wide range of student-run clubs, organizations, and on-campus initiatives
- Charter and regulate student organizations and budgets

Becoming an elected officer or serving on various committees and councils can be an exciting and empowering experience. It can give you the opportunity to have both your individual voice heard, as well as be an ally/representative for the queer community on campus. As Michael, a student at Saint Anselm explains: "I am president of my class. In addition to planning events like formal and cocktails, I want student government to become a tool for students to articulate their concerns on campus. By serving the campus as an openly queer student government leader, you can help represent LGBTQ students within the university—and sometimes even on issues that affect the local community and/or state and the country. This can lead to some challenging experiences. Thomas, a senior at Florida State University shares his story: "When I was a [first-year] in college I wanted to join Student Government but when I put in my application I was forgotten about for some time. After about a month and a half of waiting I was called to attend a committee meeting where several other candidates were also going to be interviewed. During this interview process, one of the candidates made several references to 'fags' and 'gays.' The committee turned him down. But I was forwarded to the entire Student Senate for a vote on whether or not I should be appointed as a Senator. At the meeting of the full Senate I was presented as the gay candidate by the man who did not get forwarded. Some others in the room also spread rumors that I was a Communist. After an hour and a half of debate and questioning, I was voted down." Fortunately, Thomas' story ends on a positive note: "Currently, I am the Union Board Chair of the Oglesby Union Board, which governs the Student Union at Florida State. I am also on the board of directors of the Pride Student Union, which plans and hosts events for all students on campus, but with a specific eye towards LGBTQ students."

While each student's experience will vary from school to school (for better or for worse), the important thing to remember is that there are loads of opportunities for queer students to engage in enriching experiences in student government. It may even be the first accolade in a long and storied career as an "out and proud" political leader.

Interview with Ryan Fournier: Openly Gay Student Body President at The Ohio State University[1]

Some consider Ryan Fournier to be a trailblazer as The Ohio State University's first openly gay undergraduate student government president. For Fournier, though, it's all about service. The 21-year old senior has gotten a lot of national attention since winning the election. Campus Pride contributing writers Jeff Sapp and Jill Aguilar recently spoke with Fournier about being an openly gay leader in the Big Ten.

YOU'VE BEEN INVOLVED IN MANY LEADERSHIP CAPACITIES AS A STUDENT. TELL ME ABOUT THE JOHN GLENN INSTITUTE.

I've had a lot of opportunities to travel with them to places like Boston and Washington and actually speak with those who are public officials. My main focus during my time with these officials was to find out how they successfully represented their constituents and kept them engaged and involved.

YOU'RE IN A FRATERNITY TOO. WHICH ONE AND WHY DID YOU CHOOSE THAT PARTICULAR FRATERNITY?

I joined Sigma Phi Epsilon SIGEP.org at the end of my sophomore year and I've been a member for three years. I joined Sig Ep because they had the highest GPA of any fraternity on campus. The average was

1   www.campuspride.net/ryan_fournier.asp

3.4. They were all very involved across campus and they seemed to really have a great balance between being involved and academics.

DIDN'T YOU START THE FIRST-EVER COLLEGE CHAPTER OF THE HUMAN RIGHTS CAMPAIGN?

Yes, I was in Washington once and I saw a building with a large equal sign on it and asked a friend what it was. He told me about the political advocacy of the HRC and I was hooked. At OSU at the time, there was no political LGBTQ group. There were groups that supported and helped university students who were coming out, but no group that specifically took a political view and action about LGBTQ issues. I think every gay person is political just because of who we are. I started HRC and, although I am not that involved now because of my student government position, the organization is in its third year and doing very well.

YOU'RE WHITE AND YOUR RUNNING MATE, KATE CHRISTOBEK, IS WHITE AS WELL. HOW DO YOU BRING DIVERSITY INTO YOUR TEAM? HOW DO YOU CROSS BORDERS OF RACE, CLASS, AND GENDER?

It's easy when you're the student body president because you go and speak to all kinds of groups on campus. After all, I represent the student body.

WAS YOUR POLITICAL CAMPAIGN DIVERSE?

Oh yeah. We had to have a diverse team to get elected. The diversity on our campaign team was 50/50.

WAS IT EASY TO GET OTHERS ON CAMPUS TO JOIN YOUR CAMPAIGN?

I was a little shocked at first about this. People who I had considered good friends asked me, "Do you think your lifestyle represents OSU students?" Then they told me they couldn't or wouldn't support me and it basically ended our friendship.

BELIEVING THAT A UNIVERSITY IS A MICROCOSM OF WHAT IS GOING ON IN THE LARGER SOCIETY, WERE THERE MUD-SLINGING THINGS THAT MIRRORED STATE AND NATIONAL POLITICAL CAMPAIGNS?

Oh yeah! I had some hateful name calling made about me. There was a university blog about the elections and they posted some pretty cruel things there. For instance, they did the celebrity name blending thing and took Ryan Fournier and Kate Christobek, my running mate, and made it "Fournikate."

WHAT WAS YOUR MOST NEGATIVE EXPERIENCE WHILE RUNNING FOR STUDENT BODY PRESIDENT?

I had a big surprise when I visited the College Republicans. It was in April so it was before the elections and they had invited a Republican candidate who was running for the United States Senate to speak. He spoke right before me and his speech had a lot of anti-gay rhetoric in it. I couldn't believe I had to speak right after him to this crowd of about a hundred people. He finished and was walking out when I got to the podium. I said, "Sir, you might want to stay and hear what a university student has to say about some of your comments." He agreed. I confronted things like how a lack of domestic partnership benefits deters quality faculty from coming to OSU. I gave one of the best speeches I have ever given and when I finished, there was very little applause. Another odd speech was with the Campus Crusade for Christ. I spoke and asked for questions and total silence. The other two speakers were asked all kinds of questions.

HOW DID YOU NURTURE YOUR SPIRIT DURING THOSE TIMES WHEN NEGATIVE THINGS HAPPENED TO YOU?

I'd go home at night and I'd write down the most memorable things that happened that day. Things like people on our team who stayed up all night long and were still putting flyers around campus at 6 a.m. for an event that day. Or I'd go online and look at the database of volunteers who were supporting our campaign.

WHAT DID IT FEEL LIKE WHEN YOU WON THEN?

It was a public announcement. I jumped out of my seat! It was awkward in that moment, because they sit all of the people running together and read off who is second place, runner-up, and then winner. Our team was all wearing green t-shirts and they let out a roar of a cheer.

HOW DID YOU FRATERNITY AID YOU IN THE ELECTION?

The main benefit for me is the tremendous support I receive from brothers. I'm out to all of my brothers, so they were very supportive.

Other fraternities were supportive too because they liked that someone Greek was running for office.

HOW HAVE YOU BEEN RECEIVED SINCE YOU WON THE ELECTION?

Well, I'm the first gay student government president and I realize that that is how people remember me. I wasn't okay with that. I didn't run on a singular platform of being gay. But we're starting to get things done now. Recently we got the old lighting on campus replaced at a cost of $938,000. This is a major issue for student safety. I want to be remembered as having contributed to the overall quality of students' lives.

WHAT ABOUT THE STUDENTS WHO WOULDN'T JOIN YOUR CAMPAIGN BECAUSE YOU WERE GAY? HOW DID THEY RESPOND TO YOU AFTER YOU WON?

I never received a single apology and never talked to them again. We see each other on campus, but we don't speak.

WHAT IS A MESSAGE YOU WANT TO GET OUT ABOUT OSU?

Columbus is much more open. LGBTQ people have a strong presence here. Equality Ohio recently formed here. Our Pride Festival had over a hundred thousand people. OSU is getting more accepting. You can live here and be integrated.

TO GREEK OR NOT TO GREEK? THAT IS THE QUESTION . . .

Almost half of U.S. colleges and universities offer a chance for students to "go Greek" on campus. It's a system that dates all the way back to the first chapter of *Phi Beta Kappa* formed by a small group of friends at The College of William & Mary in 1776. If joining a fraternity or sorority is something you're definitely interested in doing, it's a good thing to investigate about a school before you decide to enroll there, as the experience can be incredibly varied.

One of the best benefits of being involved in Greek life is that it's a surefire way to quickly develop a solid group of friends. You may not love all of your "sisters" or "brothers" equally, but there will be plenty of people in your fraternity/sorority that you'd like to get to know. Beyond that, you'll be bombarded with a variety of social activities and community service opportunities, and enjoy the visibility and popularity on campus that usually comes with membership.

On the downside, you may feel a certain amount of pressure to hang out with the people in your particular chapter—possibly to the exclusion of those who aren't members. This can be particularly problematic for LGBTQ members, who may feel isolated by their chapter's heteronormative events, activities, and membership. Some members also cite the enormous time commitment and the feeling of being pigeonholed as a certain "type" just because they are a part of the Greek system. You might experience strong reactions from non-members in the LGBTQ community who find out that you're involved.

LGBTQ students deciding whether to pledge a fraternity or sorority often find the decision process to be daunting and anxiety-ridden. It's no secret that some chapters have reputations as being passively disapproving or even overtly homophobic of "queerness." However, some people might see participating in the Greek system as an opportunity to help change perceptions. Ellen, a sophomore at Carnegie Mellon University notes, "I am a sister of Kappa Alpha Theta. My experience being gay and Greek has been awesome because I get to educate the Greek world on being gay and the gay world on being Greek. Oddly enough, I experience more prejudice from the LGBTQ population for being Greek than I do from Greeks for being gay. The Greek world, at least at CMU, is much more open and accepting than people like to think. My sisters like my girlfriend and they hang out with her when she comes over to the house. Fraternity boys (for the most part) respect my lifestyle, and more than one Greek student has expressed to me an interest in knowing more about being gay."

Like any decision, the choice to pledge is a personal one—one that is often informed by "family legacies," social orientations, or the fundamental need to feel like you're part of a larger and already structured social system on campus. Greek life can be life-changing—and a great route to building a core social universe on campus, but it is most assuredly not for everyone. Here are some things to consider as you make your decision.

10 Reasons to Join a Fraternity or Sorority:

- They help you build a family away from home.
- They create opportunities to make lifelong friends.
- You will have a calendar full of activities.
- You will be actively involved in community service and volunteering.
- You can develop your leadership skills.
- You will help promote campus spirit.
- You will feel like you are part of a giant social matrix of other fraternities and sororities.
- You can discover more about yourself.
- You will have built-in networking opportunities for a lifetime.
- You will be a part of a longstanding tradition.

10 Reasons *Not* to Join a Fraternity or Sorority

- You might not feel comfortable being "out" or being open about exploring your sexuality and/or gender identity/expression.
- Greek organizations can be potentially unfriendly environments toward gay, lesbian, bisexual, transgender, or queer pledges.
- They might deter social integration and contact with non-Greek students.
- They might promote a lack of individuality and discourage "out there" creative self-expression.
- Hazing or ritual initiations (which still exists on some campuses, even if under the administration's radar) can be demeaning, and emotionally, psychologically, and physically harmful.
- Obligations to the chapter can be grueling and time consuming.
- Dues can be costly.

- Senior members of the house often dictate much of what you do with your spare time during your pledge semester/year.
- Lots of parties means lots of distractions...and lots of temptations.
- If the fraternity or sorority is heterosexual in orientation, same-sex dating and relationships may be frowned upon, discouraged, or not tolerated by your fellow brothers and sisters.
- If the fraternity or sorority is queer, same-sex dating and relationships may become awkward or inappropriate.

It's clear that queer students are becoming more and more visible on campuses, and with that comes a shift in the ways many Greek organizations are dealing with the LGBTQ community. But changes are slow, and there are currently *no* national policies on homophobia in the Greek-letter system. Whatever decision you make, remember that if you pledge a mainstream Greek organization, as an LGBTQ member you will most likely be in the minority. Remember, no two Greek experiences are the same—do your research and find the best alternative for you.

QUEER & CANDID: SPEAKING OUT ABOUT GREEK SYSTEM EXPERIENCES

"As an undergraduate, I was in a sorority starting in my sophomore year. I was just coming out to myself. I had briefly dated one woman in my sorority. The house of 100-plus women was in general pretty gay-friendly (there were a lot of closeted women, some of whom I knew). There was one instance when I had (anonymously) hand-written a note about homophobia that was expressed in the house. The note was torn down a couple of times, but eventually sisters wrote on it to not tear it down and it stayed for quite awhile. I have since been back for reunions with my partner and family and have been warmly received by my classmates."

Liz, Professor, University of Illinois at Urbana-Champaign

SPOTLIGHT ON:
THOMAS MARCROFT (LEFT), JUNIOR, ST. CLOUD STATE UNIVERSITY; JOHNNY M. PACKARD (CENTER), SOPHOMORE, ST. CLOUD STATE UNIVERSITY; BEN THOMPSON (RIGHT), JUNIOR, ST. CLOUD STATE UNIVERSITY

"Being out is important everywhere you go because you'll never know how accepting people can be until you give them a chance."

—Thomas Marcroft

"Being an out gay man in a predominantly straight fraternity has really helped me and other students that wouldn't usually socialize, progress not only in a personal way but also in a completely new level of thought for central Minnesota."

—Johnny M. Packard

The Progressive Greek System

If you're itching to be a part of the Greek social scene but you're concerned about how accepting your potential brothers or sisters will be of your sexual orientation, why not join (or start) a Greek society designed specifically for the queer and questioning? Since the late 1980s, an increasing number of queer-oriented Greek organizations (often known or referred to as "Progressive") have begun to pop up on campuses across the country. The main purpose of these organizations is to provide LGBTQ students with an opportunity to be part of the Greek system—even if they do not feel comfortable with, or particularly welcomed by, traditional fraternities or sororities. These groups apply a progressive and enlightened approach that places value on both individuality and on the benefits of fostering a tightly-knit group of like-minded queer members from varied backgrounds and orientations. Here's a list of the most notable Greek organizations specifically for the LGBTQ community:

- **Delta Lambda Phi Fraternity** (www.dlp.org/main/):

  Since its founding in 1986, Delta Lambda Phi has become one of the nation's fastest growing fraternities with chapters

2 Lambda 10 Project. "What Is Lambda 10 Project?" www.lambda10.org/aboutus.asp.

from coast to coast. The fraternity is dedicated to promoting diversity, providing gay, bisexual, and progressive men with social, service, and recreational activities, and empowering members to take on leadership roles in securing LGBTQ rights on and off campus.

- **Beta Phi Omega** (www.betaphiomega.net/sitemap.html):

  This national lesbian sorority has eight chapters throughout the U.S. and is dedicated to promoting awareness, pride, love, joy, prosperity, community involvement, and, last but certainly not least, lesbian victory. Although it caters to feminine lesbian women, it does not discriminate against bisexual, heterosexual women, or women of any race.

- **Gamma Rho Lambda** (http://gammarholambda.org):

  Gamma Rho Lambda National Sorority is a woman's alternative lifestyle-focused social sorority that seeks to exemplify the qualities of tolerance, diversity, unity, and trust. Continuously developing the lifelong bonds of sisterhood, they also provide a network of assistance in the areas of scholastic guidance, emotional support, and community service.

- **Kappa Xi Omega** (http://kappaxiomega.org):

  Kappa Xi Omega is a community-oriented sorority for lesbian women developed in February 2004 in the southern United States. It does not require its members or potential members to be enrolled in an institution of higher learning. The focus of Kappa Xi Omega is to create a cohesive environment of like-minded lesbian women in a combination of business and sisterhood.

- **Omicron Epsilon Pi** (www.oepi.com/contents.htm)

  Omicron Epsilon Pi Sorority, Inc. is the nation's first and only Greek letter organization that caters specifically to the needs of lesbians of color. They pride themselves on providing services to the LGBTQ community in a variety of cities, and work hard to make life better for all women.

- **Sigma Phi Beta Fraternity** (www.sigmaphibeta.org):

  Sigma Phi Beta Fraternity is organized for and by gay, straight, bisexual, and transgender men in college. Working within the traditional Greek fraternity system, they provide a unique social and educational environment for members with plenty of career and character-building opportunities. By participating in recreational, scholastic, and community service programs, Sigma Phi Beta members contribute to a unique Greek system on campus.

QUEER-TIP: TRANSGENDER GREEKS WELCOMED!

Sigma Phi Beta Fraternity's National Board of Directors recently enacted a policy that allows transgender students to pledge and join. The policy goes above and beyond any other known policy of a national social college fraternity by allowing individuals who self-identify as male to seek membership, regardless of their sex at birth and whether or not they have obtained legal recognition of their gender identity. The policy also allows members to maintain their fraternity membership, even if at a later date, they decide to change their gender to female.

LOOKING FOR LOVE IN ALL THE RIGHT PLACES

Romantic relationships are a natural part of college life. There's something about being on campus that ignites a certain spark between fresh-faced students. While having a honey on campus gives you someone to talk to after class and a reliable date to various activities, it can also be a huge headache. Balancing a rigorous academic course load, extracurricular activities, and your parent's phone calls is stressful enough. Add the additional pressure of a relationship, and you really just might crack.

So how do you make sure that your love relationship is both fulfilling personally and non-disruptive of your academic and social routine? Well, the most important thing is to make sure that the relationship does not consume your whole being. It's okay to be into your significant other, but you have to balance the intense face-time, sleepovers, and late-night pizza runs with some time to yourself—and not just time to yourself to write papers or pull the occasional all-nighter. We're talking about time to yourself to pursue your own interests, hang out with your own friends, or just to spend some QT with *you*. So many college students get involved in unhealthy relationships in which they lose themselves completely. If this sounds like you, don't be afraid to seek out counseling at your school's student health center or to ask your partner to take a break. In the long run, your relationship will be better for it.

As an LGBTQ student you may also experience some anxiety around public displays of affection—both on campus and off. How you choose to deal with this is a personal matter. While heteronormative social standards allow for heterosexual couples to be more public in certain settings about their physical interactions with one another, to feel comfortable in your own skin and not be afraid of PDAs with whomever you may choose to share them with. Just remember that not every campus is going to be as tolerant as others when it comes to displaying your gay/lesbian/bisexual/transgender affection. On top of that, the person with whom you may be involved may still be in the closet and not "out" or comfortable with such candid behavior. While it sucks to have to think about these boundaries when you'd just like to enjoy the feeling of being in love (or at the very least, intense like), you have to balance your own desires/needs with respect for your significant other's choices, and a realistic assessment of your own sense of safety. At the end of the day, all students need to be aware of their surroundings. In fact, our research suggests that most people don't want to see queer or straight PDA.

GAYS AND GOD: LGBTQ STUDENTS AND RELIGION

Religious groups on campus are an important part of the campus life. They run the gamut, from Christian Bible Study groups, to Jewish Hillel Centers, to Muslim Student Associations and everything in-between. There are also many specific denominational groups on campus with many faiths and beliefs represented. These groups provide valuable support networks for students who wish to grow spiritually as well as intellectually at college, and they can also function as a reaffirming symbol of political and social values held by their student members.

The wonderful thing about college religious groups is the open-door policy that many of them have. If you ever want to learn more about Hinduism, Judaism, Islam, Buddhism, Christianity—you get the picture—college is a perfect time to join or attend meetings and activities sponsored by the religious group in which you are interested. In addition, many college campuses host an interfaith ministry, in which students from a variety of religious backgrounds can attend services and explore faith-based questions together. Interfaith groups are dedicated to creating a unified spiritual community on campus and exploring, with sensitivity and respect, the important similarities and differences that characterize the world's religions.

Certainly religious belief is a personal and private matter, one that many LGBTQ students struggle to reconcile with their sexual identity and/or gender identity. It does not help that religious doctrine is repeatedly invoked by some extremists as justification for homophobia or discrimination against LGBTQ people. In April 2006, The Advocate ran an article discussing a new bill pending in the U.S. Senate which would exempt some faith-based colleges from local antidiscrimination laws, allowing them to legally reject gay students.[3] The proposed amendment to the 1965 Higher Education Act would require accrediting boards to consider an institution's "religious and moral goals" during evaluation, but not require them to adhere to local nondiscrimination laws if these laws conflicted with the institution's goals. The bill passed in both the House and Senate. The Senate committee added language to the measure stating that it is "not meant to allow an institution to discriminate on the basis of race, color, religion, sex, national origin, age, or disability," leaving out sexual orientation and gender identity/expression.

While it is tempting to interpret this legislation as clearing the path for some faith-based institutions to discriminate against LGBTQ students, it is important to realize that an institution's vested interest in remaining true to its religious and moral goals, does not necessarily preclude an anti-gay discrimination agenda. The fact is many faith-based institutions are home to a vibrant community of LGBTQ students, and work hard to send students the message that religious belief and queer sexuality do not have to be mutually exclusive. But even when the campus community

3   The Advocate. "U.S. Senate Bill May Exempt Christian Colleges from Antidiscrimination Laws." April 20, 2006.
www.advocate.com/news_detail_ektid29845.asp.

has a narrow view of religion, LGBTQ students can always look off campus for faith-based support networks. Here is a list of some of the religious organizations that open their arms to queer college students:

- Association of Welcoming and Affirming Baptists (www.wabaptists.org)
- Affirmation—United Methodists for Lesbian, Gay, Bisexual, and Transgender Concerns (www.umaffirm.org)
- Dignity/USA—Gay, Lesbian, Bisexual, and Transgender Catholics (www.dignityusa.org)
- Evangelicals Concerned (www.ecwr.org)
- Lutheran Lesbian and Gay Ministries (www.llgm.org)
- More Light Presbyterians (www.mlp.org)
- The United Church of Christ Coalition for Lesbian, Gay, Bisexual, and Transgender Concerns (www.ucccoalition.org)
- Universal Fellowship of Metropolitan Community Churches (www.mccchurch.org)

In addition, the National Gay and Lesbian Task Force offers a comprehensive list of local LGBTQ-friendly religious organization as well as resources for finding a welcoming congregation. Visit: TheTaskForce.org for more information.

Queer-Tip: Soulforce

Soulforce (soulforce.org) is a national social justice and civil rights organization. It works to free lesbian, gay, bisexual, and transgender people from religious and political oppression through the practice of relentless nonviolent resistance.

A Journey of Real Faith in America: *An Overview of the Soulforce Equality Ride*

Following in the footsteps of the Freedom Rides of the 1960s, the Soulforce Equality Ride uses principles of non-violent direct action to open a conversation about faith and sexuality at colleges and universities with policies that silence or exclude LGBTQ students. At each of the nineteen schools on the 2006 Equality Ride, the young adult ambassadors of Soulforce brought this simple message to students, faculty and administrators: learn from history, end religion-based oppression. In spring 2007, the journey continued with 50 young adults traveling to 32 Christian colleges on two separate routes. At each stop, they promoted an ethic of inclusion and delivered a message of hope and healing to students suffering from doctrinal prejudice. The opportunity to get involved in the next evolution of the LGBTQ rights movement has not passed. For more information on how you can get involved in Equality Ride 2008, visit EqualityRide.com.

QUEER & CANDID:
NOTES FROM EQUALITY RIDERS

"My initial motivation was to reach isolated LGBTQ students with the life-saving message that they are not alone and deserve better than they currently receive from the Christian community. During the Ride, I've spent a bit of time each morning thinking of the many students who are on the verge of committing suicide. I put faces with my thoughts such as the face of Andy, from BYU, whose best friend shot himself under the pressures put on him by his father and his faith. I think of these beautiful people and realize they are merely a few representing thousands. "

Pam Disel

"One of the most important things we have seen on this trip is the diversity that exists within the LGBTQ community and the Christian community. No longer are we faceless abstractions, facing each other across some theological and lifestyle chasm. Rather, we are all people, striving to live with integrity in community with each other and our beliefs. "

Di Gray

"Day after day on the Equality Ride, I watch countless individuals wrestle with cognitive dissonances regarding ideas about sexual orientation and sin. Some cross over the border and become allies. Others come to conclusions closer to the truth, though still unable to affirm an LGBT person. Regardless, they are one step further toward acceptance. Others live in fear and have the opportunity to tell us so and find a healing voice from the Riders. We stand for them, and they know it."

David Coleman

A Biblical Response to the Question People Often Ask: "How can you consider yourself a Christian when you are also gay?"[4]

by Rev. Dr. Mel White of Soulforce

The Rev. Dr. Mel White is a former ghostwriter for fellow evangelicals, including Billy Graham and Pat Robertson. Inspired by the nonviolence movements of Gandhi and Martin Luther King Jr., White developed a program based on their principles to address the suffering of lesbian, gay, bisexual, and transgender people. In 1997, he was awarded the ACLU's National Civil Liberties Award for his efforts to apply the "soul force" principles of Gandhi and King to the struggle for justice for sexual minorities.

Dr. White is also the author of *Stranger at the Gate: To Be Gay and Christian in America.*

Like you, I take the *Bible* seriously!

Many good people build their case against homosexuality almost entirely on the *Bible*. These folks value Scripture, and are serious about seeking its guidance in their lives. Unfortunately, many of them have never really studied what the *Bible* does and doesn't say about homosexuality.

I'm convinced the *Bible* has a powerful message for gay and lesbian Christians—as well as straight Christians. But it's not the message of condemnation we so often hear.

4   Excerpt from "What the Bible Says—And Doesn't Say—About Homosexuality" by Rev. Dr. Mel White. Soulforce, Inc.: Lynchburg, VA, 2000. www.soulforce.org/article/homosexuality-bible-gay-christian.

In fact, the *Bible* is a book about God—not a book about human sexuality. The *Bible* is the story of God's love for the world and the people of the world. It tells the history of God's love at work rescuing, renewing, and empowering humankind. It was never intended to be a book about human sexuality. In fact, the *Bible* accepts sexual practices that we condemn and condemns sexual practices that we accept.

Lots of them! Here are a few examples:

- **Deuteronomy 22:13–21**

    If it is discovered that a bride is not a virgin, the *Bible* demands that she be executed by stoning immediately.

- **Deuteronomy 22:22**

    If a married person has sex with someone else's husband or wife, the *Bible* commands that both adulterers be stoned to death.

- **Mark 10:1-12**

    Divorce is strictly forbidden in both Testaments, as is remarriage of anyone who has been divorced.

- **Leviticus 18:19**

    The *Bible* forbids a married couple from having sexual intercourse during a woman's period. If they disobey, both shall be executed.

- **Mark 12:18-27**

    If a man dies childless, his widow is ordered by biblical law to have intercourse with each of his brothers in turn until she bears her deceased husband a male heir.

- **Deuteronomy 25:11-12**

    If a man gets into a fight with another man and his wife seeks to rescue her husband by grabbing the enemy's genitals, her hand shall be cut off and no pity shall be shown her.

The list goes on: The *Bible* says clearly that sex with a prostitute is acceptable for the husband but not for the wife. Polygamy is acceptable, as is a king having many concubines. (Solomon, the wisest king of all, had 1,000 concubines.) Slavery and sex with slaves, marriage of girls aged 11—13, and treatment of women as property are all accepted practices in the Scriptures. On the other hand, there are strict prohibitions against interracial marriage, birth control, discussing or even naming a sexual organ, and seeing one's parents nude.

Over the centuries the Holy Spirit has taught us that certain *Bible* verses should not be understood as God's law for all time periods. Some verses are specific to the culture and time in which they were written, and are no longer viewed as appropriate, wise, or just.

Often, the Holy Spirit uses science to teach us why those ancient words no longer apply to our modern times. During the last three decades, for example, organizations representing 1.5 million U.S. health professionals (doctors, psychiatrists, psychologists, counselors, and educators) have stated definitively that homosexual orientation is as natural as heterosexual orientation, that sexual orientation is determined by a combination of yet unknown pre- and post-natal influences, and that it is dangerous and inappropriate to tell a homosexual that he or she could or should attempt to change his or her sexual orientation.

While there are some people now living in heterosexual marriages who once perceived themselves to be gay, there are millions of gay and lesbian persons who have accepted their sexual orientation as a gift from God and live productive and deeply spiritual lives. The evidence from science and from the personal experience of gay and lesbian Christians demands that we at least consider whether the passages cited to condemn homosexual behavior should be reconsidered, just as other *Bible* verses that speak of certain sexual practices are no longer understood as God's law for us in this day.

PFLAG Parent Tip: How Your LGBTQ Child Can Find Spiritual Support at College

Parents who raise children with a strong religious or spiritual upbringing may wonder if their child will continue practicing their faith while they are away at college. There is no easy answer to this question. Each student's experience will vary widely depending on the school they attend and their personal commitment towards their faith. On the other hand, if the school is strongly affiliated with one faith, other religious groups may not have as much visibility as they do on campuses where a wider variety of faiths flourish. Parents with these kinds of concerns should check college websites to ascertain what religions and spiritual groups have a strong presence on the campuses of the colleges their students are interested in attending.

> "The spirit of nonviolence that Soulforce and the Equality Riders embody is the key to making the world a different place, a more just place. We create a safe space at these schools where people can ask really tough questions and say all the things they know are hurtful because we commit to loving them regardless. Students and faculty alike cannot help but see to the honest core of who we are as people because of our methods of nonviolence. A student told me that they were touched by the awesome power of the love we had not only for each other but also for the people on campus."
>
> Tommy Atz

At most colleges today, if a student wants to practice his or her family's faith, or even explore a new one, they will most likely find support. Kurt Nelson, a straight ally attending Yale's Divinity School and a multi-faith intern in the Chaplain's office, says "Finding new spirituality is something that seems to happen to virtually all people in college, whether leaving a church, joining a church, changing a religion, or disregarding religion altogether. And because there are places where the queer community is explicitly welcomed and affirmed, those are good places to start looking."

Indeed, most colleges have a wide-range of religious groups participating on their campuses. These groups can include Jewish Centers like Hillel, the Latter-Day Saints, Christians, Muslims, Catholics, the Bahá'i Faith, pagans, and more. Affiliated activities may include providing meal services like Shabbat, space for students during Ramadan, and midnight services for Buddhists. Groups like gospel choirs also grace many campuses. Many colleges also hold non-denominational services called "interfaith" which are open to everyone, and represent a wonderful melding of people of all faiths.

Guiding the religious activities on these campuses is the Chaplain, who can be contacted directly for counseling and spiritual advice. Chaplains can also perform weddings and memorial services. Often the Chaplain's office provides workshops for university employees, students, and faculty on issues like grief, depression, identity, and family illness. They are also available to talk to parents about the state of religious and spirituality activity on campus.

Parents may find it hard to understand that in the process of leaving home, their children are now more fully able to decide when and if they will participate in religious or spiritual worship. For queer college-bound students, college may be a welcome escape from their family's religion, which may not have been accepting of their sexuality. Still, it can hard for parents to let go of this part of their child's upbringing. Here's what some parents had to say about their LGBTQ children, and their faith:

"We have always gone to a very conservative Baptist church and all of a sudden she refused to go to church when she was visiting us. She found fault with the sermons and stated that she didn't believe the way we believed. I don't think I'll ever change my religious view that homosexuality is a sin."

"Anne," Texas

"I'll never forget those difficult telephone calls to the family. We are all Catholic and it has been very hard for the grandparents to accept that our daughter is a lesbian. We continually point out that the work she is doing is for all people to be treated equally.

It tends to fall on deaf ears, and they actually keep praying that she will change and fall in love with some 'nice boy . . . argh!"

"Margaret," Illinois

"My son and I have the same religious beliefs. He is a little less of a believer than I am, but I respect his right to not believe in everything I do."

"Sylvie," Massachusetts

"As a family we are currently re-evaluating our religious beliefs and convictions. I have fallen farther and farther away from the church as I see what horrific lies many fundamentalists spread about LGBTQ people."

"Jennifer," Texas

"Our biggest religious conflict came when my then-daughter (now trans son) wanted to belong to a different synagogue than the rest of the family."

"Rebecca," New York

"We have the same religious beliefs, and have worked together to find the answers that were important for our personal faith."

"Alice," Colorado

"We are not religious nor do we affiliate with any religion. If our daughter becomes a right-wing, evangelical, Christian republican we'd probably make fun of her. After all, I can't imagine that there are too many biracial, trans, right-wing, evangelical Christians out there!"

"Michelle," Connecticut

QUEER SPACES, COOL PLACES: LIFE OUTSIDE THE CAMPUS

Despite what your parents think and what your school's recruiting materials might claim, going to college isn't just about hitting the books, doing research, making friends that will last a lifetime (or at least until graduation), or going to on-campus parties and events. For better or for worse, there is life outside the hallowed walls of your university. And oftentimes, off-campus excursions offer different challenges and opportunities for spreading your wings and interacting with a larger LGBTQ community.

For many students, especially those attending large schools or liberal arts institutions, the queer scene on campus may be vibrant and jampacked with events, clubs, and members. Others may feel your campus social scene is small, lacking, or dull, so hitting the surrounding areas of your college may be one of the only ways you have to meet other queer people your age and tap into LGBTQ culture at large.

In many cities, there are "gay-friendly" coffee shops or bookstores that cater to a college crowd and eagerly welcome all sorts of alternative types. In larger towns, there may even be entire "gayborhoods" where large numbers of LGBTQ people live and work. Many offer queer gyms, restaurants, clothing stores, salons, and other retails spaces that specifically target the queer community. While some people see these "gayborhoods" as homogenized and confining city spaces, they often act like giant "Safe Zones" where members of the queer community can feel a little safer and less likely to face intolerance or homophobia.

If you're attending a school in an urban environment, or even a school on a suburban campus near a big city, you'll probably have a variety of bars, clubs, and vibrant cultural options to tap into. But if your college is in a rural area, or if it's extremely small, your options might be far more limited. In some cases, there may only be one "gay" bar (if any) in the county. In worse cases, the climate of the region may be so "anti-gay" that there are few, if any, resources or safe spaces, period. Here are some tips to help you integrate on- and off-campus life wherever you attend college:

- Ask your LGBTQ center or advisor if there are stores, restaurants, nightclubs, coffeehouses, and other hang-outs within a few miles of the university that cater to an LGBTQ audience.

- Check out any available weekly newspapers that cater to LGBTQ people in the surrounding community. Local LGBTQ-focused newspapers contain current information of interest to the community as well as a variety of listings for events such as concerts, performances, movies, and parties. These mostly free publications can point you in the direction of a vast array of resources in the area. Plus, they won't break your student budget.

- If you're attending a university within or near a large metropolitan area, chances are there's some type of LGBTQ community center within your reach where you can participate in a variety of activities, groups, and events, depending on your interests. You can also utilize these centers to find out about additional LGBTQ activities in the surrounding areas including club nights, pride events, and support groups.

Consortium Tips on Finding Off-Campus LGBTQ Resources

by Lis Maurer, Coordinator of the Center for LGBT Education, Outreach, and Services, Ithaca College

So you've moved to campus, unpacked your things, found your way to classes and the dining hall, and maybe you've made some new friends already. Now you're ready to strike out a little further, and see what else awaits you in your new surroundings. What opportunities does your new town or city hold? Connecting with local LGBTQ community resources can open up a plethora of opportunities for extracurricular fun, while at the same time putting you in touch with potential contacts for your curricular areas of study and/or career interests. Some communities have rich networks of social and educational groups, clubs, and activities. LGBTQ students may get involved in the local community for many reasons—to meet new people, try out new interests and skills, find potential internship opportunities or career mentors, or to give back to the community.

The first step to connecting with LGBTQ community resources outside your campus may be as simple as connecting with your on-campus LGBTQ Resource Center. If your campus has a Resource Center, it is usually a place with information about LGBTQ happenings both on and off campus. Campus LGBTQ Resource Centers are usually also great places to connect with like-minded people—students, faculty, and staff—who are familiar with the local area and its LGBTQ and allied offerings.

If your campus does not yet have an LGBTQ Resource Center, don't worry! There are many other ways to find out what's happening. More than 150 cities across the United States have LGBTQ Community Centers. These are similar to campus-based centers, and they offer a wide variety of resources, services, support, advocacy, and referrals for everyone in the local region. Such centers may catalog information about events, groups, and job opportunities in the area, and many offer classes and events of their own. The National Association of Lesbian, Gay, Bisexual, and Transgender Community Centers maintains a directory of community-based centers at LGBTcenters.org. Check it out to see if one is near you.

A third way to connect is to network, network, network! Talk with people you know, and let them know the types of things in which you're interested. Ask students for their suggestions, talk with out professors and staff, read the local (as well as campus) newspaper for event listings and activities. In smaller towns, sometimes businesses take on "double duty"—a restaurant or club may have an "LGBTQ night," a chain bookstore may have LGBTQ book clubs that meet regularly, or the dance studio may cater to both hetero- and same sex couples with fun events and lessons for all. Many communities also have an "Information and Referral" phone number (or sometimes a smaller social service directory) that can provide resources and referrals on everything from finding the local PFLAG chapter to learning if there is a gay bowling league in town.

Still considering what college to attend? Want to know more about the local area before deciding? Ask the campus LGBTQ Resource Center or LGBTQ student group to connect you with current students who can give you the scoop on where they go to find the local LGBTQ scene. When considering colleges, ask the Admissions Office if there is a resource for prospective LGBTQ students available that describes the climate for LGBTQ issues on campus and in the community. During campus visits, be sure to venture into town to see which businesses display pride flags or decals in their windows, to see whether you can find a local LGBTQ newspaper or events calendar, and what other services or businesses are well-known for being LGBTQ-friendly. In some communities, there are so many resources that it is difficult to choose—sport leagues, book groups, welcoming congregations, dinner clubs, knitting circles, bookstores, eateries, clubs and nightlife, and groups of just about every type that are LGBTQ or LGBTQ-friendly.

QUEER-TIP: A DATABASE JUST FOR YOU

Looking for a fantastic way to meet friends in your city, get questions answered by professional and outreach volunteers, or find support for whatever issue you are facing? QueerAmerica is a database published by OutProud, The National Coalition for Gay, Lesbian, Bisexual, and Transgender Youth. With over 5,000 entries, it's the largest collection of queer resources in the nation, and includes information on community centers, support organizations, queer youth groups, and more. You'll also be able to locate LGBTQ facilities in the vicinity of your college campus. To conduct a search, log onto QueerAmerica.com.

CHAPTER 9
DEALING WITH HOMO/BI/TRANSPHOBIA ON CAMPUS (AND OFF)

THE NATIONAL GAY AND LESBIAN TASK FORCE ON THE CAMPUS CLIMATE

In May 2003, the National Gay and Lesbian Task Force published a report—"Campus Climate for Gay, Lesbian, Bisexual and Transgender People: A National Perspective"—that documented the experiences and perceptions of anti-LGBTQ bias and harassment, along with levels of institutional support for LGBTQ people at colleges and universities across the country.[1] Based on a survey of nearly 1700 students, faculty, and staff, *Campus Climate* revealed some startling statistics:

- More than one-third (36 percent) of LGBTQ undergraduate students experienced harassment within the year prior to taking the survey, as did 29 percent of all respondents.

- Those who experienced harassment reported that derogatory remarks were the most common form (89 percent) and that students were most often the source of harassment (79 percent).

- Twenty percent of all respondents feared for their physical safety because of their sexual orientation or gender identity, and 51 percent concealed their sexual orientation or gender identity to avoid intimidation.

- Respondents felt that LGBTQ people were likely to be harassed on campus. Seventy-one percent felt that transgender people were likely to suffer harassment, and 61 percent felt that gay men and lesbians were likely to be harassed.

- Forty-three percent of the respondents rated their overall campus climate as homophobic.

The Task Force's findings reveal that homo/bi/transphobia is still a very prevalent concern for the LGBTQ campus community. This chapter discusses this topic at length, and lets you know what you can do if you are the victim of a homo/bi/transphobia act during your time at college. We'll point you toward a variety of additional resources to help you

---

1   Susan R. Rankin. *Campus Climate for Gay, Lesbian, Bisexual, and Transgender People: A National Perspective.* New York: The National Gay and Lesbian Task Force Policy Institute. 2003. www.ngltf.org.

combat homo/bi/transphobia; you'll also find candid words of support from other students and even some parents, as well as advice on how to deal with expressions of homo/bi/transphobia from your peers, teachers, and administrators should they arise.

Consortium Tips on Handling Administrative Homophobia

by Ken Schneck, Assistant Dean of Student Affairs, Sarah Lawrence College

Unfortunately, each and every day, we are all confronted with not only homophobic commentary, but with sexist and racist rhetoric that propagates bigoted thinking. Just look at what passes for our mainstream media these days and you can see that this is not a perfect world, nor is it a world that always supports us or members of other marginalized groups. Whether it's someone calling you a "fag" if you can't catch a football (how many of us had to go through that horror!) or a "bitch" if you don't put up with sexist talk, these comments and acts hit hard and have reverberating effects on us as unique individuals and collectively as a society. And while there are battles to be fought in order to secure the rights and protection of *all* underserved and at risk populations, your biggest concern right now is how to handle homophobia should you experience it during your time in college.

> "I haven't experienced [homophobia] as directed to me personally but I have felt it from my campus. There is definitely a certain attitude here that emphasizes a general regard to homosexuality as being frowned upon, even the way it is discussed in a classroom environment in a Morals and Ethics Philosophy course."
>
> Vanessa, Sophomore, Texas A&M University— College Station

Daniel Coleman, the Program Coordinator for Gay, Lesbian, Bisexual and Transgender Student Support Services at Indiana University, echoes this sentiment: "Hearing one of your peers say something homophobic is one thing. Hearing those same anti-gay words come out of the mouth of a faculty or staff member is quite another. Often our attention is focused so much on creating acceptance and sensitivity within the student population that we forget that a faculty or staff member could possibly be homophobic."

The following tips are for students who experience administrative homo/bi/transphobia:

> "In classroom debates, other students will sometimes say things such as, '*Perverts* do not deserve to have civil rights.' I just look at it as an opportunity to speak up on behalf of the entire community."
>
> Jacob, Junior, Columbia University

- **Know It's Not Okay.** It can be truly jarring to hear a faculty or staff member say something homo/bi/transphobic. After all, they are the individuals in power, the role-models who should be setting the tone of safety and inclusion for the entire campus community. The important thing to remember is that they're also just people, some of whom embody the same hostility and lack of understanding for LGBTQ issues as anyone else in the world. They could be your most thought-provoking professor or that Director of Student Activities who has really helped your organization grow. None of that makes their anti-LGBTQ comments or actions acceptable. Nor does it mean that they are entitled to have their homo/bi/transphobia ignored.

- **Know Your Allies.** Somewhere in your institution, you have LGBTQ allies. Chances are you already know who they are. Seek out those individuals and engage them in conversation about how they think you should respond to a homo/bi/transphobic staff or faculty member. It will quickly become clear whether or not they are truly allies and will assist you in addressing the anti-gay statements. If they are not offering suggestions or you feel like they're not backing you up, it's ok to back off the conversation. The hope is that they ask more specific questions and actively look to support you.

- **Know Your Rights.** The goal of every college is to protect its students from harm. Some are just more explicit in their protections for LGBTQ individuals than others. Do some research to find out what protections your institution offers for you through their non-discrimination statement and general code of conduct. Somewhere in those policies should be a method by which you can file a complaint about faculty and staff. Try to document the exact wording of the homo/bi/transphobic comment or action you observed, when it occurred and any campus officials (allies or otherwise) with whom you discussed the incident. All of this information will assist you in the grievance process.

Hopefully you will never be in the situation where you are the recipient of an anti-gay comment from a faculty or staff member. If you are, feel empowered to take some action to make sure it doesn't happen again, to you or any of your peers.

QUEER & CANDID: STUDENTS SHARE THEIR EXPERIENCES WITH ADMINISTRATIVE AND FACULTY HOMO/BI/TRANSPHOBIA

"I experienced homophobia from my former swim coach and team. My first experience occurred when my friend and captain told me that some people on the team felt uncomfortable with my sexual orientation. My second experience happened when my coach pulled aside a friend of mine and asked if it was okay that he chose her to room with me on a 'team training' trip. When she responded that I was the only one she would want to room with anyway, he was startled that not only was she okay with it, she was actually happy with his decision. I quit the team not long after that."

"Bridget," Sophomore, Carnegie Mellon University

"In some classes, professors may go on diatribes against gay marriage or homosexuality, employ philosophers who say homosexuality goes against 'natural law,' or other anti-gay views. But in general, professors are very respectful when discussing the issue."

Michael, Senior, Saint Anselm College

"Although the upper administration is not happy with visibility of LGBTQ students, students and faculty tend to be very supportive. However, the student body is not as supportive of LGBTQ students as it was two years ago when Wells was still a single-sex institution."

"Lily," Senior, Wells College

HAND IN HAND: ARE PUBLIC DISPLAYS OF AFFECTION ACCEPTABLE?

Public displays of affections, or PDAs as they are commonly known, are everyday acts that our straight friends and families take for granted. No one would bat an eye if a guy and a girl were to hold hands on the quad or kiss on the steps of the science building. But PDAs for queer students . . . well that's a whole other story. Around certain student populations, and on some college campuses, the simple and loving act of holding hands with, kissing, or hugging your LGBTQ loved one can potentially cause you to become the target of homo/bi/transphobia. But PDA among queers may also enhance and enriche queer visibility on your campus and cause peers to have to confront their own close-mindedness about "seeing" queer physical contact.

There is no question that LGBTQ students deserve, and need, to express themselves just like everyone else. Some of you may feel out and proud and want to visibly demonstrate that you have the same rights that non-LGBTQ students have. But public displays of affection do not come easily to everyone. Figuring out just how much PDA is right for you, depends on some basic factors. Ask yourself these questions:

- Do I really care what people think?
- How queer-friendly is my campus?
- Am I doing this in a safe space?
- Am I putting myself and the other person at risk?
- Am I doing it to get a rise out of people or to genuinely show affection with my partner?

During our research for this book, we asked both straight and queer students to respond to the following survey question: "Do you feel comfortable seeing public displays of affection of campus." The responses ran the gamut—from outright hostile and bigoted ("as long as it is not between gays"; "two guys kissing here would be a major event...they would get their asses kicked"; and "only between normal straight couples") to defiantly supportive of LGBTQ students' rights ("I'm proud when I see it because some couples have to be very courageous to do it"; "why should it bother me"; and "I'm pro-love, provided it's between two mature and consenting people. If someone's comfortable enough to make out in front of me, I'm comfortable enough to be in their presence/watch.") But interestingly enough, the majority of students said that they did not want to see any public displays of affections among anyone, straight or queer.

So where does that leave you? The reality is that in some settings, whether on or off campus, physical expressions of affection or attraction between LGBTQ individuals are not looked upon "favorably." On the other hand, some schools are very supportive, and their student bodies respect and support the LGBTQ population in its efforts toward visibility. Only you can gauge your school's level of tolerance and acceptance and your individual comfort level with PDAs. Whatever you do, don't forget to consider your partner's feelings first—while PDAs among LGBTQ students can certainly make a political statement, it should not be at the expense of your intimacy with one another.

QUEER & CANDID: STUDENTS SHARE THEIR EXPERIENCES WITH PEER-TO-PEER HOMOPHOBIA

"I kissed my boyfriend once at a party and we were both called 'fags.' Before it got any worse, we just decided to leave. My friend who knew the people having the party confronted them on it and really stuck up for us."

"Bobby," Junior, University of Wisconsin—Madison

"I have most definitely experienced discrimination and homophobia/heterosexism. The most prominent example I can think of was selling bracelets to fundraise for the Translating Identity Conference (TIC is a student run Trans-Identities educational conference at the University of Vermont). I explained what TIC is and how it is run and why we needed to fundraise so much. The response I got from one of the students in the group of friends that stopped was, 'So this supports trannies? [Forget] that, freak.' His friends all nodded in agreement and they walked off laughing and slapping five and patting the kid who made the comment on the back."

"Frankie," Sophomore, University of Vermont

"I have encountered biphobia on campus in many subtle, as well as some not-so-subtle, ways. I will never forget reading in my Intro to Microbiology textbook that bisexuals were to blame for the spread of AIDS in America. It has also been fairly common for me, after coming out to large groups of people both on and off campus, to have a few individuals come up to me later, usually in private, and solicit me for sexual favors or even touch me inappropriately because they assume that I, as a bisexual woman, would be promiscuous. Additionally, even in the most 'politically correct' queer circles on campus, there are always one or two members who do not believe that bisexuality exists (i.e. that it is 'just a phase' on the way to 'real' queerness or heterosexuality). More rarely, people sometimes come to one of the queer groups on campus and vocalize their disdain for bisexuals because they accuse bi people of trying to hold on to some form of heteronormative privilege. Contrary to what some people might think, bisexuals face stereotypes and hatred from not only the straight, but also in many cases, the queer, community."

Lauren, Senior, Michigan State University

Consortium Tips on Personally Handling Homophobia, Biphobia, and Transphobia

by Lis Maurer, Coordinator, Center for LGBT Education, Outreach, and Services, Ithaca College

Homophobia is the irrational fear or hatred about attraction between people of the same sex; biphobia is the fear or hatred of people with a strong sexual and emotional attraction to both men and women; transphobia is the fear or hatred of people of trans experience, including, but not limited to, transsexuals, transgender individuals, and genderqueers. Confronting homophobia, biphobia, and transphobia can be difficult. It is a challenge to remain calm, self-confident, and positive in the face of blatant (and sometimes not-so-blatant) disrespect. Here are some tips on how to deal when the going gets tough:

- **Try to keep in mind that it's not about you.**

  Even when it stings and seems like a very personal attack, remember that the roots of homo/bi/transphobia are an irrational, unreasoned fear.

- **Make sure you are safe.**

  Never challenge someone/something if you fear for your physical safety. Be sure you know of other resources on campus that can assist you with confronting homo/bi/transphobia, or with reporting potential incidents of bias or discrimination. Know your campus policies regarding non-discrimination.

- **Gently educate.**

  Sometimes people don't know the hurtful effect of their words. Because it is still difficult to learn about the history and culture of LGBTQ people, some students may arrive at college without knowledge of which terms are potentially insensitive or offensive. They cannot know this unless you educate by telling them. Try calmly saying "When you use those words or make those jokes, I feel put down," or "It sounds like you think no one is hurt by those remarks, but I am," or "LGBTQ people, people who have LGBTQ family members or friends, or classmates who have LGBTQ parents may really tune out to what you have to say when you use those types of words because they are considered insulting."

- **Pick a good time.**

  Some homo/bi/transphobic situations can come up very publicly; others arise in a small group or between just a couple of friends or peers. Deciding whether and how to respond requires you to take into account many factors, including how much time is available, where the situation takes place, how well you know the person/people, and other details. In some situations you may speak up right away, while in others you may say "I'd really like to talk about what just happened, can we make time to get together later?" Also, in some situations you may choose to just walk away.

- **Equip allies.**

  Friends and allies can assist tremendously in this work. Sometimes allies can be very powerful, especially when intervening around a dimension of diversity which they themselves do not share. Does your campus provide bystander training or some similar process (such as the National Coalition

Building Institute [www.ncbi.org] and other diversity and coalition building training models) through which students can receive training and tips for intervening in situations of discrimination or bias? Find out, or advocate for the start of a new skills building program of this type.

- **Practice!**

Practicing strategies takes time and preparation. Take the time to think through different ways you could approach situations; perhaps talk it out or role play with a friend. Some campuses offer training to help you design and refine your responses to common types of homophobia encountered in the college environment. Cultivate many different strategies and approaches.

- **Stock your toolbox with many different ideas.**

A technique as simple as modeling how to use inclusive language, or how to intervene as an ally for someone else around another dimension of diversity, can go a long way toward helping others see how they too can be role models for respect. Be intentional and thoughtful as you consider ways to counter homo/bi/transphobia while remaining calm, centered, and balanced. Encouraging people to talk about how homo/bi/transphobia affects heterosexual people may also go far to illustrate how this issue is important for everyone.

- **Take care!**

Sometimes we have the energy to address or confront homo/bi/transphobia, and sometimes we are running on empty. Evaluate whether you are mentally prepared to take on each situation. Even LGBTQ professionals sometimes need a rest or a break from confronting bias. Living in a world with homo/bi/transphobia and heterosexism can cause wear and tear on both your body and your soul. Seek support from friends, family, and allies. Take care to attend to your health and wellness needs. Develop methods to creatively channel negative feelings—talk it out, take a hike, listen to music, pound on a pillow, make some art! Identify and develop your support system, and ask for help when needed.

- **Remember: Life is complicated and messy.**

  Sometimes people need time to think through their own thoughts and feelings. Even people who are questioning whether they might be LGBTQ may engage in bias behavior—either because of the discomfort they are examining within themselves, to "fit in," or to "throw people off the track" of their own identity or their questioning process. Realize that ideas about identity are complicated, and sometimes a person may hold two beliefs or ideas that seem to be in direct opposition to each other. Sometimes people need time to reconcile or explore these ideas themselves, or with a trusted advisor or friend. Also recognize that homo/bi/transphobia and heterosexism can exist within ourselves as well as in others. Nobody's perfect, and our own internalized oppression can keep us from reaching our full potential just as much as acts of discrimination from the outside world. Recognize that being self-aware can help you act with compassion toward others' missteps or mistakes, especially if you have ever made them yourself.

- **Finally, never doubt yourself!**

  You have the right to feel safe and validated, and deserve the same freedom, dignity, and respect as your heterosexual peers. If you feel unsafe, unsettled, or targeted due to the comments or actions of others, you have the right to stand up and say so. This is one of the challenges all LGBTQ people face, living in a world where heterosexism and homo/bi/transphobia exist. You are a good, valid, and important person. You have the right to be—to be who you are, to love who you love, to speak your mind, to learn what you need to know, to get the care and attention you need, to speak up in class, and to be yourself.

PFLAG PARENT TIP: SAFEGUARDING YOUR CHILD FROM HOMO/BI/TRANSPHOBIA ON CAMPUS

LGBTQ students have all the basic needs for safety of any college student, and then some. Probably the biggest concern parents have for their LGBTQ students is their physical safety against homophobic attacks. Brett-Genny Janiczek Beemyn, the Director of the Stonewall Center at the University of Massachusetts—Amherst, suggests that parents guide their children towards schools with a supportive environment for LGBTQ students. This, Beemyn stresses, will minimize the possibility of acts of homo/bi/transphobia towards their children, and ensure that a good response system is in place for when such acts occur. Beemyn says, "While no college is immune to incidents of LGBTQ harassment . . . some schools send a strong signal, administratively and through the student culture, that such actions are inappropriate and will not be tolerated." Here is what some parents of LGBTQ college students had to say about how their families handled these concerns:

"As the parent of a gay freshman living in the dorm, I was concerned about his safety in the community showers and bathrooms, but nothing ever happened."

"Katarina," Pennsylvania

"I always advise other parents to safeguard their children from homophobia by discussing what forms it might take in college, then developing a plan to deal with it as it arises."

"Patrick," Ohio

"We are always concerned. However, we trust our [MTF] daughter's judgment and behavior. I did make her note where the panic boxes were on campus. My best advice for trans students is to move in groups and stay away from obvious homophobic scenes. And it is always best for people to know you are trans, especially in intimate situations. Things can get dangerous when others out you."

"Denise," California

"In our son's college, they had just begun a program for first-years called SPECTRUM which placed all self-identified LGBTQ students on one floor of the dorm. This was a real plus, and in addition, the university had a gay resource center with plenty of social and activist opportunities. So when he arrived on campus he had an already built in community."

"Marlena," Indiana

"Our daughter did not want to live in a dorm, instead choosing her own apartment on campus. This worked well because she made many friends in the building."

"David," Utah

"I was initially concerned about her roommate. The girl she was originally assigned to room with seemed like a great fit. But a last minute change had her paired with someone very different. But it also seems that rooming with someone you are not going to spend a lot of time socializing with has its advantages too."

"Richard," New Jersey

"Have your child join a LGBTQ campus social group. They educate students in so many ways about safety, legal rights, and even just the basic transition to college."

"Jim," Kentucky

"I did worry about our son's safety, but he is smart and stays with his close friends."

"Lonnie," North Dakota

"Your child may need to be reminded that the RA, campus counselors, and other resources are there to help them, but for the most part they are so glad to be on their own they will handle whatever comes up and it gives them something to talk about at length with their new friends."

"Ruth," New York

"Because our daughter was targeted by an adult hate group while she was still in high school, everything that happened after that seemed so much easier to deal with. And she has always had our unconditional love and support."

"Andie," Texas

"I would recommend your child not being so out that everyone knows, just trusted friends. It is a safety issue, not a denial of who they are."

"Mimsie," Massachusetts

"I cautioned her as I did all my daughters to travel in groups, let friends know their whereabouts, and their expected time of return. Very important to have students exchange phone numbers of their friend's parents, including home and work numbers, and cells. Just a little reassurance that someone will get in touch if there's a problem."

"Sophia," Tennessee

"He has been fortunate to have either gay or gay-friendly roommates with the exception of his first year, and during that time I was a frequent visitor to his residence hall so any problems he had with his homophobic roommate were kept to a minimum."

"Sandra," New York

"High school was such a terribly homophobic environment for my son that college turned out to be an incredibly liberating experience for him. There are so many types of people there, all of different races, religions, genders, and sexual preferences. My son tells me as a result, most people just don't care who he loves. They are so wrapped up in their own activities they don't have time to harass others."

"Grace," Texas

"Our trans son lived in off-campus housing after his first year to avoid the whole bathroom privacy issue."

"Kenneth," New Mexico

"On-campus homophobia was not the problem. Rather, community-wide 'queer politics' can be the issue, and even on a LGBTQ-friendly campus, your child can wind up on the wrong side of prevailing queer issues."

"Marianne," Arizona

"I was very worried about our son's safety at first, even though I knew his school was pretty liberal. I was afraid someone would target him for being gay and try to hurt him physically. But he's handled this by being smart and cautious."

"Darla," Texas

> "I used to tell her not to wear any buttons that would let people know she was a lesbian and make her a target. I doubt she listened to me but it made me feel better to say it."
>
> "Suzanne," Alaska

Whatever your concerns, the first step is for you to talk about them with your child. Together you can come up with preventative steps that will ease your anxiety and help ensure that your LGBTQ child is as protected as possible from the violence often associated with homo/bi/transphobia.

TRANS-SENSITIVE U: SCHOOLS IN STATES PROTECTING TRANSITIONING STUDENTS' RIGHTS ON CAMPUS

Individuals of trans experience are often faced with some of the most violent reactions in our communities. Yet, on the collegiate front, it seems as if sensitivity and support of transitioning students is moving in the right direction at many leading institutions across the country. According to the most recent data available from the Transgender Law and Policy Institute, there are currently seventy-nine colleges and universities and one law school in the United States that have non-discrimination policies that include gender identity/expression.[2] The following is a list of affected schools with the year the policy change went into effect, if known.

- **Arizona**

  Arizona State University (2004); University of Arizona (2005)

---

2   Transgender Law and Policy Institute. "Colleges and Universities with Non-discrimination Policies that Include Gender Identity/Expression." www.transgenderlaw.org/college/index.htm#policies.

- **California**

  California College of the Arts; California Institute of Technology (2004); City College of San Francisco (2005); Foothill-DeAnza Community College District (2006); Golden Gate University School of Law (2005); Harvey Mudd College (2005); Occidental College (2006); University of California system (2004); University of Southern California (2004)

- **Colorado**

  Colorado State University (2004)

- **Connecticut**

  Connecticut College (2005); Wesleyan University (2002); Yale University (2006)

- **Florida**

  New College of Florida (2006)

- **Illinois**

  Knox College (2001); Parkland College (2006); University of Chicago (2004); University of Illinois system (2005)

- **Indiana**

  DePauw University (1999)

- **Iowa**

  Central College (2005); Drake University (2004); Iowa State University (2005); Southwestern Community College (2003); University of Iowa (1996)

- **Maine**

  Colby College (2005); Rockport College (2000); University of Maine system (2006)

- **Maryland**

  Goucher College (2006); Johns Hopkins University (2005); University of Baltimore (2006)

- **Massachusetts**

  Brandeis University (2006); Harvard University (2006); Massachusetts Institute of Technology (2003); Suffolk University (2006); Tufts University (2005); Western New England College (2006); Williams College (2006)

- **Michigan**

  Kalamazoo College (2000); Kalamazoo Valley Community College (2005); Western Michigan University (2006)

- **New Hampshire**

  Dartmouth College (2006); University of New Hampshire (2005)

- **New Jersey**

  Princeton University (2006)

- **New Mexico**

  College of Santa Fe (2005)

- **New York**

  City University of New York system (2002–2003); Columbia University (2006); Cornell University (2005); Ithaca College (2006); New York University (2005); Rochester Institute of Technology (2005); Sarah Lawrence College (2006); Syracuse University (2005); Vassar College (2006)

- **North Carolina**

  North Carolina State University (2005)

- **Ohio**

  Case Western Reserve University (2006); Ohio State University (2004)

- **Oregon**

  Oregon State University (2005); University of Oregon (2005)

- **Pennsylvania**

  Carnegie Mellon University (2003); Lehigh University (2003); Moravian University (2006); Muhlenberg College (2005); Pennsylvania State University—UNiversity Park (2006); University of Pennsylvania (2003)

- **Rhode Island**

  Brown University (2001–2002); Bryant University (2005); Community College of Rhode Island; Rhode Island College; University of Rhode Island (2003-04)

- **Vermont**

  Middlebury College (2003); University of Vermont (2005)

- **Washington**

  Central Washington University (2005); The Evergreen State College (2006); University of Puget Sound (2002–2003); University of Washington; Whitman College (2001)

- **Washington, DC**

  American University (2002)

- **Wisconsin**

  University of Wisconsin system (2005)

While not on the list, Rutgers University and the University of Michigan state in footnotes to their policies that discrimination based on "sex" includes transgender people or gender identity/expression. According to Brett Genny Janiczek Beemyn, Director of the Stonewall Center at the University of Massachussetts—Amherst and Jessica Pettitt, CAMPUSPEAK Speaker, changing the nondiscrimination policy to reflect gender identity/expression is only the first step toward creating trans-inclusiveness on campus as the study they conducted of 25 colleges and universities who adopted trans-inclusive nondiscrimination policies prior to 2005 revealed. "We were particularly interested in examining areas of campus life in which transgender students often report experiencing discrimination: having access to safe and appropriate bathrooms and locker rooms; being housed in keeping with their gender identity/expression; having access to appropriate medical care, including hormones for transitioning students; being able to change the gender designation on campus records; having trans-inclusive gender categories on institutional forms; and offering trans-related programming," says Beemyn and Pettitt. They discovered that few changes had occurred as a result of the changes to the schools' nondiscrimination policies and said that "given the amount of time required to construct new restrooms and the brief time that most of the campuses have had a trans-inclusive policy, this finding is not surprising."

That said, even in areas where institutions might be able to implement changes more quickly, progress has been slow. For example, "None of the colleges and universities in the study offered the option for students to self-identify beyond 'male' and 'female' on all institutional forms." On the upside, "Most of the institutions surveyed were trans-inclusive [when it came to] providing transgender-related programming." Beemyn and Pettitt suggest that the general lack of progress on transgender inclusion sends an important message: "All colleges and universities have work to do on transgender issues, and no campus is so far behind other institutions that it cannot catch up." They encourage colleges and universities to "assess their progress in meeting the needs of transgender students and begin dialogues that can lead to further trans-supportive changes." For more information about their study and to find out more information about how universities are working towards improving the rights of its trans students, visit www.transgenderlaw.org/college/index.htm#practices.

QUEER & CANDID: A Trans Student Speaks
Out about Transphobia

"I see institutional discrimination in many ways through my activist work on campus. Though we succeeded last April in changing our university's non-discrimination policy to protect against discrimination on the basis of gender identity and expression, there are currently no official policies on this campus that ensure that trans students have access to safe housing, access to counseling services, access to the health center, access to insurance coverage, access to adequately trained and trustworthy police services, access to public facilities, or recognition in the language used on written policies, forms, general information, and publicity on this campus. I currently do not have access to the same resources that every other senior has through the career center, as the new program they just purchased that electronically conducts personality and career assessments and provides online resources to students requires that one select a "gender" to sign up, the only choices being male or female. I brought this to the attention of the Director of the Career Center and was promised that he would personally look into this problem for me, but he resigned before I ever heard back. We have a lot of out queer staff, administrators are generally supportive, there are a couple of queer electives taught here, and we have student activities funding for the LGBTQ organization, but in my opinion this disconnect just serves to illustrate how often people are ignorant to all of the ways that homophobia adds up and also how often the T in LGBTQ is a silent T."

Marcus, Senior, Brandeis University

TAKE ACTION: FACILITATION LEGAL AND ADMINISTRATIVE RESPONSES TO HOMO/BI/TRANSPHOBIA

Some of you may think that there's nothing you can do if you are the victim of homophobic actions. Others may think that you can single-handedly bring down the system. The truth actually lies somewhere in the middle. Fortunately there are many organizations working to improve queer student rights on campuses across the country. Hayley Gorenberg, Deputy Legal Director for Lambda Legal explains: "Lambda Legal has worked on a variety of issues on college campuses from defending gay supportive campus groups to fending off attacks on domestic partner benefits for university employees." Gorenberg adds that "currently Lambda Legal has two open cases relating to LGBTQ issues on campus. Lambda Legal represents Professors Jean Lynch and Yvonne Keller, after the domestic partner benefits offered by their employer, Miami University (OH), came under attack by the antigay Alliance Defense Fund (ADF). The ADF, along with ultraconservative

Ohio legislator Thomas Brinkman, is suing the university, claiming that its domestic partner benefits violate Ohio's constitutional amendment, which limits marriage to a man and a woman."

In the second case, "Brett Timmerman, a student at University of Wisconsin at Platteville, was about to walk into a local sandwich shop when his attackers called him a 'faggot.' Then Oden Waite and Enove Urias slapped and spit in Timmerman's face and struck him in the head before pushing him to the ground. Though Timmerman said he felt safe while on campus, he felt unsafe in the surrounding community."

Most of you will never have to deal with such extreme experiences as a queer college student, but if you are a victim—no matter what the scale—remember that there is support out there. These cases prove that while we have come a long way toward advancing the rights of LGBTQ people, there is much, much more to accomplish. Remember, *you don't need to be a victim*. Take great pride in who you are and if you find yourself in a situation that needs legal action, contact Lamda Legal to find out how they can put you in touch with the right advocates.

CHAPTER 10
STAYING HEALTHY, FIT, AND FABULOUS AT COLLEGE

SOUND BODY, SOUND MIND

There's a reason university health insurance is a mandatory part of your tuition and fees at most colleges, and you're required to show proof of a gazillion immunizations before you're even allowed to step foot on campus. It's because campus life can be a virtual cesspool of germs. Think about it: You're living in close quarters with dozens of students where wheezes and sneezes are as transferable as lecture notes. Your class schedule, extracurricular activities, and social calendar keep you constantly on the go, and you're fueling it all with a not-so-well-balanced diet of late night pizza, soda, and the occasional beer. Not to mention the stress that comes with college life in general. Together these form just the right conditions for a not-so-healthy lifestyle. It's inevitable that as a college student you will get sick, and you won't have mom and dad around to stroke your forehead and bring you soup. Fortunately, your University Health Center is well-equipped to handle the minor aches and pains that come with college life. But there's an even better strategy for dealing with these concerns. Have you ever heard the old adage: "An ounce of prevention is worth a pound of cure?" The truth is there are some basic things you can do that will go a long way toward helping you stay healthy at college:

- **Maintain a positive attitude**

  The first step toward maintaining your physical health at college is to maintain a positive attitude about college life. While you're sure to miss your family and your old GSA buddies, campus life will bring with it plenty of opportunities to forge new friendships and connections. While you might be unsure about whether you can handle the academic rigors of college, remember that there are plenty of resources available—tutors, study groups, advisors—to help you succeed; you just have to seek them out. If you still find yourself feeling blue, talk to someone. Your University Health Center will offer counseling services, and the LGBTQ Resource Center on campus is a great place to go for help and advice about queer-specific concerns. If you can succeed in staying positive, everything else has a tendency to fall into place.

- **Diet**

  Everyone has heard about the dreaded "Freshman 15." It's not just the grilled cheese sandwiches and chicken fingers on the menu in your school's cafeteria that helps students pack on the pounds. It's also their on-the-go lifestyle that contributes to the weight gain. As your routine becomes more and more hectic you'll find yourself eating at irregular times and grabbing whatever snacks might be available. In order to avoid the Freshman 15 you're going to have exercise some restraint: Cut out the late night pizza runs, drink lots of water, increase your intake of fresh fruit and vegetables, and eat smaller portions throughout the day. Having a healthy diet is not just about avoiding the Freshman 15. Your diet directly affects your energy levels which impacts your immune system; in other words, eat a healthy diet and you're less likely to get run-down and become sick.

- **Exercise**

  Regular exercise is a crucial component of maintaining a healthy lifestyle on campus. Fortunately, many college students—through participation in intercollegiate or intramural sports teams or simply walking, running, and biking across campus to make it to their next class—get lots of exercise without even trying, but many others get far too little. Like diet, exercise can directly affect your energy levels. Tuition fees at most colleges include the cost of membership at the on-campus gym, so why not take advantage? These campus gyms are often pretty cushy affairs, offering classes like yoga, Pilates, fencing, kick-boxing, swimming, free-weights training—you name it! If hanging out at the campus gym isn't your thing, there are plenty of little things you can do throughout the course of the day to get your blood pumping. Take the stairs instead of the elevator, or walk into town instead of taking the bus. Organize a pick-up game of Ultimate Frisbee, or have your LGBTQ student group sponsor an all-night dance-a-thon. Get the picture? Whatever you decide to do for exercise, make sure that you eat a light, healthy snack first, and drink plenty of water.

- **Get those Zzzzzs**

  While eight hours of sleep a night might be asking a bit much, you should still try to get a regular sleep routine down. Whether you're an early riser or a night owl, the key is to sleep *restfully*. This means avoiding working to the point of exhaustion before collapsing into a sleep-induced coma, and occasionally skipping a circuit party in order to stay in and get your beauty rest. When you're eating right and exercising properly, it's easier to sleep well. If you're having trouble sleeping in a noisy dorm, consider investing in one of those noise-silencing headphones; you'll be sleeping like a baby in no time.

While these are important preventative measures, your health at college is about more than diet and exercise and beating the occasional cold. In the following sections we discuss more serious student health concerns—stress, depression, sexually transmitted diseases and infections (STDIs) and sexual health—that require you to take a more active role in educating yourself and seeking out resources to help you deal with these issues should any problems occur. Whether you've got a toothache or you're struggling with an STDI, the important thing to remember is that there is help out there—even if you have to look off campus to find it.

Consortium Tips on Health and Wellness for the LGBTQ Student

by Lis Maurer, Coordinator, Center for LGBT Education, Outreach, and Services, Ithaca College

Many people only think of their health when they feel a cold coming on, but did you know there are several different kinds of health and wellness that are important for college students (and everyone!) to pay attention to? Students in college may be aware of their physical health, and perhaps their intellectual health, but the six Dimensions of Wellness model reminds us to be attentive to six distinct yet interconnected areas of health and wellness.[1] They are: physical wellness, emotional wellness, social wellness, intellectual wellness, spiritual wellness, and occupational wellness.

1 Dr. Bill Hettler. "The Six Dimensional Wellness Mode."The National Wellness Institute. www.nationalwellness.org/index.php?id=391&id_tier=381.

While the six dimensions of wellness are important considerations for all college students, LGBTQ students may face additional factors that can be challenges, or perhaps even opportunities, for their health. Some LGBTQ students arrive on campus and hit the ground running, getting involved—and even taking on important leadership roles—in on-campus LGBTQ groups as well as other student groups. This involvement can pose both challenges and opportunities for health. On the positive side, feeling connected to your new campus and fellow students, experiencing the excitement of bringing an idea to fruition, and enjoying the sense of being part of something bigger on campus, can all support dimensions of health and wellness in many ways. On the other hand, pulling all-nighters to get that publicity plan ready for the next big event, or trying to work on ideas and issues with people who may have differing, yet just as passionately held views, may impact a student's health and wellness too. LGBTQ student leader burnout can also be a real issue—so real that some campuses hold specially-tailored sessions to help LGBTQ students recognize the warning signs and create strategies to stay healthy and on track.

Other LGBTQ students experience challenges to their health in the form of homophobia and heterosexism. Confronting stressful or negative events can sometimes wear down even the most prepared and self-confident student.

As an LGBTQ student, what can you do? Cultivate strategies to increase and maintain your health in all six key areas. Take a walk, try to eat nutritious foods, pay attention to your body's need for sleep as well as leisure pursuits, spend time with friends and allies, connect or reconnect with your faith community, seek mentors and role models, and remember the importance of study breaks. Develop coping strategies for both overt and covert (or sometimes unintentional) discrimination (see Chapter 9 for more tips on this topic).

Try to keep worry at bay, or at least set aside a certain brief time (once a day, once a week, etc.) to purposefully think about concerns and create proactive strategies to address them. Stressed out about declaring a major or choosing a possible career path? Contact the career services office on campus, find out about internships or job shadowing opportunities in fields you are considering, learn whether there is a mentor program that can match you with a current student or alumni in similar professions. Trying to find your niche? Go to a student group meeting, presentation, or event on a topic in which you are interested; bring a friend with you for instant camaraderie. Not sure how to address a homophobic remark made by a class-mate? Talk with a trusted friend, or check out on-campus or community LGBTQ resources.

Remember to be aware of health concerns of particular import to LGBTQ people. Some LGBTQ people put off going to the doc-tor because they are worried their health practitioner might not be supportive. Good information about important health issues for LGBTQ people, for patients as well as practitioners, can be found by accessing local resources, or through the websites GLMA.org and LGBThealth.net. Rates of tobacco smoking are also higher within LGBTQ communities than those of the gener-al population. Consider quitting or cutting back if possible.

Pay attention to your health—spiritual, occupational, physical, emotional, social, intellectual—and you'll be equipped to tackle the most difficult tasks, whether in class or out in the world!

MANAGING STUDENT STRESS

The college years, once thought of as a time of fun and freedom, have become characterized by a heavy level of stress. Balancing intense academic loads with internships, work, extracurricular, and social life is nearly impossible to accomplish stress-free. The American College Health Association cites stress as the number-one impediment to aca-demic performance in its national college health assessment.[2] College administrators and support groups alike agree that stress is an almost unavoidable hurdle for students, with consequences that are significantly worse than a botched exam or a couple of missed classes.

Stress is a particularly tricky issue because its source can't always be precisely defined and quickly eliminated. As of today, there is no drug

2 American College Health Association. "National College Health Assessment: Spring 2003." Baltimore: 2003. www.acha.org/newsroom/pr_ncha_11_03_03.cfm.

that eradicates the symptoms caused by stress and no vaccine that prevents them. In an academic environment, pressure to succeed is an obvious stressor, but there are other factors that can contribute to a frazzled state. Is your family life a stressor? Are you having relationship trouble? Are finances a concern? What about your lifestyle? Are you going out too much, consuming too much caffeine and/or alcohol, or not getting enough sleep or exercise? All of these factors can directly affect stress levels. Students who are always feeling run down or constantly fighting a cold should consider how stress is affecting their physical health.

As professors continue to pile on the work and demands in and out of the classroom increase, students have to take stress management into their own hands. Acknowledging that stress is actually happening is the first step to controlling it. Carve out personal time for yourself. Balance your academic workload and social commitments with purely relaxing activities, whether that means taking a walk, reading the paper, or sunbathing on the quad. One of the best ways to avoid spiraling into a stress-induced nightmare is to make a strong connection with your university. Most colleges offer students support via peer groups—some schools even have "queer peers," or fellow LGBTQ students trained as peer counselors—and one-on-one counseling with a psychologist. Your LGBTQ Resource Center will also likely have counselors on hand to help you deal with stress-related issues. They key is to catch it early: Seek out help as soon as you feel that stress might be interfering with your life.

Consortium Tips for Handling Student Stress

by Michelle Vaughan, Counselor, Longwood University Counseling Center

While all students encounter stress adjusting to new responsibilities and opportunities associated with college life, queer college students must navigate these challenges while developing a positive identity as a sexual minority. Although colleges and universities are often perceived as relatively open and accepting environments for queer students, the campus climate can vary widely between campuses and within a given campus, creating additional stress.

Students are often excited by the promise of greater freedom and autonomy at college. However, they often underestimate the mixed emotions they may experience as they leave friends, family, partners, and familiar surroundings for unchartered territory. Working to find safe places and people on campus, queer students must also learn, often for the first time, how to juggle relationships (friends, family, roommates, partners), academics, activities/clubs, work, and decisions about visibility. Students within more conservative institutions and those with limited social support may be especially likely to struggle with managing stress.

Coping with college student stress begins with recognizing one's own unique physical and emotional responses to stress. Changes in appetite and sleep, decreased energy, and muscle tension are common among stressed students. Others may struggle more with the emotional consequences of stress, finding that they are more irritable, numb, sad, frustrated, and/or anxious. Similar to other college students, queer students may find themselves turning to alcohol and/or drugs to cope with stress, leading to other risky behaviors. Here are some strategies for coping with stress:

- **Seek Support**

  Emotional and social support from queer-friendly family, friends, and faculty/staff is essential for coping with stress for sexual minority college students. Relationships built on trust, warmth, and openness foster a sense of closeness and connectedness that is invaluable in times of stress. Staying in contact with supportive others on-line or via phone can be very helpful, although in-person contact is even better. For queer students who have few existing supports, connecting with a campus/community LGBTQ group or the campus counseling center can provide the support, encouragement, and affirmation they need in a safe, supportive environment.

- **Learn How to Say "No"**

  Students often feel internal and external pressure to "do it all" in college, and can quickly find themselves overwhelmed with the demands of academics, extracurricular activities, work, dating, friendships, and activism/advocacy work. With so many interesting opportunities and new people with whom to spend their time, students often find themselves overcommitted, booked solid from early morning to late night. No matter how exciting or rewarding, almost all students find it helpful to set aside at least an hour every evening that is entirely their own to relax, hang out with friends, journal, read, or listen to music.

- **Keep physically healthy**

  As discussed earlier, students often take their physical health for granted in college. However, taking care of your physical health can be essential to helping your body cope with stress. Eating regular, healthy meals, getting moderate exercise, and building in adequate time for relaxation and sleep all help to maintain your immune system and keep you emotionally healthy. Relying on alcohol, caffeine, nicotine, or other drugs to cope with stress often backfires over the long haul. Making your physical health a priority can help to reduce anxiety and tension, minimize mood swings and help you feel more in control of your life.

QUEER-TIP:

NATIONAL YOUTH ADVOCACY COALITION

The National Youth Advocacy Coalition (NYAC) is the only national organization focused solely on improving the lives of lesbian, gay, bisexual, transgender, queer, and questioning youth through advocacy, education, and information. Chock full of weblinks, publications, reports, and directories on countless topics, it is a virtual compendium of facts and resources that a queer student may use to find answers to their sexual, physical, and mental health concerns. For more information, log onto NYACyouth.org.

DEALING WITH DEPRESSION

Whether you're male or female, LGBTQ or straight, in college or trying to make it in the "real world," fighting depression is a universal concern. It happens to everyone, and the triggers can be as varied as a low grade on a midterm exam to a feeling of isolation on a not-so-queer-friendly campus. College is filled with new experiences that require new coping strategies. The pressure to fit in socially and remain academically competitive is great. This, compounded by distance from the family unit's support system, can easily lead to feelings of isolation and hopelessness. LGBTQ students face several additional issues that may contribute to depression, including the stress associated with the coming out process, experiences of homophobia, fatalistic perception of long-term relationship potential, feelings of alienation from both the straight and LGBTQ communities, history of or experience with early anti-gay harassment, and HIV-related illness or fears. In fact, the number of students on campus who experience problems with mental health is startling. In a 2004 report, the American College Health Association found that 14.6 percent of college students had been diagnosed with depression. Of those, over 40 percent said they felt so depressed they could barely function, and 10 percent said they had seriously considered suicide.[3]

So what should you do if you feel yourself spiraling down into a depressed state? The first step is to acknowledge that you need help. There is no shame in admitting that you are in need of counseling services. Your privacy is protected under the Family Educational Rights and Privacy Act (FERPA) which states that schools cannot share your educational records with anyone (not even your parents) unless you provide written consent.

Any record that contains personally identifiable information that is directly related to the student is an educational record under FERPA. Students can change what personal information is made public. While medical records are not covered under FERPA, most state laws and professional ethical codes prohibit universities from sharing student medical information and counseling records with third parties, including parents, without the student's consent. These confidentiality requirements are supported

3   American College Health Association. "American College Health Association Survey Shows Increase of Depression Among College Students Over Four-Year Period."
www.acha.org/newsroom/pr_ncha_11_18_04.cfm.

by the proven therapeutic benefits associated with encouraging students to talk openly and candidly with a physician or counselor—without fear of their conversations being reported to others. But it's important to be aware that this confidentiality is not absolute. Parents may be notified if staff members determine that a student possesses an imminent danger to self or others, as well as conduct violations like illegal drug and alcohol use.

Moreover, your counseling will not remain a part of your permanent transcript, and prospective employers are prohibited from asking questions about mental illnesses or emotional crises. While almost every college will offer some sort of counseling service, it's important to do your research beforehand to make sure that the specific services offered cover a wide spectrum of needs.

QUEER-TIP: QUEER ONLINE HEALTH RESOURCES

- **National Coalition for LGBT Health (www.lgbthealth.net)**

  The National Coalition for LGBT Health is committed to improving the health and well-being of lesbian, gay, bisexual, and transgender individuals and communities through public education, coalition building, and advocacy that focus on research, policy, education and training.

- **LGBT Health Channel (www.lgbthealthchannel.com)**

  Developed and monitored by physicians and written especially for health care consumers, this comprehensive site includes tons of information, articles, and news on dozens of LGBTQ health topics.

- **Gender Education and Advocacy (www.gender.org)**

  Gender Education and Advocacy is a non-profit that provides information about a variety of transsexual and transgender issues including health concerns.

Lesbian Health Concerns Q & A

Dr. Patricia Robertson is Professor of Clinical Obstetrics and Gynecology in the Department of Obstetrics, Gynecology, and Reproductive Sciences at the University of California at San Francisco. She co-founded Lyon-Martin Women's Health Services in 1978, while doing one of the earliest studies on STDIs in lesbians. She has been providing medical care to lesbians for many years, and lectures on this topic to clinicians around the country. She is also a perinatologist, taking care of high-risk pregnant women, as well as Director of Medical Student Education for her university. Here is what she had to say about lesbian health concerns:

Why is it important for college campuses to address the health needs of LGBTQ youth?

LGBTQ youth have risk factors for health which have the potential to interfere with academic productivity, and each college needs to optimize the environment for learning for all youth. Specifically, for those youth who are questioning or are just starting to come out, the campus atmosphere needs to be especially supportive so that these youth do not encounter hostility or discrimination.

How does lesbian health differ from women's health in general?

Lesbians between the ages of 20 to 40 have increased rates of smoking, alcohol consumption, drug use, and depression compared to heterosexual women of the same ages. Lesbians exercise more than heterosexual women, but also have increased body mass index, which puts them at risk for health issues such as diabetes.

Lesbians in the past have not easily transmitted sexually transmitted infections (STIs) such as gonorrhea, syphilis, or chlamydia, but now we know that the Human Papilloma Virus can be transmitted between women. This virus is associated with abnormal pap smears and cervical dysplasia. The herpes virus, hepatitis, and HIV can also be transmitted between women, so precautions need to be taken against their transmission (e.g. updated vaccination for hepatitis B, use of female condoms in the initial phase of a female to female sexual relationship until 6 months of monogamy, and proof of both partners' negative HIV status).

Since many lesbians do have sex with men, it is important that protective measures for pregnancy prevention and STDIs be taken. If unprotected intercourse happens, there are two morning-after pills available: Preven and Plan B which can now be taken up to 96 hours after the unplanned intercourse to prevent pregnancy.

What are the most important health issues facing lesbian teens today?

Smoking is the most important health issue facing lesbian teens. The rate of smoking among lesbian teens far exceeds the rate of smoking for heterosexual female teens. Health consequences may include lung damage which could lead to chronic pulmonary obstructive disease and emphysema, as well as lung cancer. More immediate effects are more frequent incidences of bronchitis and pneumonia, as well as facial wrinkles!

How can queer female students locate LGBTQ sensitive health resources off campus?

The Gay and Lesbian Medical Lesbian Association (GLMA) maintains a list of LGBTQ sensitive health providers (www.glma.org).

The Lesbian Health and Research Center also maintains a list of lesbian sensitive health providers mostly in the San Francisco Bay Area, but can also can help you locate one throughout the country through its relationship with the Women in Medicine organization, an organization of lesbian physicians from across the country. In addition, sometimes HMOs like Kaiser have LGBTQ sensitive provider lists. Also, check with other LGBTQ people on campus, and ask them whom they use.

In large urban areas (Boston, New York City, Los Angeles, Washington, DC, San Francisco) there are LGBTQ community clinics. If there is an LGBTQ Center on campus, check with them for a local list of sensitive providers.

QUEER-TIP: HEALTH CONCERNS FOR QUEER STUDENTS OF COLOR

Dr. Robertson agrees that "LGBTQ youth of color have many challenges and their own set of health concerns. Depression is higher. Homophobia by their communities of origin is so strong, that many youth of color who are LGBTQ decide not to be out at home. There is much pressure to adopt a traditional lifestyle/family path, so some of the youth lead a 'double life' which is particularly draining, and takes away from the focus of their studies." If you are a queer student of color and want to find out more about your specific health concerns, check out the "Youth of Color" resource page on the National Youth Advocacy Coalition's website at NYACyouth.org.

PEFLAG Parent Tip PARENT'S TIP: Helping Your Child Stay Healthy

Any child leaving home for the first time needs encouragement and information on how to stay healthy. LGBTQ and non-LGBTQ students alike should be prepared to make choices that are in the best interests of their health. These include including getting enough sleep, eating well-balanced meals, exercising regularly, not overindulging in the party scene to the detriment of health or grades, and staying safe sexually. In addition, students should also be able to prevent and recognize sexual harassment and sexual abuse, and know how to avoid date rape. Whether they are currently sexually active or not, LGBTQ students, like all students, should know where they can get safe sex supplies on campus.

Students should know specifically who to contact in case they get sick or feel overwhelmed. Is it the floor RA, their roommate, their parents, or their student health center? They should also understand that emotionally, they're not expected to handle everything alone. As one mother explains, "We have made ourselves available for many long phone calls and sometimes last minute trips to her campus for the weekend." Another parent stressed the importance of "keeping the conversation about health care open, and of being willing to provide whatever they need, especially in the way of counseling services."

Lis Maurer, Coordinator of the Center for LGBT Education, Outreach and Services at Ithaca College, says that for all college students, "Health and wellness present a complex web of interconnected factors. For LGBTQ students in particular, find out what resources are available to support your specific needs for physical, emotional, social, spiritual, and mental health. Sometimes there are more resources available than you might expect. And if there are gaps or areas in which you believe there could be more helpful resources, ask for what you need."

Brett-Genny Janiczek Beemyn, the Director of the Stonewall Center at the University of Massachusetts—Amherst says, "Parents can push colleges to hire health care providers who are knowledgeable about the health care needs of LGBTQ students;

to require regular LGBTQ education sessions for all medical and counseling staff; to have therapists who can provide informed, supportive counseling for students coming out or transitioning, and to offer safer sex and STD information and anonymous HIV testing." Beemyn also notes that colleges need to understand that they should "provide and cover hormones for transitioning students under student health insurance," which is generally not the case.

These PFLAG parents weighed in on how they encouraged their LGBTQ students to stay healthy:

"I caution [my daughter] against casual sex, pointing out that although she isn't having intercourse she still needs to be careful and take steps to avoid physical and emotional harm."

"Laticia," Rhode Island

"Since transition, our trans child has been encouraged to live an extremely healthy lifestyle by his doctors. We help by paying for his gym membership."

"April," New York

"We've arranged periodic counseling sessions for her at college as she goes through tough transitions."

"Sarah," Washington

"Our child was transitioning from female to male and arranged all his own medical care, using the Fenway Clinic in Boston. He now gets all his own hormones via mail order pharmacy."

"Greyson," Maryland

"We read a lot about depression among his peers, and we deal with problems—whether emotional or physical—together."

"Neil," Hawaii

"We encourage physical exercise and healthy eating habits. I have encouraged our son to date others who are active like we are so that the four of us can enjoy the same active lifestyle together."

"Sara," Colorado

As a parent you can assist your child in developing a healthy lifestyle by encouraging good eating and sleeping habits and regular exercise, and by providing social and spiritual support while your student is away at school. You play a large part in helping your child develop the self-confidence to ask for what they need during their college years, and the courage to hold their schools and local community accountable for providing the support services they—like any other college student—deserve.

QUEER-TIP: TRANSGENDER CONCERNS AND TRANSITIONING FACILITATION

Dr. Robertson also notes that "Trans and transitioning youth need student health insurance to cover the costs of medication, surgery, and therapy to support them through this process. Very few colleges cover these expenses. Some very preliminary research shows that it is better to transition early: Names do not then need to be changed on degrees, support systems are formed." Dr. Robertson also warns however, that "Some youth are taking hormones without medical supervision through the Internet: These hormones can be dangerous and can have permanent side effects, which can be distressing if a youth changes their mind about gender identification. Trans and transitioning youth have an increased risk of intimate partner violence, and need education about this as well as exit plans as needed. Depression is higher in trans and transitioning youth. It has been shown that GPAs can drop a whole point due to depression, and of course suicide can also be the result of depression. There is effective treatment for depression, so depression needs to be recognized."

QUEER YOUTH AND SUICIDE

Although it is still an open question as to whether LGBTQ youth are more at risk for suicide than their heterosexual peers the statistics concerning queer youth and suicide are revealing. According to a 2002 report prepared by Dr. Michael J. Feldman of the Association of Gay and Lesbian Psychiatrists, and the Lesbian and Gay Child and Adolescent Psychiatrists of America, "Most gay, lesbian, and bisexual youth *never* attempt suicide and never have other serious substance use or mental health problems" such as depression and anxiety.[4] However, Feldman also notes that:

- LGBTQ youth are up to six times more likely to have serious substance use or mental health problems that are known risk factors for attempted suicide.

- LGBTQ youth may be at greater risk for attempted suicide if they experience difficulties expressing their sexual identity and/or gender identity/expression in a hostile environment.

- Additional risk factors for suicide include gender nonconformity, early awareness of homosexuality, lack of social support, school dropout, family problems, homelessness, and suicide attempts by family members or friends.

- Young men are at greater risk for suicide attempts due to sexual minority status as compared to young women.[5]

According to Feldman, it is still not known whether/how the risk of suicide correlates with race or ethnicity, and neither is it clear whether sexual minority youth experience an increased risk of suicide between the ages of 15—25 years.[6] What these statistics suggest, however, is that queer youth may experience many of the "at risk" factors associated with suicide at higher rates than their heterosexual peers. What does this mean for you? What can you do if you or someone you know becomes at risk for suicide and needs help?

---

4   Dr. Michael J. Feldman. "Fact Sheet on Suicidal Behavior in GLBT Youth." Association of Gay and Lesbian Psychiatrists. www.aglp.org/pages/cfactsheets.html.

5   Ibid.

6   Ibid.

Seeing Signs, Getting Help

According to The Trevor Hotline, the following are some warning signs you should look out for when dealing with an LGBTQ individual you suspect may be at risk for a suicide attempt:

- A tendency toward isolation and social withdrawal
- Increasing substance abuse
- Expression of negative attitudes toward self
- Expression of hopelessness or helplessness
- Loss of interest in usual sources of pleasure
- Giving away valued possessions
- Expression of a lack of future orientation: "It won't matter soon anyway."[7]

According to Trevor counselors, when someone who has been very depressed is experiencing that depression begin to lift, the individual may be at increased risk of suicide, because he or she may now have the psychological energy to follow-through on suicidal thoughts.[8]

---

7   The Trevor Project. "Suicidal Signs: Warning Signs." www.thetrevorproject.org/suicidalsigns.aspx.
8   Ibid.

Fortunately, there are things you can do to help a suicidal LGBTQ college friend. If you're dealing with a queer individual who you fear is at risk and requires an intervention, The Trevor Helpline recommends that you take the following steps:

- Listen to them. Many teens and adults who are at risk for suicide complain that they are not understood by and/or not taken seriously by others. Address this concern by taking the time out to listen to them.

- Accept the person's feelings as they are. Do not try to cheer the person up by making positive, unrealistic statements.

- Do not be afraid to talk about suicide directly. You will not be putting ideas into the person's head. Most of the time the person has already experienced suicidal feelings. It is dangerous practice to avoid asking a person directly if they are feeling suicidal.

- Inquire if they have developed a plan of suicide. The presence of a well-developed plan indicates a more serious intent.

- Remind the person that feelings of depression do change with time.

- Express your care for the person and your hope that he/she will not choose suicide.

- Point out that death is irreversible.

- Develop a plan for helping the person. If you cannot develop a plan and a suicide attempt is imminent, seek outside help.[9]

Emergency intervention is available at a hospital, mental health clinic, or through The Trevor Helpline. For further information on how to educate others about LGBTQ Youth Suicide Prevention on your college campus, in your classroom, or through your LGBTQ support center, log onto TheTrevorProject.org.

9   The Trevor Project. "How Can You Help a Suicidal Person." www.thetrevor-project.org/howtohelp.aspx.

LET'S TALK ABOUT SEX

Let's face it: Sex is an active part of the lives of most college students. Why should queer students be any different? Considering that statistics on heterosexual and gender-typical student sexual activity are hard to come by, it's no wonder that data chronicling the sexual habits of LGBTQ students is practically non-existent. So where does that leave you? Well, despite what your parents may want you to do (or *not* do), it's a personal choice to decide to have sex and it's ultimately your perogative as an adult to engage in it as much or as little as you want. Just be sure to educate yourself about the risks involved and the ways that you can engage in harm-reduction and safe sex practices. There are lot of resources that provide information on the risks that queer individuals, specifically gay men, need to take into consideration when it comes to sexual activity, the influence of drugs and alcohol on sexual behavior, and the psychological and emotional impact of engaging in unsafe sex. One of the best sites available to specifically address queer youth sexual health issues is YouthResource.com/index.htm. Here are some additional websites that also provide loads of information about LGBTQ sexual topics:

Advocates for Youth

(www.advocatesforyouth.org/glbtq.htm)

The Body: The Complete HIV/AIDS Resource

(www.thebody.com)

Sexual Health—Public Information Resource

(www.sexual-health-resource.org)

Coalition for Positive Sexuality

(www.positive.org)

Gay Men Play Safe

(www.gaymenplaysafe.com)

About: Lesbian Life

(http://lesbianlife.about.com/od/lesbiansex/a/FirstTimeSex.htm)

QUEER-TIP: QUEER STDI 101

While many of you may have learned about sexually transmitted diseases back in the 9th grade, many of you did not. Whether your parents or teachers addressed them or not, STDIs (sexually-transmitted diseases and infections) do exist and they do affect queer students of every shape, size, race, gender, and sexual orientation. If you are going to be sexually active, take control of your health and make sure you learn how to protect yourself. Here's a quick lesson on sexually transmitted diseases and infections that you should know about:

- **AIDS:** A disorder of the immune system caused by HIV. AIDS or Acquired Immune Deficiency Syndrome affects the proper functioning of the immune system, increasing a person's susceptibility to contracting viruses or cancer. AIDS is transmitted through bodily fluids such as blood, saliva and semen. There is currently no cure for AIDS.

- **Chancroid:** A treatable bacterial infection that causes painful sores.

- **Chlamydia:** A treatable bacterial infection that can scar the fallopian tubes, affecting a woman's ability to have children.

- **Crabs:** Technically known as pediculosis pubis, crabs are parasites that live on the pubic hair in the genital area and cause irritation.

- **Genital Herpes:** A recurrent skin condition that can cause skin irritations in the genital region (anus, vagina, penis).

- **Gonorrhea:** A treatable bacterial infection of the penis, vagina, or anus that causes pain or a burning sensation, as well as a pus-like discharge. Also known as "the clap."

- **Hepatitis:** A disease that affects the liver, with more than four types. A and B are the most common and most commonly transmitted via sexual contact.

- **HIV:** Stands for Human Immunodeficiency Virus, the virus that causes AIDS.

- **HPV:** Stands for Human Papillomavirus, a virus that affects the skin in the genital area, as well as a female's cervix. Depending on the type of HPV involved, symptoms can be in the form of wart-like growths, or abnormal cell changes and even certain forms of cancer in women. HPV is also referred to as genital warts.

- **Nongonococcal Urethritis (NGU):** A treatable bacterial infection of the urethra (the tube within the penis) often associated with chlamydia.

- **Pelvic Inflammatory Disease:** An infection of the female reproductive organs by chlamydia, gonorrhea, or other bacteria. Also known as PID.

- **Scabies:** A treatable skin disease that is caused by a parasite.

- **Shigella:** A bacterial infection that causes serious stomach cramps and diarrhea that can easily be spread from one person to another through oral-anal contact and from oral contact with contaminated skin including skin in the groin area, the testicles, and the penis.

- **Syphilis:** A treatable bacterial infection that can spread throughout the body and affect the heart, brain, and nervous system.

Most of these STDIs are treatable, especially if caught early. If you are showing symptoms or suspect that you may have contracted an infection, consult a physician immediately.

Of course, the best form of prevention is abstinence. But should you decide to abstain from abstaining it's extremely important to practice safe sex with all of your partners. Fortunately, there are a number of safe sex methods to choose from. Your University Health Center and LGBTQ Resource Center should have plenty of information on hand to educate you about how to use these methods in order to maintain your sexual health. In the meantime, here's a breakdown of some specific safe sex methods you should know about:

- **Condoms:** The most common safe sex method, condoms are a device, usually made of latex, worn by men during sexual contact to prevent the exchange of bodily fluids.

- **Dental Dams:** Dental Dams are latex barriers that help reduce the risk of catching and spreading STDIs. These are used during intimate oral, vaginal, and anal contact to serve as a barrier from bodily fluids that can transmit STDIs.

- **Female Condoms:** A polyurethane sheath or pouch worn by a woman during sex. It lines the vagina and helps to prevent pregnancy and STDIs. At each end of the condom there is a flexible ring—one that holds the condom in place inside the vagina and another that sits outside the entrance to the vagina.

- **Finger Cots:** A latex device resembling a male condom used to cover the fingers during sexual contact involving the fingers. While finger cots are effective in preventing the transmission of STDIs, surgical gloves are considered more effective for such sexual contact.

- **Gloves:** Latex surgical gloves function in the same manner as finger cots but provide coverage for the entire hand, and help prevent the transmission of STDIs during sexual contact involving the fingers.

Remember: Safe sex is about making responsible choices. Empower yourself by making sure you understand all your options, so you can choose the best methods for you *and* your partner.

National Gay and Lesbian Task Force Tips on HIV/AIDS and the College Student [10]

The AIDS epidemic is a problem confronting all Americans, including members of college and university communities. Since the NGLTF Campus Project addressed issues of AIDS on campus in its first *Organizing for Equality* newsletter in 1988, increasing numbers of college and university administrations have undertaken serious programs to stem the spread of the disease and respond to its aftermath. Still, misconceptions about AIDS—along with fear and hatred associated with certain AIDS "risk groups"—have often slowed the official response to the problem both on and off campus. If colleges and universities are to meet the challenge of AIDS, then sound programs and policies are needed to protect the entire campus community. In the absence of such programs, LGBTQ students, faculty, and staff, and others concerned about AIDS, may need to take the lead by lobbying for official action and initiating their own education and support programs.

The AIDS epidemic affects college campuses in several ways. As in the rest of society, there still remains considerable spread. Some people may take extreme precautions based on irrational fears of casual AIDS contagion, while others often mistakenly assume that they can engage in unsafe sexual activity without risk to their health. Combating AIDS on campus is made more difficult by the fact that many students are just beginning to explore their sexuality and often only have meager knowledge of sexually transmitted diseases and other reproductive health issues. Oblivious to the risks associated with unsafe sex, some students have become infected with the Human Immunodeficiency Virus (HIV)—commonly believed to be the cause of AIDS—and growing numbers have developed full-blown AIDS. Without a cure or a vaccine expected in the near future, and an extremely high mortality rate for those afflicted with the disease, it is vital that AIDS education be a high priority on campus. As institutions devoted to higher learning, colleges and universities offer an ideal environment for a successful public health campaign—one on which lives depend.

---

10 Excerpted from *Lesbian, Gay, Bisexual, & Transgender Campus Organizing: A Comprehensive Manual* by Curtis F. Shepard, PhD; Felice Yeskel, EdD; and Charles Outcalt. National Gay and Lesbian Task Force. 1995. www.thetaskforce.org/downloads/reports/reports/CampusOrganizingManual.pdf.

The college or university administration should assume primary responsibility for promoting AIDS awareness and combating AIDS discrimination. LGBTQ student and alumni/ae organizations should be among those involved in the planning and implementation of AIDS education programs and policies. As members of a community hard hit by the disease, LGBTQ people have a right to expect action and to have a say in decisions that will affect their lives. Although lesbians are not considered to be at high risk for AIDS, they nevertheless confront discrimination associated with the disease and should be encouraged to participate in efforts to combat it. In the absence of a full scale effort to combat AIDS, both LGBTQ and non-LGBTQ student and alumni/ae groups should encourage and assist college administrations in acting responsibly. They should meet together with campus officials to urge both the adoption of an unofficial policy on HIV infection and AIDS, and the establishment of a full scale AIDS education program. Some possible AIDS initiatives are suggested below:

- Request the establishment of an official policy on HIV infection and AIDS that includes a focus on such issues as health care, housing and employment. (For more information about model AIDS policies, contact the American College Health Association at the address listed in Appendix C.)

- Request that the administration hire a health education coordinator who would have responsibility for planning a comprehensive education program focusing on AIDS and other LGBTQ health concerns. A growing number of colleges have already hired such staff.

- Request that the student health center provide free condoms and safer sex kits. A safer sex kit might contain, for instance, two condoms, a latex barrier, K-Y Jelly, and a pamphlet explaining safer sex guidelines

- Request that the health center offer in-depth AIDS education training for volunteer peer AIDS educators. Some type of AIDS education should also be part of the standard training for resident advisors and medical and counseling staff.

Some schools may be receptive to proposals and involvement by LGBTQ groups. Others will not, and may require pressure—from individuals both on and off campus—to deal with AIDS in a cogent and compassionate way. If the school is reluctant or unwilling to take appropriate measures, students may need to organize for change. Meetings, petition drives, resolutions from your student government association, calls and letters from supportive parents and alumni/ae, and—as a last resort—direct action (demonstrations, sit-ins, etc.) may be necessary to foster action.

PROGRAMS SPONSORED BY LGBTQ CAMPUS GROUPS

Whether or not colleges take official action, LGBTQ students should educate themselves about AIDS and provide support for those trying to cope with surviving this epidemic. A number of projects focusing on AIDS that student and alumni/ae groups may want to initiate are listed below. Of course, the scope of your efforts will depend upon your resources—both human and financial.

- **Offer AIDS referrals.** LGBTQ campus organizations can act as a clearinghouse, directing people on campus to local AIDS service agencies, hotlines, doctors, HIV testing sites, and counseling and support groups.

- **Set up a resource center.** Collect AIDS educational materials from other campuses and from AIDS service organizations. Develop a small library of these materials in the LGBTQ student group office (if one exists) or somewhere accessible to students needing such information.

- **Distribute AIDS information pamphlets and literature.** Busy public places such as student unions, residence halls, and health centers are often ideal places to hand out or leave information pamphlets. Campus media such as newspapers, radio, or television can run stories on AIDS issues.

- **Hold special events on AIDS.** These can be short programs or day- or week-long events devoted to exploring AIDS issues. Programs may include guest speakers, panel discussions, group discussions, theater and film presentations, and workshops. When scheduling a series of programs—as in the case of an "AIDS Awareness Week"—keep the topics diverse in order to meet the interests and needs of the community. Evaluate topics covered. Are issues of particular concern to women, the disabled, and people of color being addressed? Remember that in order to reach the widest possible audience, your programming should reflect the diversity of your community.

- **Run a rap group for gay students on AIDS.** AIDS has created enormous stresses for everyone and raises all kinds of issues—from internalized homophobia to safer sex. Consider running a peer group or ask a counselor whom you trust if s/he could facilitate such a group.

- **Document AIDS and gay-related discrimination and violence and report such incidents to the university** (allowing for anonymity, if the victim wishes). Keeping track of such incidents will help in promoting college action on AIDS and homophobia.

See Appendix C for a list of AIDS support and advocacy resources.

DEALING WITH DRUGS AND ALCOHOL ON CAMPUS

College is full of temptations and experimentation, and while most students are relatively safe and stay clear of illegal substances, there are those who fall victim to vices. In fact, the combined findings of the 2002 and 2005 National Surveys on Drug Use and Health (NSDUH) conducted by the Substance Abuse and Mental Health Services Administration (SAMHSA) of the U.S. Department of Health and Human Services, provide some startling statistics:

- 57.8 percent of full-time college students aged 18 to 20 used alcohol in the past month[11]

- 40.1 percent engaged in binge alcohol use, and 16.6 percent engaged in heavy alcohol use[12]

---

11 The National Survey on Drug Use and Health. "Underage Alcohol Use among Full-Time College Students." *The NSDUH Report.* Issue 31, 2006. www.oas.samhsa.gov/2k6/college/collegeUnderage.htm.

12 Ibid.

- Among full time college students aged 18 to 20, males were more likely than females to have used alcohol in the past month (60.4 percent versus 55.6 percent), binge drink (46.9 percent versus 34.4 percent), or drink heavily (22.7 percent versus 11.5 percent)[13].

- The rate of current illicit drug use was similar among full-time college students (21.2 percent) and among other persons aged 18 to 22 years, which includes part-time college students, students in other grades, and non-students (21.8 percent). [14]

Perhaps because of these disturbing statistics, most universities now provide confidential and discreet referral services for those who may require help dealing with alcohol and drug problems. But increasingly, campus recovery centers are beginning to appear on-site at colleges and universities across the country, providing 12-step meetings, addiction recovery education, and other services. Some even host AA and other 12-step meetings specifically designed for LGBTQ students who may find a queer-inclusive or dedicated space safer to explore recovery. The point is that help is out there.

Following are some handy search portals that can help you locate drug and alcohol rehabilitation centers, treatment options, and 12-step recovery programs that are available wherever you may be attending college:

- **Alcoholics Anonymous**

  (www.alcoholics-anonymous.org)

- **Drug Rehabs.org**

  (www.drug-rehabs.org)

- **Marijuana Anonymous**

  (www.marijuana-anonymous.org)

- **Narcotics Anonymous**

  (http://portaltools.na.org)

For more statistics and information on NSDUH findings, log onto: OAS.samhsa.gov/nsduh.htm.

13 Ibid.
14 The National Survey on Drug Use and Health. "College Enrollment Status and Past Year Illicit Drug Use among Young Adults: 2002, 2003, and 2004." *The NSDUH Report.* October 21, 2005. www.oas.samhsa.gov/2k5/College/college.htm.

The Meth Epidemic and Queer College Students

Since the mid-1990s, methamphetamine use has risen steadily in America. While all ethnic groups, genders, and demographics have been rattled by this epidemic, use and dependency among gay men (including queer college students) has skyrocketed. In fact, studies have found that meth use among gay and bisexual men is up to ten times higher than in the general population. One especially dangerous corollary of methamphetamine use is the very high rate of unsafe sex among gay men who use the drug. According to a 2003 study by the Chicago Department of Public Health and Centers for Disease Control and Prevention (CDC):

- Approximately 10 percent of gay men had used methamphetamine at least once in the previous year, compared with 0.7 percent of the general U.S. population.[15]

- Of those gay men who reported using meth, 20 percent were using at least once per week.[16]

- 20 percent of young gay and bisexual men had used crystal meth in the previous six months, with 6 percent reporting daily use.[17]

The good news is that according to a National Survey on Drug Use and Health Report (www.oas.samhsa.gov/2k6/stateMeth/stateMeth.htm) college students are less likely to use methamphetamine than those in their age cohort who are not enrolled in school. If you or someone you know is struggling with this crippling addiction, there is help out there. Your university's health center or LGBTQ resource center should have information on hand to you to help you get the assistance you need. But if they don't, or if you feel uncomfortable talking to someone on your campus, contact your local LGBTQ community center or check out some of these meth-use prevention and harm reduction sites for information about dealing with meth-related dependency:

---

15 Medical News Today. "Crystal Meth Addiction Still A Problem For Gay And Bisexual Men, USA." June 26, 2006. www.medicalnewstoday.com/medical-news.php?newsid=45855.
16 Ibid.
17 Ibid.

- **Tweaker.org** (http://tweaker.org)
- **The Lesbian, Gay, Bisexual and Transgender Community Center** (www.gaycenter.org/Surveys/crystal/yres)
- **Crystalneon.org** (www.crystalneon.org)
- **Crystal Meths Anonymous** (http://crystalmeth.org)

QUEER-TIP:
NATIONAL TOLL-FREE QUEER COUNSELING HOTLINES AND INTERVENTION RESOURCES

GLBT National Youth Talkline

800-246-PRIDE (800-246-7743)

www.GLBTNationalHelpCenter.org

Operating Monday thru Saturday from 9:30pm to Midnight, ET, this junior program of The GLBT National Help Center offers teens and young adults up to the age 25 free access to peer volunteers trained to discuss coming-out issues, relationship concerns, parent issues, school problems, HIV/AIDS anxiety, safer-sex information, and much more. The GLBT National Youth Talkline maintains one of the largest resource database of its kind in the world, with over 18,000 listings on social and support groups, as well as gay-friendly religious organizations, sports leagues, student groups, and other topics of interest.

Peer Listening Line of Fenway Community Health Center

800-399-PEER (800-399-7337)

The Peer Listening Line provides an anonymous and confidential forum where young people can get help, information, referrals, and support on a range of issues. Young people up to 23 years of age can talk to a peer without being judged or rushed into any decision they are not prepared to make. Issues include sexuality and safer sex practices, coming out, HIV and AIDS, depression and suicide, and anti-gay/lesbian harassment and violence.

National AIDS Hotline

800-342-AIDS (800-342-2437)

This 24-hour hotline, sponsored by the Centers for Disease Control (CDC), provides information on AIDS and its prevention, local testing facilities, and medications for treatment.

Gay Men's Health Crisis Hotline

800-243-7692

www.GMHC.org

Gay Men's Health Crisis (GMHC) is a nonprofit, volunteer-supported, and community-based organization committed to national leadership in the fight against AIDS. Their mission is to reduce the spread of HIV disease, help people with HIV maintain and improve their health and independence, and keep the prevention, treatment, and cure of HIV an urgent national and local priority. The GMHC Hotline responds to over 35,000 phone calls and Internet requests yearly in both Spanish and English and offers an expansive referral service that includes over 10,000 service providers.

Pride Institute

800-54-PRIDE

www.pride-institute.com

Pride Institute operates a leading inpatient drug and alcohol treatment facility for gay men and lesbians and specializes in providing addiction and mental health treatment to the LGBTQ community.

CHAPTER 11
BREAKING AWAY: WHAT TO DO WHEN NOT AT SCHOOL

SHOOL'S OUT

By now you've got a feel for the rhythms of college life. Each semester begins at a hectic pace—you've got to register, pick your classes, buy your books—and ends on a similarly intense note with final papers and exams. But just when you think that you're about to explode from the stress of trying to balance a full course load with your extracurricular involvement, activism, and/or part-time job, you get a break. Literally. Anyone will tell you that one of the best things about being a college student are the days, weeks, and even month-long breaks you can look forward to throughout the academic year. Not to mention the three-month long summer vacation that you get when the academic year comes to a close. While you can—and should—use these breaks to catch up on your sleep, read a book for fun, or just chill out with friends, you should also think about other things you'd like to do with your time off. Maybe you'd like to travel? Volunteer for a nonprofit organization? Complete an internship? All of these activities can enrich your college experience. This chapter will help you get started thinking about things you can do to make the most of your time off from school—from letting your hair down on a fun spring break getaway to landing a coveted internship that will get your foot into that post-graduation door.

TRAVEL

There won't be another time in your life when traveling will be so easy. Sure, you're a broke college student, but your penury is the very thing that works in your favor. Think about it: All you need is a backpack, a place to lay your head, and a ticket, and you're there. You'll get invitations from roommates and friends to hang out at their parents' cribs on three-day weekends and holiday breaks; someone you know might invite you to visit them over the summer or join them on a winter break road/ski/hiking trip. The many getaway opportunities that inevitably crop up in a college student's life often come with free food and lodging—all you need to do is find a way to get there. But even when you're looking to do something a bit more structured or would like to travel on your own, you'll find that your college student status makes doing so easy and affordable.

In other words, there are some serious benefits to being a student traveler. Your age and student status will garner you tons of discounts on non-school sponsored trips. STA Travel (www.statravel.com) has been a leading force in youth travel since the 1970s. They specialize in student travel discounts and even offer various study and volunteer abroad programs. Check out their website for deals on airfare, vacation packages, hotel and hostel rates, and more. Another great discount offer for college students is Airtran's X-fares program (www.airtranu.com/airtran_u.aspx), which allows students under the age of 25 to fly standby on any of its domestic flights for only $69—$89 each way. Even Greyhound Bus Lines (www.greyhound.com/deals/student_discount.shtml) offers student discounts on regular fares. Do your research. Pick up a few travel guides for tips on where to stay and what to see wherever you're going, and then do some follow-up calling to find out about special student rates or discounts. As long as you're willing to pack light, fly standby, and bunk at hostels where you'll probably have to share a bathroom with a dozen other student travelers, chances are you can afford to take a trip anywhere you'd like to go. Of course, LGBTQ student travelers, like those studying abroad (see Chapter 6) should also be especially mindful of safety concerns. Is your destination city/country a welcoming environment for LGBTQ people, or does it have a reputation for intolerance and homo/bi/transphobia? You'll want to consider this carefully before finalizing your travel plans. There are tons of resources out there that can help you plan your trip with these concerns in mind.

Queer Travel Resources

Whether you're looking for a getaway, or you're doing a simple search for a cheap flight home, chances are you'll need some help sorting through your options to find the best bargain for your buck. There's no shortage of travel sites, publications and organizations catering to the LGBTQ community. Here's a list of the top ones to check out:

- **Gay Travel News** (www.gaytravelnews.com)

  Gay Travel News (GTN), a division of Los Angeles-based Instinct Publishing, is an online travel information clearinghouse. GTN offers tons of gay-friendly tourism information, as well as lists of gay and lesbian travel agents, tour operators and other travel links.

- **International Gay & Lesbian Travel Association**
  (www.traveliglta.com)

  Founded in 1983, IGLTA is a 1000-plus member strong organization of gay, lesbian, and community-friendly travel professionals. They can help you locate LGBTQ-owned, operated, or sensitive travel companies that support the queer community.

- **Lonely Planet** (www.lonelyplanet.com)

  Since the early 1970s, Lonely Planet has continually pushed the boundaries of travel journalism by publishing over 600 travel guides in English covering every corner of the planet. By drawing on its adventurous, globe-trotting young writers and focusing on super budget-conscious travel tips, the guides are a college student's no-frills dream. Plus, since Lonely Planet does not accept endorsements or advertising in its guidebooks and the authors don't accept kickbacks, payment, or favors in return for positive reviews, you can rest assured that the opinions are often spot on. Their guidebooks often feature information of interest to intrepid LGBTQ travelers, and their website offers hundreds of free articles on any number of destinations. Lonely Plant also offers a "Gay & Lesbian Travelers" branch on their Thorn Tree online discussion forum. Log onto ThornTree.lonelyplanet.com.

- **Passport Magazine** (http://passportmagazine.com)

  "America's #1 Gay and Lesbian Travel Magazine" *Passport* provides tons of information about the latest queer travel hotspots, special deals and offers, along with a plethora of videos, multimedia, and articles on unique destinations around the world.

- **Planet Out Travel** (www.planetout.com/travel)

  PlanetOut travel section offers a near-encyclopedic library of articles and resources on queer vacations, interesting destinations and off-the-beaten-path travel options. So whether you are planning a spring break getaway on a student budget or flying off to Asia for a month-long backpacking adventure, check out some of the comprehensive information they offer for free. They also offer an extensive list of links especially for women at PlanetOut.com/travel/vacations/women.

- **Travelocity**
(http://leisure.travelocity.com/Promotions/0,,TRAVELOCI-
TY|935|gaytravel,00.html)

  Travelocity offers loads of special packages and booking options of interest to the LGBTQ community. They also offer toll-free numbers where you can talk to a queer travel expert who can help you build out the best vacation to suit your needs.

QUEER-TIP: WHAT DOES TAG APPROVED MEAN, AND WHY SHOULD I CARE?

Travelocity has recently partnered with Travel Alternatives Group, an organization founded in 1992 whose main mission is to rate the world's gay-friendliest hotels, resorts, and inns and provide reliable and accurate prescreened information for LGBTQ travelers. TAG Approved properties:

- Enforce non-discriminatory policies including "sexual orientation."

- Treat heterosexual and domestic partners equally in personnel policies.

- Provide diversity and sensitivity training for employees.

- Employ staff that reflects the diversity of the community, including LGBTQ employees in all levels of employment.

- Empower customers and employees to be "watchdogs" of its LGBTQ business practices.

Making the Most Out of Mainstream Queer Travel Guides

Travel guides are there to prepare and inform. They are often college students' first point of contact with their backpacking/road-tripping adventure. Travel guides let you know about the culture of your destination city or country, give you an idea of how much money you can expect to spend, provide tips on how to find good deals, and, most importantly, describe points of interest that you might want to check out during your stay, covering everything from major tourist destinations to hidden gems off-the-beaten-path. In addition to the *Rough Guides* and *Lonely Planet* travel books, you might want to look at *Fodor's* and *Frommer's*. These guides often include short sections on queer travel options. *Fodor's* has recently started publishing a series of *Gay Guides* to the USA, Amsterdam, Los Angeles, New York City, San Francisco, the Pacific Northwest, and South Florida.

However, the books in the *Time Out* City Guide series are the hippest and trendiest of all the travel guides out there. They offer guides to forty-eight worldwide destinations, each featuring a comprehensive section for queer travelers. But remember: While *Time Out* may be super queer friendly, some of the featured destinations may not so be LGBTQ-friendly or tolerant. Do your homework and read up before jetting off to the latest hotspot.

QUEER-TIP: SUGGESTED QUEER TRAVEL GUIDES

Damron Men's Travel Guide, Gina Gatta (Editor)

The Damron Women's Traveler, Leila Walker (Editor)

Fodor's Gay Guide to the USA, 2nd Edition: The Most Comprehensive Guide for Gay and Lesbian Travelers, Andrew Collins

Gay Travel A to Z: The World of Gay & Lesbian Travel Options at Your Fingertips, Marianne Ferrari (Editor)

Is Spring Break for Queer Students?

Of course it is! Spring break is an institution for most college students and LGBTQ students are no different. For many college students, this much-anticipated break following the stress of spring semester midterms is a time to gather a horde of your closest friends, pack your swimsuits and tanning lotion, and head off to the beaches of one of the notorious spring break paradises in Florida or the Bahamas. Others may want a mellower getaway where thay can decompress from the pressures of the school year. Whatever you choose, remember that as an openly queer traveler, you may feel more welcome in some places than others. Choosing to book LGBTQ-friendly hotels and finding LGBTQ vacation and cruise deals or packages might help ensure that you feel more comfortable in your destination vacation spot and may relieve some of the anxiety that goes into booking travel plans. Here's a partial list of some of the LGBTQ-owned and/or operated travel outfits that offer unique vacation packages catered especially to queer travelers:

- **Alyson Adventures, Inc.** (www.AlysonAdventures.com)
- **Atlantis** (www.AtlantisEvents.com)
- **Coda International Tours** (www.Coda-Tours.com)
- **EuroBound/TahitiBound** (www.eurobound.com)
- **Footprints** (www.footprintguides.com)
- **Hanns Ebensten Travel, Inc.** (www.hetravel.com)
- **Hermes Tours** (www.hermestours.com)
- **Journey Out** (www.journeyout.com)
- **Olivia** (www.oliviacruises.com)
- **Out In Alaska** (www.outinalaska.com)
- **OutWest Global Adventures** (www.outwestadventures.com)
- **Pied Piper Cruise** (www.davidtravel.com/piedpiper-gay-group-cruises.html)
- **RSVP Vacations** (www.rsvpvacations.com)
- **Toto Tours** (www.tototours.com)
- **Undersea Expeditions** (www.underseax.com)

Shop around and see what they offer and before you know it you'll be planning the spring break of your dreams!

CONSIDER AN "ALTERNATIVE BREAK"

Alternative breaks are, in many ways, the polar opposite of "traditional" summer, fall, winter, weekend, or spring breaks. If you're not into the idea of jetting off to sun-soaked vistas to work on a tan and party it up, rest assured that there are some interesting alternatives available to you.

In the spring of 2006, an estimated 35,000 students across the nation participated in alternative break experiences. Many of those students traveled to New Orleans to assist with clean-up and rebuilding efforts in the wake of Hurricane Katrina. Alternative break programs organize teams of college and high school students and place them in a variety of locales across the country where they can participate in and benefit from community service and experiential learning opportunities. The purpose of this type of program is to engage students in community-based service projects so that they may learn about the problems faced by members of communities with whom they may have otherwise had little or no direct contact. LGBTQ college students and their allies often work on a wide range of projects for community agencies that need assistance in educating others about important issues such as HIV/STDI prevention, literacy, homelessness, and the environment.

These organizations position their programs as springboards into lifelong active citizenship in which community involvement becomes a priority in an individual's life decisions. One of the leading organizations working in volunteer-based college student travel is Break Away. Established in 1991, this Tallahassee, Florida outfit encourages college students to make the most of their vacations by organizing and offering unique alternative breaks to students who are more interested in making a difference in the world. Break Away's mission is to train, assist, and connect campuses and communities in promoting quality alternative break programs that inspire lifelong active citizenship.

For more information on Break Away's unique programs, services and trips, log onto AlternativeBreaks.org.

Volunteering Your Way Across the Globe

For many students, volunteering in a foreign country may provide a safe and satisfying way to explore the world while also learning about the lives of different people across the globe. Some of the benefits of international volunteering include personal growth, finding a new sense of purpose and independence, connecting with people from another culture, and seeing a country from the inside-out. Organizations like the Red Cross routinely organize teams of volunteers to assist with disaster relief efforts across the globe. But, as when making any travel plans, you should remember that some countries are more LGBTQ-friendly than others. Whatever you choose to do and whichever overseas volunteering outfit you decide to go with, be sure to ask about LGBTQ safety and try to get testimonials from other queer volunteers about their experiences before you go.

QUEER-TIP: CROSS CULTURAL SOLUTIONS

Since 1995, Cross-Cultural Solutions has been a leader in the field of international volunteering and has helped more than 10,000 volunteers participate in programs around the world. Cross-Cultural Solutions offers short- and long-term internships and volunteer opportunities for high school and college students as well as adults of all ages. Their unique *Insight Abroad* program offers one-week volunteer placement in Brazil, Costa Rica, Guatemala, Peru, and Russia. For more information about how you can get involved, log onto CrossCulturalSolutions.org.

HEADING HOME FOR THE SUMMER?

You should really start thinking about your summer plans as early as winter break. Are you going to look for a job, try to find an internship, make travel plans, or volunteer with a community service organization? Whatever your plans are, you should try to finalize them by late Spring, so you can begin planning your campus exit strategy. If you're planning to head home for the summer, you'll need to let your parents know, so they can help you coordinate things like transportation and finding summer storage for your things.

For many college students, making the adjustment back to life at your parents' home can be a jarring experience. You've spent nine months on your own, setting your own curfew and following your own rules. The transition back to the more structured environment of your parents' home can be a difficult one. The key to making this transition successfully is to keep the lines of communication open. Be willing to chip in around the house by doing the dishes, cleaning out the garage, or taking the trash out. You should also be willing to talk about your grades and academic plans—your parents will want to know about the courses you've taken, the ones you're thinking about signing up for next year, and how you're adjusting to college life in general. These conversations are an important step in feeling out your new relationship with your parents, one in which your newfound interests and independence can make it seem like you're getting to know one another for the very first time.

LGBTQ students heading home for the summer may face a unique set of issues. Some LGBTQ students don't have a home to go to. Other LGBTQ students come out for the first time to their parents, childhood friends, and neighbors, during the summer break. If you are a newly "out" student heading home, remember to engage your parents in a conversation. The news may or may not upset them or catch them off guard. Be honest with yourself and be as honest as you can with them. Check out the "coming out" tips provided in Chapter 1 for helpful suggestions on how to deal with the process.

PFLAG PARENT TIP: ADJUSTING TO YOUR CHILD'S HOMECOMING

Like most parents, parents of LGBTQ college students enjoy visiting with their children over weekends and school breaks. However, some do find that unusual situations crop up when their LGBTQ child is back at home. Some parents may find it hard during such visits to reconcile their child's sexual orientation and/or gender identity/expression with hometown values or religious attitudes. Still others welcome their child's LGBTQ friends into their home, especially if these students have nowhere else to go.

Following are some tips to help parents and family members make sure that their LGBTQ student's homecoming is a welcome trip back to the hearth:

Before the visit...

- Practice in advance if you are going to be discussing your family member's sexual orientation or gender identity with family and friends. If you are comfortable talking about it, your family and friends will probably be more comfortable too.

- Anticipate potential problems, but do not assume that reactions will always be what you expected.

- Consult with your LGBTQ loved one when coordinating sleeping arrangements if he or she is bringing home a partner.

- If your family member is transgender, practice using the correct pronouns.

During the visit...

- Treat a LGBTQ person like you would treat anyone else in your family.

- Take interest in your family member's life. He or she is still the same person.

- Ask your LGBTQ family member about his or her partner if you know they have one.

- Don't ask your LGBTQ family member to act a certain way. Let them be their natural selves.

- If your LGBTQ family member is bringing a partner, acknowledge him or her as you would any other family member's partner.
- If your LGBTQ family member is bringing a partner, include him or her in your family traditions.

Here's what some parents told us about what it's like to have their LGBTQ child "home for the holidays":

"I love to have my daughter at home for breaks! Of course, when she brings a [girlfriend] with her, I don't get as much personal time with her as I would like to have. She does usually respect my request for some one-on-one time with her, if the length of the visit allows for this."

"Patrice," Indiana

"Our (trans) daughter comes home on weekends. We all get along well and enjoy each other's company. And as a college student, the lure of getting your laundry done at home has proven irresistible."

"Sarah," California

"My daughter divides her time up during longer breaks, often bringing along a friend or two for short visits. She also works part-time. Sometimes she goes to visit friends on the weekends. All the parents of her friends are very welcoming."

"Roxanne," Connecticut

"Both our daughters love coming home whenever possible. College students should always know they are welcome at home."

"Frank," Washington

"My daughter's practice of bringing home same-sex lovers and transgendered lovers can be difficult for other family members, who are uncomfortable with varieties of sexual expression."

"Devi," Florida

"[Our daughter] comes home to visit us during breaks more than I thought she would, but I've noticed that she likes to spend more and more time at school and with her friends there."

"Theresa," Colorado

"My daughter says she feels uncomfortable at family reunions and when she sees her old acquaintances at home. It's very conservative where we live and I would not want her moving back here. Her lesbian lifestyle would not be accepted in our town."

"Faith," Texas

"We have hosted several holiday dinners at our home for LGBTQ youth who were no longer welcome at home over break or during holidays."

"Roger," Pennsylvania

"We always love having our son home, but if he had a better plan, say an internship or travel plans, we would not force the issue."

"Michelle," Louisiana

"We have always encouraged our daughter to travel and see other places. But we also discuss the importance with her of traveling to places that are 'gay-friendly' for safety's sake."

"Renata," Illinois

"When my daughter came home from school with a girlfriend we sometimes had to tell her to cool it when they were making out on the front porch or in the bedroom, where her younger sister was trying to sleep. But again this isn't any different than we would speak to her sisters about if they were making out with boys on the front porch!"

"Lillian," Rhode Island

Whatever your specific experience is, it's clear that simply providing your child with a safe and welcoming place to return home to will go a long way towards increasing your child's self-confidence when he or she is away from the hearth.

Taking Classes in the Summer

It is becoming more and more common for students to graduate in six years or less with a bachelor's degree. That said, college is expensive, many students can't afford *not* to finish in four years. For this reason, taking summer classes is an increasingly popular option for college students on summer break. Think about it: If you could knock out that math requirement with a course at your local community college or state school for $1,200 as opposed to $4,200 at your regular college, wouldn't that make the idea of summer classes sound much more appealing? Or, let's say you're a few credits off from making a degree in four years a reality—wouldn't you rather take a summer class than have to pay a semester's worth of tuition just to complete one course? For these and many other reasons, college students on summer break often choose to take classes while they're at home for the summer. These classes are often more laid-back than regular academic-year courses, and there is the added benefit of being able to focus your attention on one course, rather than several at a time. Taking classes during the summer will help keep your academic skills sharp, and may provide you with an opportunity to explore new themes and interests. Perhaps your school doesn't offer an extensive queer studies curriculum, but your local state school has a great "Queer Cinema" course you're dying to take. Whatever your objective is, the key is to do some pre-planning and talk to your advisor beforehand to get advice on transferring credits and to find out what type of courses are eligible. It would be awful to spend all that time in class during the summer only to find out later that you can't get the credits to count towards your degree. On the other hand, if you're interested in taking a class just for the fun of it, you should by all means do so. Personal growth and interest are just as valid reasons for signing up as anything else.

Working During the Summer

Working during the summer is the only option for lots of students. Independent LGBTQ students who are footing the bill for their education often have no choice but to take advantage of summer vacation to work as much as possible for as much money as possible. Even students who have their parents' financial support have an incentive to find a summer job to help finance travel plans, pay off credit card bills, or just defray the costs of any number of personal expenses. If you are thinking about working over the summer, your first stop should be the Career Services Office on campus. Stop by to get help with your resume and interviewing tips. The staff will also be able to give you leads on different job opportunities, both locally and out-of-state. If you worked while you were in high school, you might want to follow up with your old boss to find out if you can get your job back for the summer. Competition for local summer jobs can be fierce though, so get started early.

FINDING A GREAT SUMMER INTERNSHIP

An internship is a position held within an actual company that will offer you hands-on experience with the type of work you may eventually choose to do. The benefits of summer internships are innumerable: Internships can provide you with a plethora of valuable opportunities for both practical work experience *and* personal growth. According to the National Association of Colleges and Employers, employers extend job offers to more than 70 percent of their interns.[1] While the benefits of completing a summer internship might be self-evident, landing one is not nearly as easy.

The trouble with awesome summer internships—editorial intern at *Time Magazine* or *Rolling Stone*, apprentice writer for NPR, tour guide at the Art Institute of Chicago—is that many of them are unpaid. This means that the best internships end up going to people who can afford to sail through months without an income. This gives an advantage to students who are supported financially by their parents. If you have a healthy trust fund from which to draw, you're good to go for any internship. But the truth is that most people don't have trust funds. So what are you to do?

The good news is that there are actually a few different ways around this obstacle. First off, the assumption that all internships are unpaid is a false one. It really depends on the field you're targeting. Many large companies offer paid internships, along with other perks like housing, travel, and cars. Ford, Pepsi, Microsoft, and Time Warner are just a sampling of major *Fortune* 500 companies to offer paid internships.

1 College Recruiter. "College Students Find Internships Can Pave Way to Job." www.collegerecruiter.com/weblog/archives/2006/11/college_student_1.php.

In addition, many corporations sponsor diversity programs especially for students of a certain ethnic or cultural group, or for students who need financial assistance. Inroads (www.inroads.com) and Sponsors for Educational Opportunity (www.ny-seo.org) are just two examples of such programs. Many LGBTQ media groups such as Logo and Here! Networks and advocacy groups such as the Human Rights Campaign and the National Gay and Lesbian Task Force also offer internships to members of sexual minority groups. You might also be able to receive a grant from your school or a private organization for working an unpaid internship. The Foundation Center in New York City is a useful place for researching grants and nonprofit funding (www.foundationcenter.org). Also, an exhaustive online search could net some surprising funding sources.

The unfairness factor really kicks in when students are trying to land coveted internships in Hollywood or on Capitol Hill, since very few paid internships are available in these fields. In general, movies, television, and politics are such popular career routes that finding interns willing to work for nothing is easy, and the competition is stiff. Even so, there are options. For those interested in Hollywood internships, the Academy of TV Arts and Sciences (the producers of the Emmy Awards) offer a ten-week program stipend, and on Capitol Hill, the WISE program for engineers and science-oriented interns offers financial assistance.

Landing the right internship can be a career-bolstering opportunity. If money is a concern, consider working another part-time job while you complete your unpaid internship. Part-time jobs such as waiting tables, bartending, working for catering firms, moving furniture, painting houses, and driving a cab can pay $150 to $300 per shift; if you work two or three nights a week and share an apartment with a couple of other interns or friends, you should be able to pay your rent, eat, and have some spending money left over for the double espressos you'll be slamming to stay awake. And who knows? Your night or weekend gig could turn out to be more fun than you can imagine. If you wait tables or bartend in a good restaurant, you'll have the added benefit of delicious staff meals to boot.

Queer Tip: 15 Reasons to Pursue an Internship

- Exposes you to the interviewing process early on.
- Offers a low-risk way to explore a possible career path.
- Provides you with work experience to build your resume.
- Gives you the chance to practice networking skills.
- Presents opportunities to learn and practice your communication and interpersonal skills.
- Supplies you with earned money and/or academic credit.
- Exposes you to real-world corporate and professional culture.
- Provides environments to learn more about yourself and your areas of interest.
- Presents a perfect opportunity to test how comfortable you are being either "out" or "closeted" in the workplace.
- Helps you develop time management skills.
- Conditions you to the pace and energy of certain industries.
- Provides you with a structured environment in which to develop specific job skills that can't be taught through books and schoolwork.
- Allows you to experiment with the idea of working for a LGBTQ-owned or sensitive company.
- Provides you with "real world" responsibilities.
- Helps you build your self-confidence!

Landing an Internship

Whether they're paid or unpaid, competition for internships can be stiff. To be sure, some internship programs impose a minimum grade-point-average, although such requirements are relatively rare. The CIA, for example, seeks undergraduates with at least a 2.75 GPA, while the Environmental Protection Agency draws the line at a 3.0 GPA. Moreover, a few programs also scrutinize the coursework of their applicants. The auction house Butterfield & Butterfield favors art history majors, and the *Washington Post* seeks out students who have taken classes in journalism. And every now and then, one runs across an internship that seems to have a disproportionately high representation of students from the Ivy League and other top schools.

But with most internships, application requirements are typically looser and coordinators care about more than just a stellar GPA and enrollment at a top-ranked school. The deciding factor is often an applicant's attitude. Specifically, internship coordinators use cover letters and interviews to gauge an applicant's motivation and energy. Organizations want interns who are fired-up and who will accept all assignments or ask for more during slow periods. Inquisitive and enthusiastic applicants routinely beat out those who look better on paper. Along with a "go-getter" attitude, applicants must also display diplomacy and discretion. Interns have to know when to check their enthusiasm and assume the role of low-key team-player in a sensitive, hierarchical institution. The key for internship applicants is to play up not only their enthusiasm, but also their professionalism and maturity. As the internship coordinator at Lucasfilm in San Rafael, California, says, [companies] "don't want people with pixie dust in their eyes."

Building Your Own Internship

For those dissatisfied with the internship chase, there remains a long neglected but potentially winning route to a dream internship: Make your own. Rather than apply only to pre-established programs, internship seekers should consider persuading an organization or person who does not normally hire interns to offer an "ad hoc internship." Here's how: Think of six or so accomplished people whose shoes you would love to fill. It could be a bigwig advertising executive, a documentary filmmaker, a renowned park ranger, a compelling author—the sky's the limit. Just make sure it's not someone so famous that a letter from you would hit the trash before it ever reached your quarry's desk. After deciding upon a handful of people worth writing, it is time to research them thoroughly. Go online and look up what that journalist (or cardiologist or ski racer or pilot) was doing last week, last month, and last year. Use biographies, databases, magazine indexes, annual reports, the Internet, or anything else that will tell you exactly what your potential mentor is all about.

Then, write each person an earnest letter that not only introduces you, but convinces him or her that hiring you as an ad hoc intern would be mutually beneficial. Play up your best qualities—abilities either directly related to your potential mentor's work (e.g., your fluency in French if you are writing to the French ambassador) or traits suggesting that you would be a valuable assistant (emphasize your enthusiasm, discreetness, diligence, etc.). Be sure to customize each letter, showing each person that you have done your homework by incorporating into the letter choice bits of information unearthed during your research. Convey why his work is exactly the kind with which you want to be involved or why her organization is singularly important to your career aspirations.

Chances are that your six letters, voraciously researched and carefully written, will yield at least one internship opportunity. There probably will be no other interns, giving you the pick of possible projects and undivided accessibility to your mentor, forging a professional connection that may last a lifetime.

CHAPTER 12

WELCOME TO THE REAL WORLD

THE GRADUATION BLUES (AND LAVENDERS)

It seems like it was just yesterday when you arrived on campus with stars in your eyes, eager for all the exciting adventures that awaited you at college. You've survived homesickness, first-year anxiety, roommate drama, heteronormativity in the classroom, discovered your activist "you," and maybe even had a few "queer-fabulous" experiences along the way. Now all of that is coming to a close. Your senior year in college will bring with it lots of conflicting emotions as you prepare to end a key stage of your personal and educational development. While you may be thrilled to get on with your adult life and leave your university days behind, try to remember that adjusting to life after college can be a tough process that requires patience and time on your part. The fact is that shifting from college student to the "real world" of working, independence, and obligations can often be just plain hard. Fortunately, at the end of the day, after you've turned in your thesis and taken your final exams, you'll have a whole new chapter of your life to look forward to, one that involves as many ups and downs (if not more) as your transition to college life. Get ready for a bittersweet celebration and a party to end all parties as you prepare to close out your college career. Whether you're planning on finding a job, taking time off, or applying to grad school, this chapter will let you know how to get started and give you tips to help you along the way.

Consortium Tips: What is a Lavender Graduation?

by Dr. Ronni Sanlo, Director, LGBT Resource Center, University of California—Los Angeles

Lavender graduations honor the lives and achievements of lesbian, gay, bisexual, transgender, and queer students in colleges and universities. Lavender graduations tell LGBTQ students that they mattered to their institution. For many LGBTQ students, a lavender graduation is viewed as their reward for remaining in school despite the hardships, marginalization, and isolation they may have experienced. It is an opportunity for their college institution to acknowledge their unique accomplishments.

The first lavender graduation was held at the University of Michigan in 1995. Dr. Ronni Sanlo, then director of the

University of Michigan LGBT office, noticed the ethnic celebrations during Michigan's 1994 June commencement and decided to create a similar celebration for LGBTQ students. The event was named "lavender graduation" to commemorate the history of LGBTQ people from Nazi Germany who were forced to wear the pink triangle (if they were gay) and the black triangle (if they were a lesbian) in the concentration camps, and the courageous leaders of the LGBTQ civil rights movement of the 1970s who merged those hateful triangles into a symbol of pride and community.

The significance of lavender graduations quickly became evident and by the spring of 1999, 18 institutions sponsored lavender graduation events. The celebration continued to grow annually. In 2006 there were over 60 such events nationwide.

The process of hosting a lavender graduation celebration is unique to each campus. Keynote speakers, music, leadership awards, recognition of donors, LGBTQ Studies Minor certificates, and especially the recognition of graduates are all components of lavender graduations at many institutions. At UCLA, for example, Lavender Graduation is a collaborative event involving the LGBTQ Campus Resource Center, the LGBTQ Studies Department, the LGBTQ Faculty-Staff Network, the Lambda Alumni Association, and LGBTQ student organizations, as well as local community organizations. At many institutions, each graduate receives a rainbow tassel and a certificate.

Because LGBTQ students are of every race, nationality, gender, ethnicity, socioeconomic background, and ability, it is an opportunity for institutions to acknowledge the diversity of the LGBTQ population on campus, to provide LGBTQ students with a respectful exit, and to invite them to return as valued and generous alumni. If you are an administrator or student who is interested in hosting a lavender graduation on your campus, please visit the Consortium's website at LGBTQcampus.org/faq/lavender_graduation.html for more information.

I Have No Idea What I Want To Do With My Life!

You've done your fair share of internships; worked all summer, every summer; volunteered your butt off with various extracurricular groups on campus; and you've lost a bevy of beauty sleep and sanity trying to keep your GPA at a suitable level. Despite all that, you *still* have no idea what you really want to do with your life.

Take heart: It's perfectly okay, in fact, it is absolutely normal, not to know what you want to do with your life at this moment in time. We can all but guarantee that the majority of college graduates—even those now happily situated in great careers—felt a wave of helplessness wash over them around graduation time. You have a few options. First, you can take a break to think it over. This is an attractive option for the short term. In many cases, however, while it may sound like a good idea at the outset, it can end up backfiring when you slide deeper into uncertainty at the sight of all of your friends moving into the next phase of their life while you sit at home watching reruns of *The Simpsons*. Whatever your post-graduate plans might be, there are some things you can do beforehand to help make your exit as cleanly as possible, and prepare you mentally and emotionally for the next step, whatever that might be.

- **First, take a deep breath.** While college graduation does represent the end of a phase in your life, it does not mean that you can't keep in touch with all the friends you've made along the way. Get your MySpace and Facebook profiles together, and make sure that your alumni e-mail is activated. When all the dust settles you'll be surprised by just how "in touch" you all managed to stay.

- **Thank your professors.** Although by now you're probably ready to hightail it off campus, before you go, remember to take a moment to thank the folks who made it all possible: your professors. This actually serves a dual purpose. As you're thanking your favorite professors for an amazing academic experience, don't be shy about asking them to write you a recommendation. It doesn't matter if you have no clue what you're going to be doing after graduation. Having this generic recommendation from them will make it that much easier to approach them down the line when you need a recommendation for grad school, a fellowship, or job opportunity.

- **Visit the Career Services office.** This might be obvious, but if you're planning on looking for a job after graduation, make sure you stop by the Career Services office on your campus and speak to a career counselor. Not only will they be able to provide you with leads on jobs and internships, but you'll also be able to get valuable help and advice on resumes and interviewing.

- **Take advantage of the community.** Join your school's LGBTQ alumni network. These social and professional organizations for LGBTQ alumni connect old friends, help new friendships develop, and aim to keep LGBTQ alumni involved with the current LGBTQ campus happenings. Alumni groups also sponsor social events and provide opportunities for professional networking.

- **Talk to your parents.** Think long and hard if you really want to go back home (if that's even an option) or if you want to find a place to live on your own or with roommates. Whatever your decision is, talk to your parents about it. Your plans also affect them, whether through a return to the nest or the financial and emotional support you'll inevitably need when striking out on your own.

- **Get your credits (and credit cards) in order.** Make sure you have all the credits you need to graduate! There's nothing worse than discovering in senior spring that you're two credit shorts of walking across that stage with your peers. Plan ahead so you are not put in this position. You also need to give your financial situation some special attention. Those student loans, credit card bills, and other living expenses are going to start adding up. Take the time to learn how to start managing your finances without your parents' assistance.

If you take these preparatory steps, you'll be ahead of the curve when it comes time to figure out just what your next step will be. Remember that you're not the only college student who has questions, fears, and doubts about your ultimate career path or life in general after college. For most of you, life after college will require a deep examination of where you are, where you want to be going, and where you need to start in order to get there. It's a common experience that all but the most focused undergrads face when finishing up their senior year of study. There's no reason to believe that life is a nice, neat bundle that's always going to go according to premeditated plans. Sometimes there simply is no plan. You have to design a roadmap and do the best you can navigating the thorny and often daunting challenges that await.

PFLAG PARENT TIP: RETURN TO THE NEST

Current wisdom states that about half of all college graduates plan to move back home after graduation. Like other students, some LGBTQ students finish school with high expectations, low bank balances, and a fuzzy sense of what to do next. For these graduates, returning home may be just the safe haven they need to figure out the next phase in their lives. The free food and laundry service are nice perks, too.

Other LGBTQ students, used to a fairly high level of independence, perhaps in part due to their sexual identity/gender identity, plunge easily into the "real world" after graduation. Working to pay the bills, sharing an apartment with roommates to split expenses, and enjoying their newfound freedom from school may come naturally to many LGBTQ students. For these young people, there is never any question that they will become "boomerang" kids, returning home after graduation.

If it's your child who isn't quite ready to be on his or her own, would you take them back? Should you? Professional opinion varies, with some experts urging sympathy, and others urging a more tough-love approach. Only you and your family can decide what the best tactic is for your recent graduate. If your child does move back in, be sure and discuss finances, household bills and responsibilities, and the duration of stay you'd like your child to agree to—before the bags get unpacked.

Some PFLAG parents let us in on how they really feel about this issue, and what's happened, or is likely to happen when their own child graduates:

"After graduation, my son plans on living at home and helping to pay off some of his school loans. This is his choice, and as a single mother, I welcome it. If and when he does leave home for good, it will be when he's ready."

"Zada," New Mexico

"Both of my gay sons have graduated college and live far away from home, one in New York City and one in Melbourne, Australia. I love them but absolutely wouldn't want them living at home."

"Deborah," Illinois

"My (trans) son worked through all school breaks and vacations. He hasn't ever lived at home since (s)he left for college. It's one of the things I'm most proud of."

"Daren," Wisconsin

"[My daughter's] cousin is studying abroad in the Netherlands this year and has asked her to come stay for an extended visit. We're encouraging her to do this."

"Nadine," Pennsylvania

"I would never want my daughter to come back to our small hometown. It's very conservative and not only is her lesbian lifestyle not accepted here, it is considered a disgrace. However, I do want her to live within a reasonable distance from us so we can visit each other."

"Stacy," Georgia

"I have always welcomed adventure and encouraged my children to practice making decisions early so they would be comfortable on their own."

"Tasha," Oregon

"We are in a situation of 'interrupted college' and she will be finishing college later, as an independent adult. She came home for a while during this time but now lives on her own, with some financial support from me."

"Laurie," Rhode Island

"My (trans) son recently came home after graduation. It's fine with him living at home for awhile but I know that after being on his own for five years he'll be happier once he has a job and can share an apartment with a friend, rather than his parents."

"Dawn," Massachusetts

"Will my son live back at home after he graduates? Not for more than a day or two!"

"Dustine," Arkansas

QUEER-TIP:
SUGGESTED POST-GRADUATION READING

Looking for some guidance after graduation? Hit your local library or search your favorite bookstore for these popular titles:

- *10 Things Employers Want You to Learn in College: The Know-How You Need to Succeed* by William D. Coplin
- *A Car, Some Cash and A Place to Crash: The Only Post-College Survival Guide You'll Ever Need* by Rebecca Knight
- *Guide to Your Career* by Alan B. Bernstein and The Princeton Review
- *How to Survive the Real World: Life After College Graduation: Advice from 774 Graduates Who Did* by "Hundreds of Heads" by Andrea Syrtash
- *Life After School Explained* by Jesse Vickey

I Was a Queer Studies Major . . . Am I Employable?

Many students feel pressure to find and land a job that will make use of their college degree. While this seems intuitive, the fact is that your undergraduate college major may or may not have anything to do with your chosen career path. Sure, we know English majors who've gone on to be book editors, but we also know women's studies majors working as management consultants, and history majors working in financial services. There are tons of career opportunities out there for students in all majors, some that are obvious matches and many more that are not. In other words, your major—except for those fields that require specific, specialized knowledge like computer science—should not in any way determine or prevent you from pursuing the career of your dreams. The more important thing for you to figure out—with some self-reflection and the aid of a career counselor—is the specific skill set your undergraduate major provided you with. For many liberal arts majors, that means learning the "market value" of "soft skills" like analytical ability, research and writing skills, and communication skills. Once you understand your particular value in the job market, you can articulate your abilities to friends, relatives, total strangers, and, most importantly, the people who may want to hire you.

Finding That Perfect Job[1]

While many colleges and universities sponsor recruiting events on campus, especially for the financial services and technical industries, most students are not lucky enough to have a job sown up before graduation. While the pressure to have your plans firmed up can be intense, it is important not to lose sight of the big picture. In all likelihood, your first job will have little to do with your last job. Taking a job is not an irreversible trip down a one-way career path. In fact, for many recent graduates, the function of a first job is merely to help them figure out

---

[1] Excerpt. Klein, Rachel, and Lisa Vollmer. *What to Do with Your Liberal Arts Degree in English and Communications*. New York: The Princeton Review, 2007.

what they don't want to do. It's an experiment, almost like picking a major, but in some ways less important. After all, you have much longer than four years to figure out what you want to be when you grow up.

Finding a job can take several months. In order to figure out what jobs might be right for you, the first step is to have some idea of what you want. Ask yourself: What do I like? What do I do well? What are my passions? You might also consider taking a career quiz, but be careful. Career quizzes can be found all over the Internet but most cost a lot of money and some make the results difficult to interpret. The Princeton Review offers a free career quiz that helps you find careers that may be great matches for your interests, skills, and disposition. Log onto PrincetonReview.com for more information.

Once you have determined general areas of interest, the next step is for you to come up with a daily routine of networking, scanning the classifieds and online job listings, and sending out resumes. Follow up on each resume that you send out. Talk to other people who are going through the same thing; that's networking too. Shamelessly exploit your college's career office (you're an alumnus now). In fact, they will tell you that the importance of networking when it comes to finding out about that perfect job opportunity can not be overstated. Think of networking as research that allows you to leverage the richest source of information at your disposal: other people. Networking allows you to tap into the "hidden job market"—the universe of available jobs that are not formally advertised. If you want your job search to be successful—and by successful we mean that you not only land a great job, but that it doesn't take you longer to find it than it took to complete your degree in the first place—you cannot rely on job boards and company websites alone. You have to find out about jobs before the rest of the world does. There are many career books out there that will give you tips on how to network. The most important thing to remember is to let people know you are looking for a job. Spreading the word involves talking to family members, close friends, former classmates, teammates, professors, advisors—anyone who knows you well. Not only should you make sure these folks know you're looking for a job, but you should let them know—with as much specificity as possible—what you're looking for.

After you've networked with the right folks, hopefully you'll be invited for an informational interview. This is an opportunity for you to learn more about the company and position(s) in which you are interested, and make a good impression with someone who can get your resume in the right person's hands. Prepare for it by developing a specific idea of what you hope to learn. Of course, the types of questions you'll ask will depend on what stage of the job-research process you're at. The research you've done up until this point (whether online, at your career-planning office, or through other informational interviews) should also help you decide which questions to pose. Always remain conscious of your contact's time; these individuals are not your personal career consultants, nor should you feel as though you can enlist them to support your case with recruiters.

QUEER-TIP:
BOOKS ON QUEER WORKPLACE ISSUES

- *Lavender Road to Success: The Career Guide for the Gay Community* by Kirk Snyder
- *Sexual Orientation in the Workplace: Gay Men, Lesbians, Bisexuals, and Heterosexuals Working Together* by Amy J. Zuckerman and George F. Simons
- *Straight Jobs Gay Lives* by Annette Friskopp and Sharon Silverstein

How Do I Know if That Perfect Job Is LGBTQ-Friendly?

Finding a job that allows you to be open and safe as an LGBTQ employee is one of the most important tasks that you will face when entering the workforce. While countless companies actively support the rights of queer people in the workplace, many do not. You'll need to ask yourself if a hostile work atmosphere, or one in which you will need to remain closeted, is the type of environment in which you'd like to end up. There are many ways you can determine whether the job or company you're interested in is supportive of its LGBTQ employees. The career advisors at Lawrence University in Wisconsin (http://www.lawrence.edu/dept/student_dean/career/glbt/resumes.html) recommend researching the following issues:

- **Non-Discrimination Policies:** The first place to look for information about a potential employer is in their non-discrimination clause. This policy will usually be prominently displayed in the company's promotional materials and job listings. Look to see if sexual orientation and gender identity/expression is included in their statement.

- **State regulations regarding discrimination:** Several states specifically include sexual orientation and gender identity/expression in their employee non-discrimination laws. Not only does this give you an added measure of protection should something happen, but it also sets a general tone of acceptance, or at least tolerance, throughout the state and the businesses which operate there.

- **Domestic Partner Benefits:** Many employers, particularly large companies or organizations, currently extend to employees' domestic partners benefits that have traditionally been offered only to spouses of employees. These benefits include health and life insurance, educational grants, and access to recreational facilities. These benefits may not be important to you right now, but they may become very important to you in the future when you are in a serious relationship. At the very least they demonstrate the organization's commitment to diversity. Although information regarding domestic partner benefits is often very easy to find, it may not be discussed until you are offered a job, when benefits typically are discussed. Use some of the resources provided by your school's Career Services Office to research organizations' policies before an interview.

- **LGBTQ Employee Groups:** Some major employers offer formal or informal LGBTQ groups. Human resources personnel can tell you whether the company has such a group and provide you with contact information for some of its members. Contacting alumni who work in the organization is a great networking tactic, particularly if they were active in the university LGBTQ group while a student.

See Appendix D for a list of LGBTQ career resources.

RESUME, COVER LETTERS, AND INTERVIEWS[3]

If networking gets your foot in the door, resumes, cover letters, and interviews close the deal. Packaging is everything—once you've taken the time to figure out exactly what you have to offer a potential employer, you've got to present your qualifications in a compelling, convincing way. The first step is to figure out which specific attributes the organization is looking for as it evaluates your candidacy. While every organization uses its own unique set of criteria, employers across industries mention the same qualities over and over again. Those qualities include communication skills, teamwork skills, analytical skills, and leadership ability. Many of the skills that were most critical to your success as a student are the ones employers prize most highly. The key to creating a good resume and cover letter, and having a great interview, is to demonstrate the core skills every employer is looking for.

When it comes to effective resumes, there's no single magic formula that guarantees success in every circumstance. However, the best resumes have a few things in common: They are concise, results-oriented, and clearly presented. Together, your resume and cover letter introduce your qualifications to recruiters and hiring managers. An effective resume has—at most—three sections: "education," "experience," and (sometimes) a third section for relevant information that doesn't fit into either of the other two categories. The optional third section goes by a few different names: "activities," "additional information," "interests," "other," or "personal," depending on what you've included in the section. It's worth asking family and friends—especially those who are

2   Ibid.

already working in the industry you hope to break into—for guidance. If you are job hunting in more than one field, or considering different types of positions within the same field, you will need to have more than one version of your resume. Your school's Career Service office is a great place to get help with your resume. As an alumnus of the school, you will be able to use their services even after you graduate.

Unlike you resume, your cover letter is seldom read closely. It should never be more than one-page long, and should be concise, well written, polite, at least somewhat personalized, and error-free. It should include all the required information: the position to which you're applying, the primary reason for your interest, and a brief overview of the one or two qualifications that make you a compelling candidate. At the end of the letter, you should politely suggest a possible next step—usually a brief telephone conversation or an in-person meeting.

If the primary purpose of a great cover letter and resume is to get an interview, then it seems as though the point of the interview would be to land the job. But, in reality, that's only half right. One of your goals during the interview process is to tell a compelling story—to present your life (educational, extracurricular, and otherwise) as an entirely logical series of decisions in which this particular job is the obvious next step. The other (equally, if not more important) objective is to learn as much as possible about the position for which you're applying, the culture of the organization you're interviewing with, and the extent to which the job fits with your personal and professional goals. The key to having a great interview is preparation. You can predict the vast majority of the questions you will hear during an interview—provided, of course, you've done your homework on the industry, the organization, and the position you've got your eye on. Some questions (e.g., "Why are you interested in this job?") arise so frequently in one form or another you'd be foolish not to take the time to outline your responses well in advance. Approach the interview as a learning experience, and ask questions that will teach you something you didn't already know about the position and/or company. Always remember to follow-up after the interview with a thank-you note.

QUEER-TIP: TEN TIPS TO LANDING THE PERFECT FIRST JOB

1. Network—make a list of your contacts (professors, family, friends, etc.) and don't be shy about reaching out to them.

2. Attend career fairs.

3. Join professional associations.

4. Create a concise, error-free, reader-friendly document that can be easily scanned.

5. Stick to the truth—don't pepper your resume with skills you don't actually have or jobs you never had. It's not worth the consequences if your potential employer finds out (and he or she probably will).

6. Prepare for your interview—take the time to learn about the company you are targeting.

7. Dress to impress.

8. During your interview always show your excitement and enthusiasm about the position.

9. Send a post-interview thank you note.

10. Don't give up! Rejection is common as you start looking for your first full-time job. Be proactive, be persistent and remain confident.

Being Out in Your Resume and Interview

Of course, if you majored in LGBTQ studies or have a bunch of courses listed on your transcript covering LGBTQ themes, there's a chance that you will be "outed" on your resume and application materials. For some students, this is a non-issue, but for other individuals this is a very real concern. The Career Services center at Lawrence University offers these suggestions regarding being "out" on your resume when looking for jobs[3]:

3 Lawrence University. "Sexual Orientation and Career Decision Making—Resumes and Interviews."
www.lawrence.edu/dept/student_dean/career/glbt/resumes.shtml.

1. If you feel strongly about being "out," use your resume as a tool to screen potential employers. Check out the company's non-discrimination policies and domestic partner benefits to determine whether it fosters an LGBTQ-inclusive culture.

2. For those who do not want to be "outed" early on in the job hunt, a simple strategy is to not include any reference to any LGBTQ organizations or affiliations on your application materials. However, the question of how you spent your time as an undergraduate and the skills you've developed outside the classroom will inevitably come up. If you were the president of a your campus' LGBTQ student group and took on an active leadership role organizing conferences and recruiting members, potential employers will want to know about it, as it demonstrates valuable leadership and organizational skills.

3. If you are concerned about being outed on your resume, try focusing on the skills and accomplishments you developed through your activities, rather than the specific affiliations. For example, you could list the LGBTQ organization as "Anti-Discrimination Organization," and then document the duties or skills you gained during this experience. Another option is to just use the name of the group (e.g. Pride). Many college students across the board use a "functional" or "skills-based" format for their resumes that takes the focus off the organization or employer, and emphasizes the skill set gained.

4. No matter how you choose to document your participation in a LGBTQ organization, you must be prepared for pointed questions in an interview. An interviewer might ask you to describe the organizations you were involved with in college. If you have decided to be out, you can respond with a simple description. If you have chosen not to be out, you may want to refer to it as an anti-discrimination organization and then focus on the skills or achievements you have as a result of your involvement.

5. As with any interview situation, the key to dealing with issues of sexual orientation and gender identity/expression is to practice, practice, practice. Try not to be taken off guard by a question concerning your LGBTQ activities. Take advantage of mock interviews at your college's Career Center, and

schedule individual appointments with a career counselor to help you determine your approach for these types of questions.

For more information and tips, log onto Lawrence.edu/dept/student_dean/career/glbt/resumes.shtml.

QUEER & CANDID:
A Lesbian Leader Shares and Cares

Alina Wilczynski is graphic designer, artist and the Co-founding Board Member OP/LYNX, the Women's Network of Out Professionals.

If there is one thing I know for certain, it is that personal truth is the conduit by which success travels. My college years were experienced among a group of artistic vanguards, passionate thinkers, and compassionate soulmates. We challenged each other to be imaginative and expressive, and to be unafraid to question or to experiment. Our professors recognized and nurtured our ambitions, and helped many of us become leaders and agents of change on campus.

I trusted my intuition, followed my heart, and at 25, I opened my first business. I learned to take creative risks and to "come out" as an entrepreneurial spirit and as a lesbian. Running a business is a trial by fire for every belief you have about the world and the relationships that enrich your learning each day. When I look back at the times when I experienced discrimination, I now understand that under the surface I was not fully accepting of deep-rooted aspects of myself.

In recent years, I've reconnected with my vanguard beginnings and have sought out communities of forward-thinkers who are unafraid to question and experiment within the framework of their life's work. In a roundabout way, I found the LGBTQ business community. From the connections made here have come trusted alliances, inspiring mentors, fulfilling work opportunities, as well as true friendships and rewarding ways to give back. When you find a community that supports your highest vision of yourself, the boundaries by which you initially define your career, personal goals and desires, philanthropy, and leadership begin to expand in ways you cannot imagine.

In 2004, I co-founded OP/LYNX, the Women's Network of Out Professionals. By recognizing a need within the community, and by following a persistent vision, we have done something no other organization has been able to accomplish in New York City. Through presentations and discussions, workshops, events, research projects, and social gatherings, we have invited the lesbian business community to become active co-creators of a resource-sharing hub, as well as to be recognized on a national scale and valued by the greater business community. Being invited to introduce the work of a respected avant-guard filmmaker at MoMA is a moment I will forever cherish. It was a direct result of living my personal truth openly and honestly.

QUEER-TIP: BLOW THE WHISTLE

Workplace discrimination against LGBTQ people and those with HIV occurs in every corner of this country, but we don't often hear these stories. Lambda Legal's Workplace Discrimination campaign empowers LGBTQ people, people with HIV, and the public at large by providing information and advocacy opportunities to fight employment discrimination based on sexual orientation, gender identity, and HIV status. Become part of a national network of thousands of people who are working to fight discrimination at work. Sign up for Lambda Legal's "Blow the Whistle" e-mail list at http://GA4.org/lambdalegal/join.

RIDE ON THE PEACE TRAIN: VOLUNTEERING AND NONPROFIT WORK

If you are interested in a career in the nonprofit sector, considering doing long term volunteer work, or looking for an organization with whom to do an internship, the Idealist is the place for you. Established in 1996, the Idealist is as an extension of Action Without Borders, a nonprofit group founded on the idea of building a network of neighborhood contact centers that would provide a one-stop shop for volunteer opportunities and nonprofit services in communities around the world.

Over the years, the Idealist has become one of the most popular communities of nonprofit career and volunteering resources on the web, with information provided by over 57,000 organizations in 165 countries, and visits from thousands of users every day.

In addition to searching and browsing, you can use the Idealist to:

- Define what information you'd like to receive by e-mail from among the job openings, volunteer opportunities, internships, events, and resources posted there by organizations all over the world.

- Design the perfect volunteer opportunity for yourself by setting up one or more Volunteer Profiles with your interests, skills, and schedule. These profiles can then be searched by organizations in Idealist.

- Find people around the world who share your interests, goals, and ideas.

For more information, log onto Idealist.org/career/career.html.

QUEER-TIP: A CONFERENCE JUST FOR YOU

OUT for Work, is a national lesbian, gay, bisexual, transgender and ally undergraduate student career conference. OUT for Work's mission is to prepare LGBTQ individuals for the challenges they face in the workplace. Diversity Change Agents is the founding sponsor of OUT for Work. OUT for Work is the only national non-industry specific career conference for LGBTQ undergraduate students, bringing together students, allies, and representatives from America's top companies and LGBTQ advocacy groups. Best of all, the conference is FREE. To register for OUT for Work, download the application at OutForWork.com.

A YEAR OFF ON THE ROAD: BACKPACKING AND EXTENDED TRAVEL

Many recent college graduates choose to take a year off year immediately after graduation. This time is often spent travelling, and can encompass work experience, extended study, volunteer work, or just time spent roaming around experiencing different cultures and environments. It is an opportunity to construct an adventure that can yield amazing memories, a wide network of friends, and a greater sense of self- confidence.

Moreover, time off spent travelling will make you stand out to employers and graduate schools. The fact that you have traveled extensively and have engaged with a variety of people from different cultures can make you a strong candidate for many jobs. Most importantly, it provides a much-needed respite from a grueling undergraduate experience and is a great opportunity to do and see things you have always dreamed of before jumping into the workforce.

But for many students, money is the biggest obstacle to taking time off. How much do you have? How much do you need? How much do you need to have left over when your backpacking adventure comes to a close? Do you need to make money, break even, or will you be able to spend some money from your savings or family along the way? Because one or both of your parents are probably involved in this issue, you should discuss your financial situation with them at the very beginning of your decision to take time off. Your financial status may make taking time off more difficult, but it does not have to be an insurmountable obstacle.

Most student loans have a built-in grace period that begins when you leave school. If you take time off, this period may expire, interest will kick in, and you will have to begin making payments. Obviously, it makes sense to plan for this possibility. In some instances, taking a class during your time off (and retaining your status as a student) will postpone the need to begin paying off your loan. If your only financial need is to break even, there are numerous ways to accomplish this. Some people work for six months to make money, and then travel or spend time doing volunteer work. Many opportunities also exist for people who are willing to work for just room and board. People who need to save money will probably have to live at home. Working part-time, or even full-time during your time away or finding a paid internship to support yourself and your quest are other options worth looking into.

YEAR OF SERVICE PROGRAMS: IS THE PEACE CORPS RIGHT FOR ME?

Year of service programs are often "in the trenches" jobs that involve teaching or working in the community. These programs are very highly regarded by both employers and graduate schools and can give you serious hands-on experiences with which to shape your graduate school and career objectives. Moreover, participants may be eligible for federal loan forgiveness and/or loan deferment programs.

Maybe the idea of jetting off to some developing country to work for nearly two years in often squalid, and almost always difficult, conditions (with little, if any, money in return) may not be the first thing that comes to mind when thinking about your next step after graduating college. But some of you may feel the need to do some long-term travel that involves more than backpacking—and joining the Peace Corps might be a good option to consider—one that can offer amazing and life-affirming experiences that can only come from living abroad and helping those who are in need.

Peace Corps volunteers work in the following areas: Education, youth outreach, and community development; health and HIV/AIDS; agriculture and environment; business development; and information technology. Within these areas, the specific duties and responsibilities of each volunteer can vary widely.

All Peace Corps volunteers commit to 27 months of training and service overseas. The Peace Corps provides volunteers with a living allowance that enables them to live in a manner similar to the local people in their community. The Peace Corps also provides complete medical and dental care and covers the cost of transportation to and from your country of service. When you return from your 27 months of service, you will receive just over $6,000 toward your transition to life back home.

A Worldwide Network of Brothers and Sisters

One great online resource for students considering the Peace Corps is the Lesbian, Gay, Bisexual and Transgender U.S. Peace Corps Alumni. Founded in Washington, DC in 1991, their mission is "to promote Peace Corps ideals and the legal, political, and social rights of gay, lesbian, bisexual and transgender people around the world."[4] Members are gay, lesbian, bisexual, transgender people and others who are Peace Corps alumni, current volunteers, former and current staff members and friends, as well as hundred of members throughout the country and around the world who have served the Peace Corps since its beginning in 1961.

One of this group's most important and successful outreach and recruitment initiatives is the LGBT Mentor Program. Started in 1995, the program connects Peace Corps applicants and invitees with members to discuss life as a gay or lesbian volunteer. If an applicant has been assigned to a particular country, the group will try to connect him or her with someone who has served in the same country. Each year this group receives more than 250 requests from lesbian, gay, and bisexual people who are interested in joining the Peace Corps but seek advice and

4   Lesbian, Gay, Bisexual and Transgendered U.S. Peace Corps Alumni. "Our Purpose." www.lgbrpcv.org.

opinions about queer Peace Corps experiences before making a decision. For more information about the Lesbian, Gay, Bisexual and Transgender U.S. Peace Corps Alumni, log onto LGBRPCV.org.

QUEER & CANDID: WHY A QUEER MAN JOINED THE PEACE CORPS

"Why on earth would a queer person want to join the Peace Corps?" I asked myself that very question on so many occasions. I asked the question when the local mothers in my host country tried to wed me to their terrifying daughters. I asked the question when I didn't get to bathe for weeks at a time, measuring funkiness on an exponential scale. I asked the question when I had my second helping of meat JELL-O with hoof bits because I was the good guest who ate the *first* serving of JELL-O. I definitely asked the question when I didn't get to experience any gay intimacy for almost two years.

More to the point, why would anyone want to join the Peace Corps? Yes, there is that great motto about it being the toughest job you'll ever love, and it is the only American corps where you aren't trained to kill someone overseas. But aren't there a lot of people in need right here in America? Why leave the comforts of a relatively liberal and wealthy country and go to places that have diseases that have been eradicated everywhere else? It's terrifying to go somewhere where no one speaks your language, somewhere where people might have problems with you being queer, and somewhere where every day poses a new challenge.

Putting a personal, positive face on the "American from television" is one of the main goals of Peace Corps. Right now, public opinion in other countries in regards to America is negative. Totally changing your life, learning a new language, merging into a new culture, having that experience expand your own limits and horizons—these are the personal goals. People in your host country will learn firsthand what an American is like, and a volunteer learns what they are truly capable of achieving. When you make that first step, you learn so much about yourself and your own abilities. It's a bit like coming out of the closet.

Yes, Peace Corps is tough. However, it is a chance to do some good in the world, see a country in a way that is impossible to do on a tour, and learn a language or two. You add or refine skills that are useful back in the states, meet fascinating friends, and most importantly, have something interesting to say when you're trying to impress someone.

Glenn Bunger was a member of the Peace Corps from 2000–2001, and currently teaches high school geometry at the Eagle Academy in Bronx, New York.

THE LIFELONG LEARNER: CHOOSING TO GO TO GRADUATE SCHOOL

While some of you may have been planning since you were 10 to be pediatricians, courtroom litigators, or biochemists, most of you probably only have a vague idea of what you want to do when you graduate college. After four years of studies and stress, toiling on for several more years in a Master's or PhD program may be the last thing on your agenda. But graduate studies are an important option to consider, especially if you have the financial resources, the time, and the academic stamina. Allowing you greater creative freedom to engage in new and exciting research or theoretical writing, a graduate degree is a fantastic opportunity for you to learn more about what you "enjoy." Mind you, it isn't an easy process and is not a decision to be entered into lightly.

A happy graduate student is an informed graduate student. Weighing key factors such as time and financial commitment as well as the content and objectives of each program will help you avoid most pitfalls. The purpose of graduate school is to explore the body of knowledge in a particular field. As a graduate student, you will have a very different academic experience than you had as an undergraduate. While you may have been encouraged to explore several different academic paths as an undergraduate—trying on various majors to see if they fit with your skills and interests—graduate school doesn't offer the same level of flexibility. In graduate school, the stakes are higher—and the cost of changing your mind is much, much higher.

To ensure you get as much as possible out of the investment—and the experience itself—be sure to give serious thought to whether grad school is the right choice for you. Are you going because you have to in order to obtain the licenses and certifications necessary for your career? Or is a graduate degree required for you to advance in your career of choice? Another thing to consider is timing. Many people spend the years between college and graduate school exploring professional options—and doing some important self-exploration, too. Because you've had a few years in the workplace, you'll probably bring a greater sense of clarity and focus to your academic pursuits. You might also have saved a little bit of money during your working years—or at least been able to pay down some of your undergraduate debt, if you had any. On the other hand, many students find it difficult to transition back into school mode after taking time off to work or pursue other interests. The longer you wait, the more likely it is that personal commitments—a spouse or partner, a significant other's job, children, or a mortgage—may complicate your decision to enroll. While there's no magic formula when it comes to deciding whether to take time off between your undergraduate and graduate studies, the only absolute guideline is that you go to graduate school when you're absolutely certain it's what you want or need to do.

More Schooling Means More Money...Usually

There is quite a disparity in salary when it comes to workers who hold additional degrees and those who do not. Take look at these national averages: The average professional degree holder makes roughly $81,540 while someone who holds an advanced degree such as a master's degree makes around $63,229. Your average worker with a bachelor's degree earns around $40,478, and the typical worker with just a high school diploma makes around $22,895.[5] But be extra careful if your motive for applying to graduate school is to increase your earning potential. Depending on the specific graduate degree you're pursuing, the dollar increase in your new salary might not be enough to offset the cost of obtaining the degree. You'll need to conduct a pretty thorough cost-benefit analysis to figure out whether the enhanced earning potential justifies the substantial costs. It's possible to land a job easily after earning an advanced degree and still struggle to pay back your loans. It's also possible to complete a graduate program with no debt and still have trouble finding work. Many people would find each of these scenarios unacceptable. To avoid any nasty surprises, spend some time researching the probable cost of your graduate program and study the state of the job market in your field. The most important aspects of the job market are the availability of positions and the salary range. Together, these pieces of information give you some idea of what your professional future (and loan-paying power) might look like. The more information you dig up, the better you'll be able to appraise the financial obstacles to graduate education.

Choosing a Grad School

If you thought that choosing a four-year college was tough, then hold on tight during the search for a graduate school. Filling out applications is a huge demand on your time and energy, and whether you're taking undergraduate exams or holding down a job, you probably can't afford to spend weeks dealing with a large pile of applications.

It pays—in time and money—to narrow your field down to four or five good target schools. With only a handful of slots open each year in any field of study, finding a school you can afford, can get into, that wants you, and that is in a geographic region that has a reasonably-sized LGBTQ cultural scene might be analogous to finding a needle in a haystack. To figure out which institutions make the cut, you'll probably want to consider the following six factors:

---

5   Patti L. Harrison and Carl F. Williams. "The Benefits of a Graduate
     Education." University of Alabama Graduate School.
     http://graduate.ua.edu/publications/slides/benefits/benefits.ppt.

- **Academic fit:** How well-suited is the school to the research you want to do? Find out which schools have the best programs in your area(s) of interest. Make sure they have faculty who share your research interests, and who will become involved in your work and involve you in their own.

- **Reputation:** When it comes to reputation, the excellence of a particular program doesn't always correspond to the institution's overall reputation—or the strength of its undergraduate programs. Harvard, Princeton, and MIT might vie for the top spots of the various undergraduate rankings each year, but when it comes to department-specific rankings, there's a lot more variety. Check out annual rankings for specific graduate school programs. Be warned, however: Rankings only tell part of the story. You'll need to speak with professors and actual students to get a clearer picture of whether a program is right for you.

- **Job Placement:** When you're considering which programs to apply to, be sure to visit the Career Center and ask what resources are available to graduate students. Many students enroll in programs assuming job placement—or at least career counseling—is part of the deal, and they're unpleasantly surprised to find out how few resources actually exist. In the end, you may not lean on the resources your program provides or even use them all. But it's still important to be informed about what you can expect.

- **Students:** Talking to currently enrolled students is the best way to figure out if a particular program might be a good fit. Ask them to describe the good points and the bad points of the department and the school. Ask students about their quality of life, too. Are there opportunities to socialize, and is there a strong sense of community among LGBTQ graduate students? If you take the time to gather qualitative and quantitative information like this, you'll make a much more informed decision than you would if you relied on rankings alone.

- **Geography:** The geographic location of the university should influence your decision to attend. Does the home state of the institution have supportive LGBTQ legislation? Is there a thriving off-campus LGBTQ culture? But the question of geography isn't just about personal preferences—there are practical implications, too. For example, depending on your field of study, it might be considerably easier to secure part-time jobs (or jobs between academic years) in some parts of the country than in others. If you have a partner who's going to accompany you, your partner's career prospects in each of the locales you're considering will also influence your decision.

Getting In

Before you start your graduate school applications, take some time to consider all the application pieces and set a schedule with realistic deadlines. Due to differences in departmental requirements, it is difficult to make generalizations about applications, but most require a general information form, standardized test scores, transcripts, recommendations, and a personal statement. Some programs may have additional requirements, such as an interview or portfolio. Here are some things to be mindful of:

- **Deadlines.** This is one of the most important details of the application process. You don't want to be rejected from a school simply because you were late in filing your application. Check with each individual department to which you are applying to find out their specific deadlines. Also be aware that there may be separate (usually earlier) deadlines for those students seeking financial aid.

- **Test Scores:** Almost all graduate schools require applicants to take the GRE General Test, a GRE Subject Test, or the Test of English as a Foreign Language (TOEFL). Check with individual departments to ensure you meet their specific requirements. Preparing for these standardized tests may require the single biggest investment of time when it comes to applying for graduate school, so get started early. While the weight placed on your GRE score in relation to the other factors admissions committees consider will vary from school to school and from program to program, it's never insignificant. In addition to influencing admissions decisions, GRE scores are an important factor in the awarding of teaching and research assistantships and merit-based financial aid.

- **Transcripts:** All graduate schools require official transcripts of your grades from any colleges you attended. Contact the registrar's office (at every undergraduate institution you have attended) to request that your transcript be sent either to you or directly to the school to which you are applying.

- **Letters of Recommendation:** These letters are one of the most influential aspects of your application. Keep this in mind when choosing your recommenders. Their words will (hopefully) help set you apart from the other applicants. Most schools require two or three letters. Try to get three, or even more, in case one is lost or submitted late. If you've been out of school for a few years, you might find it difficult to approach professors from your alma mater for recommendations. This is why securing generic recommendations from them before you graduate from college is so important. They'll always have that to refer to when it comes time to recommend you for a specific job, grad program, or fellowship. If it's too late for that, consider drafting a sample letter—or even an outline— that can serve as a map for the person writing your recommendation. In it, you'll want to cover specific academic achievements—in his class or otherwise—and the topics of any research projects you undertook during the class. Give your recommenders plenty of warning when you ask them for letters! If you ask the week before the letter is due, chances are your professor (or manager or co-worker) won't be able to devote enough time to crafting a compelling letter. Also, remember to follow up to make sure letters have been sent.

- **Personal Statement:** While applicants to medical, law, and business school are often asked to submit fairly lengthy essays about their motivations, goals, greatest achievements, character flaws, and/or solutions to hypothetical problems, applicants to other graduate programs are usually asked to submit a personal statement only. Admissions committees use it to evaluate how clearly you think, how well you have conceptualized your plans for graduate school, and how well your interests and strengths mesh with their programs.

Fellowships

Imagine being paid as a student to do research and produce articles on the images of queer people in media, to present your dissertation at a conference on gender studies surrounded by intellectual luminaries, or being courted for an editorial position at *The Advocate* due to a summer spent right in the belly of a newsroom. These are some of the joys a fellowship brings. Fellowships allow you to pursue your research interests and learn directly from some of the most prominent leaders in your field. More importantly, they can help fund your graduate education. Most fellowships are sponsored by the academic department to which you're applying and are intended to provide particularly gifted students with the time and resources to immerse themselves completely in their areas of study. In order to qualify, you must create and present a fellowship proposal, a sometimes rigorous process during which you must defend the importance of your prospective research and explain the unique qualities you possess that would help further the project.

Some of the most prestigious fellowships, however, are privately funded. These fellowships often come with larger stipends, and more exciting fringe benefits. Beware, however: The competition for these fellowships is at a national level and is *fierce*. Fortunately, there are literally thousands of opportunities available. Using searchable databases is probably the easiest way to identify private fellowship opportunities. Keep in mind that most fellowship deadlines are during the fall of the year *preceding* the year when you need funding.

AFTERWORD

It's hard to imagine that, even a few years ago, the idea of publishing a book solely dedicated to the needs of LGBTQ college students would have been a radical and unlikely enterprise. And although times are changing and positive public perception and support of queer individuals and their rights is growing, there is still much to be done. Like racism and sexism, homo/bi/transphobia and its countless tentacles is still placing a stranglehold on individuals across America and around the world. While many adults can face these challenges on their own, our children need all of the nurturing and support we can give them. Our goal was to provide them and their allies with a roadmap to their college years; a dependable primer to help them educate themselves, their parents, their peers, and their counselors about the rich, varied, and wonderful experiences and perspectives that they as LGBTQ students bring to the table and to the campus.

Whether you are a high school junior looking to find out what schools are queer-friendly, a graduating senior looking for tips on landing a job, or a parent or counselor looking for advice and words of support, we hope that this book has provided assistance. In pointing you toward tons of resources, offering some reasonable advice, and providing you with loads of unique viewpoints, we sought to make a (small) a difference in your life by letting you know that you can rely upon a far-reaching and supportive community when you feel alone, scared, or in need.

We hope we succeeded, if even on even the smallest scale.

—John Brez, Jennifer Howd, Rachel Pepper,
and The Staff of The Princeton Review

MORE QUEER
AND CANDID QUOTES

On GSAs . . .

"I did not participate in a GSA in high school, since one did not exist. However, when I found out that a GSA was started at my high school 4 years after I graduated, I immediately offered to come speak about my experiences as a successful queer leader and student at Michigan State University."

Lauren, Senior, Michigan State University

"I was a student leader of my high school's fairly active GSA. It introduced me to more diverse views and opinions and taught me how to communicate effectively about my sexual orientation, stand up for myself, and work with school administrators on somewhat controversial issues."

Tiana, Junior, Franklin W. Olin College of Engineering

"I founded the GSA at my high school, and later was part of a consortium of regional GSAs. The organizational skills I learned there have been essential as I continue my activism."

Ellen, First-year, Princeton University

On "coming out" on the application . . .

"I discussed my involvement in my school's GSA on my college applications, but I didn't outright declare my sexual orientation. I also was awarded a PFLAG scholarship at the end of high school, which I told my college admissions office, since it had a bearing on my financial aid situation. "

Tiana, Junior, Franklin W. Olin College of Engineering

"In my primary application essay, I made a point of expressing my sexual fluidity without explicitly identifying myself. In the essay, I broke my 'self' down into different elements, including sexuality."

"Stacey," Yale University graduate

"I wrote my admission essay on being bi, but more specifically on how the process of discovering and accepting my sexual orientation has empowered me to live my life by my own standards, not those imposed on me by one community or another."

"Randi," First-year, Princeton University

"I was always honest about what I was interested in and what my activities were. This ended up identifying me as queer, but it's part of who I am, not what I am. Ideally, I think this approach is best. The purpose of the application process is for schools to identify who would succeed at their institution. For them to make the best decision, they should know as much about you as possible."

"Donna", Senior, Yale University

"I discussed my coming out to my parents in my admissions essay. I also talked about my involvement in my high school GSA."

Doug, Sophomore, University of New England

"My college admissions essay was about the grueling process it took me to come out of the closet and how coming out affected the relationships I had with my friends and family at the time."

Rachel, First-year, University of Rochester

On Being Queer in the Residence Halls . . .

"Queer 'housing?' In my entire class, I'm one of two students who identify as LGBTQ. So, no [we don't] have queer housing]. Since Olin is a tiny school (less than 300 students), everything is naturally on a smaller scale than you'd find elsewhere, and certain things seem wildly irrelevant."

Roland, First-year, Olin College of Engineering

"My freshman year I opted to live in queer housing in a suite-style dormitory. My first coming out experience on campus was in an environment that felt very safe in a suite meeting (of seven or eight people) and as we introduced ourselves to each other we indicated how we identified."

Chris, Sophomore, University of Vermont

"During the summer my roommate created a list of 'room rules' (that's what she called them). These rules were composed of things we 'agreed' would occur or not occur in the room. Since she was extremely against my 'lifestyle' her rules consisted of ideas such as, 'Respecting each others beliefs and values: No sexual/suggestive activities or pictures in the room,' and letting the room be a 'sanctuary from temptation.' She also told me that girls are meant to date guys and that I shouldn't hit on her (since all lesbians want to flirt with every girl they see). Once I arrived on campus my roommate brought boys into the room, stayed out late, and I have even walked in on her making out with a boy in the room. However, when I have anyone in the room, especially a girl, whether straight or gay, my roommate makes a big deal out of it, because she doesn't feel comfortable. Anytime my roommate and I are in the room at the same time, she keeps the door open, so that if I make any advances, she can scream and someone can help her."

Rachel, First-year, University of Rochester

On Finding LGBTQ Resources On Campus . . .

"The student GSA, OUTLoud, is a very strong student group on campus, while most clubs only have half a dozen to a dozen active members, OUTLoud regularly fills the room with anywhere from 15–40 students. The queer community is much larger than that as well."

Amy, Junior, Hollins University

"There's a bi-weekly Queer Alliance meeting and a bi-weekly film viewing [at Reed College]. Our Queer Alliances co-chairs have also organized the Greater Portland Inter-Collegiate Queer Society, linking the other LGBTQ college groups in the city."

Kyle, Junior, Reed College

"I am an officer for The Pride Alliance, Princeton's LGBTQ student organization, as well as a member of the Queer Radicals. I help brainstorm and run events. As bisexual and queer, I have found that the G and the L all too often dominate the LGBTQ community and its visibility, so I do a lot of speaking up for the rest of us, and trying to help my community better engage in and understand the importance of inclusive language."

Ellen, First-year, Princeton University

"I am the general coordinator of Triskelion, the campus GLBTQSA Alliance. My job is to oversee the committees of the organization and hold office hours in the Queer Resource Center. Because the university hasn't yet hired a staff person to specifically deal with queer student needs, the organization and I play the important role of being a key resource for those students. Additionally, I network with faculty, staff, and students to ensure there is a consistent awareness of the LGBTQ presence on campus and seek out ways the university can work with everyone to show its support."

Scott, Sophomore, Brandeis University

On Conservative Campuses . . .

"My school doesn't give any special recognition to LGBTQ students on campus. Most of the other students poke fun at the LGBTQ students when they advertise/present activities, such as The Day of Silence. I think this is mainly because I live in the 'Bible Belt.'"

"Bianca," Junior, University of Tennessee

"I think that if the students and faculty were to be educated more, that maybe they would be more open to my sexuality. Right now it just seems like they're a lot of people that are unaware of how to handle my lifestyle."

"Tara," Sophomore, Doane College

"There are no LGBTQ resources. It is an issue that the college will not touch."

Michael, Senior, St. Anselm College

"We cannot have an LGBTQ group on campus due to it being Catholic and our campus ministry fights groups that try to start [one]."

"John," Senior, Clarke College

ON ON-CAMPUS ACTIVISM . . .

"We live in a tiny quiet village on a beautiful lake. On National Coming Out Day our picturesque campus is chalked in the colors of the rainbow declaring support for LGBTQ persons in leadership roles and in the entire campus community. The ally community is also quite strong here."

"Melissa," Senior, Wells College

"Our LGBTQ campus club, OPEN, is one of the most active and well-respected clubs on the Olin campus. We find that targeting our events towards 'everyone,' of 'all sexualities,' is very helpful in uniting our campus together in acceptance and tolerance."

"Peter," Senior, Franklin W. Olin College of Engineering

"The University of Iowa GLBTAU (undergraduate student LGBTQ group) puts on a wide variety of social and educational programming events that are really cool. They're really involved in the university community. The GLBTAU hosts an annual Drag/Costume Ball for Halloween and a Queer Kickball tournament among other events."

"Kent," Senior, University of Iowa

"We have a Drag Show each year, a picnic for National Coming Out Day, we participate in the National Day of Silence, we raise money for the AIDS Walk among other things."

Jessica, Junior, Oglethorpe University

"I get is teased every once in a while, but nothing too serious."

Caylena, Freshman, Ithaca College

"Last year there was a big to-do on campus when Phelps of GodHatesFags.com came to Galesburg to protest at a soldier's funeral. I didn't go myself, but some of my friends were among those who stood in the rain to block him and his gang from the mourners' sight. Similarly, this year I was a little shocked—Knox is a very liberal campus—to hear someone arguing the case against homosexuality's being permitted by God, nature, morality, the Constitution and/or common sense."

Corinne, Sophomore, Knox College

"An LGBTQ 'Safe Zone' sticker was stolen from my dorm room door."

Chris, First-year, University of New England

"I have experienced discrimination in small, everyday things that most people don't notice, like flyers about an event that tells girls to 'bring your boyfriends' and stuff like that—things that assume heterosexuality. And of course, the checkboxes on forms that allow you to be male or female, with no other option. I usually leave those blank unless it's an online form that won't let me complete it without checking one of the boxes."

Mallery, Senior, Sasquehanna University

"A drunk college student tailgated into my dorm hall. At the time, I had a Pride flag hanging on my door. He saw the flag and aimed several homophobic epithets at my door. I went out in the hall and simply asked him to stop. He did, but a few minutes later a friend of mine was coming to see me and I realized that the drunk guy had stolen my flag."

Leisha, Senior, University of Maryland—College Park

"Although Brown's campus is generally tolerant, there have been instances of discrimination and homophobia on campus...Brown police and Providence police officers have not shown proper sensitivity to LGBTQ students and have not responded to hate crimes as vigorously as they ought."

Robert, Sophomore, Brown University

"I personally have not experienced discrimination or homophobia, but two years ago, there was a huge incident on campus where a lesbian couple was barricaded in their room by bed frames. The white board on their door also had 'dykes' scrawled across it. As far as I know, nothing happened to the two or three guys on the baseball team who did it. There was a campus-wide Speak Out about a week or so later, held right in the middle of campus for people to share their opinions on the incident, and/or other incidents of discrimination based on sexuality. A lot of people were there: students, staff, faculty, and local community members. The incident really outraged a lot of the students, and yet nothing happened to the boys who did it. There have been 'Safe Zone' training workshops, where students (especially resident assistants), faculty, and staff are trained to help LGBTQ students deal with discrimination, but that has really been the only response to the incident."

Peggy, Senior, Wheaton College, (Illinois)

"During my freshman year in college, I was frequently harassed by some of my roommates. They would pound on my door and humiliate me by making rude and obscene comments. I realized that I was treated very differently, and I became very isolated."

"Roger," Senior, Santa Clara University

GLOSSARY

A-Gays

Affluent, successful gay men and women in positions of power.

Aberzombie

A slang term for a gay man who tends to lack originality in his conformist appearance.

AIDS

A disorder of the immune system caused by HIV, Human Immunodeficiency Virus. AIDS or Acquired Immune Deficiency Syndrome affects the proper functioning of the immune system, increasing a person's susceptibility to contracting viruses or cancer. AIDS is transmitted through bodily fluids such as blood, saliva, and semen. There is currently no cure for AIDS.

Ally

Non-queer individual who supports the rights of LGBTQ individuals.

Alternative Lifestyle

A generic term used by both the LGBTQ community and its allies (and sometimes its foes) to describe a "queer" lifestyle that the majority of the population at large does not participate in. This can also refer to many subcultures and groups that prefer to engage in non-traditional behavior or lifestyles (such as body modifiers and tattooists, non-conformists, commune dwellers, etc.).

Androgyny

Exhibiting both (or neither) male and female behavior, physical traits, and gender. Can be used as offensive term for a person who fails to abide by traditional roles of gender expression.

Birthgender or Birthsex

Term used to refer to the biological sex you are born with but may not necessarily identify with.

BIPHOBIA

The fear or hatred of people with a strong sexual and emotional attraction to both men and women.

BISEXUAL

Individual who is sexually, romantically or emotionally attracted to both men and women and possibly to transgender or intersex people.

BUTCH

Slang for an individual who has or exhibits behavior or traits traditionally considered as masculine. Often used within the gay male community to designate hierarchical "manliness" and in the queer women's community to refer to lesbians who are more clearly masculine.

CAMP

Term used to describe the intentionally exaggerated actions, appearance, or behavior for comic effect.

CIVIL UNION

Term used by various branches of the government to refer to the legal partnership agreement between two individuals.

COMING OUT

Coming out currently refers to the process by which one understands and accepts a level of same-gender-loving feelings and begins to disclose them to friends, family and others. It has been shortened from "Coming out of the closet." The idea of "coming out" dates back to the late 1860s when Karl Heinrich Ulrichs, a German gay activist, called for homosexuals to reveal themselves in an act of political visibility.

CROSS-DRESSER

A person who wears clothes commonly associated with another gender. Many people automatically connect cross-dressing behavior to transgender identity or LGBTQ sexual orientation, but the term cross-dressing itself does not imply a specific sexual orientation.

Down Low (DL)

Slang term originating from the African American community often used in the context of "keeping it on the down low." Refers to something that is private and secret and is often used to describe men who have sex with other men in a clandestine way, but who do not identify themselves as gay or bisexual.

Drag

Term used to describe the act of wearing the clothing and performing the role of the opposite gender for a variety of reasons.

Drag King

A woman, most likely queer, who dresses and acts like a man for entertainment purposes and who usually does not self-identify as a transgender individual or live as that gender.

Drag Queen

A man, most likely queer, who dresses and acts like a woman for entertainment purposes and who usually does not self-identify as a transgender individual or live as that gender.

Dyke

Historically a derogative term for lesbians, it has been reclaimed as a term of familiarity and empowerment by lesbians. Primarily used by younger women as a term of self-identification.

Ex-Gay

Term used to describe (or self-describe) a LGBTQ individual who has removed themselves (or been forced from) from their previous queer lifestyle. The term is most often associated with the Exodus Movement, a controversial movement built on the efforts of several conservative religious groups seeking to alter the sexual orientation of queer individuals and facilitate their efforts to become straight.

FTM

(Female to Male) A person born or assigned at birth as biological-ly female, who identifies as a male and who adopts the sex, gender, and identity of a male through a variety of acts including male clothing, mannerisms, behavior, hormone therapy, and possibly, but not always, gender reassignment surgery.

FAG

Historically a derogative term for gay men, it has been reclaimed by some as a term of familiarity or empowerment. It is mainly used as slang and is not common in ally usage.

FEMME

Slang for an individual who has or exhibits behavior or traits tradi-tionally considered as super-feminine. Often used within the gay male community to designate hierarchical "girlieness" and in the queer women's community to refer to lesbians who are more clearly feminine.

GAY

Either a noun or adjective referring to typically male same-sex sexual orientation. Gay is also often used as a broad meaning for "homosex-ual," regardless of gender.

GAY COMMUNITY

Umbrella term often used to refer to the entire LGBTQ community and the infinite number of individuals who may be included within it.

GAY PRIDE MONTH

The Clinton administration designated June as lesbian, gay, bisexual, and transgender Pride Month in commemoration of the historic Stonewall uprising on June 28, 1969.

GAYDAR

Short hand for "gay radar," gaydar is often used to describe the nonscientific, intuitive ability to figure out if another individual is LGBTQ or queer.

Gay Marriage

The union of two individuals of the same biological sex (or gender). Often referred to as same-sex marriage or equal marriage.

Gay-Straight Alliance (GSA)

A type of student organization, found primarily in American high schools and universities, that is intended to provide a safe and supportive environment for lesbian, gay, bisexual, transgender and queer or questioning youth and their straight allies.

Gender

Generic, and often limiting, term used to refer to the biological division of animal species into male and female according to chromosomal determinants. This is a loaded term within the queer community and to many queer individuals and scholars as it reduces gender and gender expression to only male and female constructs.

Gender Blind

Broad term often used to define the act of ignoring gender. Within the academic landscape, it is used when referring to universities that accept and house people together without discriminating on the basis of gender.

Gender Expression

Term that loosely refers to the myriad ways a person communicates gender identity to others through their behavior, clothing, hairstyle, voice, and/or the emphasis or masking of bodily characteristics. Gender expression is not an indicator of sexual orientation.

Gender Identity

Refers to the gender with which an individual most closely identifies with. Not necessarily parallel with that person's gender expression.

GENDERQUEER

Term used to refer to an individual who identifies as other than "man" or "woman," or someone who identifies as neither, both, or some combination of "man" and "woman."

GENDER ROLE

A set of cultural rules based on external economics, religion, ethnicity, and social factors that force an individual to align with traits and behavior of one gender or another.

GAY UNTIL GRADUATION (GUG)

Tongue-in-cheek phrase that refers to the practice of engaging in same-sex relationships, sexual activity, or experimentation during college but reverting to heterosexual practices after graduating. Women who engage in these practices are sometimes referred to as LUGs (Lesbian Until Graduation).

HATE CRIME

Hate crimes (also known as bias crimes in the legal arena) are violent illegal actions, crimes, acts of vandalism, or abuse toward another individual motivated by hatred of that individual's perceived social identification group.

HETEROFLEXIBLE

A recently coined and increasingly used term used to describe a very slight homosexual attraction or curiosity about non-heterosexual experimentation.

HETERONORMATIVITY

A concept often discussed in queer and gender theory that refers to the beliefs about gender and sexuality reinforced by social institutions and their policies.

HETEROSEXISM

The act of having bias against, or hatred of LGBTQ-identifying individuals, couples, or groups.

HETEROSEXUAL

Individual who is sexually, romantically or emotionally attracted to an individual of the opposite gender.

HIR (SEE ALSO "ZE")

A gender-neutral pronoun used by some individuals of trans experience who feel that "he" and "she" do not fully reflect all potential gender identities.

HIV

Stands for Human Immunodeficiency Virus, the virus that causes AIDS.

HOMOPHOBIA

Irrational fear of gay people and of homosexuality.

HOMOSEXUAL

Individual who is sexually, romantically, or emotionally attracted to an individual of the same gender.

IN THE CLOSET (OR "CLOSETED")

Not open or revealing about one's sexual orientation.

INTERSEX OR INTERGENDER

A person who is born with or develops mixed sexual physiology (an abnormally small penis, large clitoris, closed vaginal opening, separated scrotum, etc.). If discovered at birth, the child's gender is decided either by the surgeon or by the parents. Some intersex individuals do not discover they are intersex until they reach puberty.

LAVENDER

Color often associated with the LGBTQ community because it is a combination of the stereotypically symbolic "female" pink and "male" light blue.

LESBIAN

A lesbian is a female who is exclusively emotionally, sexually, and romantically attracted to other females.

LGBTQ

An umbrella term often used as an abbreviation to collectively refer to Lesbian, Gay, Bisexual, Transgender and Queer and/or Questioning people. Many variants exist, and some variants use two Qs to represent both Queer and Questioning, an A for asexual or allies (and sometimes 'S' for Straight Ally), an I for Intersex or Intergender and/or a P for Pansexual or Polyamorous. Some also add an O for Omnisexual or Other.

MTF

(Male to Female). A biological female who lives life as or has transitioned to a male. During transition, sex reassignment candidates undergo a series of hormone and other therapies that aid them in their transition to living as another gender.

NATIONAL COMING OUT DAY

Observed each year on October 11, this is a day when members of the LGBTQ community and their allies wear identifying symbols to demonstrate LGBTQ visibility and unity.

NEG

Slang term used to refer to negative HIV status.

NON-OP

Term sometimes used to describe a transgender individual who has made the conscious decision not to undergo sexual reassignment surgery in their transition to a desired gender and/or identity.

LIPSTICK LESBIAN

A gay woman who dresses in traditionally "feminine" clothing and makeup.

LUG

Acronym for "lesbian until graduation," a phrase used to describe the experience of college women who adopt a lesbian sexual orientation during their years at college.

Omnisexual

Individual who is sexually, romantically, or emotionally attracted to an individual of any gender. Also referred to as pansexual.

Out

Open or revealing about one's sexual orientation, specifically LGBTQ.

Outing

Slang term that refers to taking an individual "out of the closet" and then publicly announcing and promoting that they or someone they know is LGBTQ.

Pansexual

A sexual/affectional orientation characterized by an attraction to people of any sex or gender, including transsexual, transgender, genderqueer, and intersex people.

Passing

Term used to refer to the act of successfully assuming a gender role and gender expression that is different from the one one was born with or assigned at birth. Passing is often used to refer to transgender individuals who can publicly be "read" as the gender they choose. It is also used to refer to closeted gay, lesbian, or bisexual people passing as straight.

Pre-Op

Term sometimes used to describe a transgender individual who has not yet undergone sexual reassignment surgery in the transition to their desired gender and/or identity.

Post-Op

Term sometimes used to describe a transgender individual who has undergone sexual reassignment surgery in the transition to their desired gender and/or identity.

Pos or Poz

Slang term used to refer to positive HIV status

Queer

At one time, a derogatory term used to describe gay or homosexual people, "queer" has since been taken back by the LGBTQ community and is now often used as an umbrella term for Lesbian, Gay, Bisexual and Transgender individuals or experiences.

Questioning

Refers to the experience of a person unsure of, or exploring, their sexuality or gender-loving feelings.

Safe Space or Safe Zone

Typically found on college campuses, safe zones are easily identifiable spaces where LGBTQ people can find support, and where intolerance and discrimination are not tolerated.

Same Gender Loving (SGL)

Term used by an increasing number of non-heterosexual African Amercians who believe that other terms, including gay and lesbian, are Eurocentric linguistic constructs that do not represent people of color.

STDI (Sexually Transmitted Disease or Infection)

Any disease or infection transmitted or contracted through sexual contact or exchange of bodily fluids.

Sexual Orientation

Term generally used to define the direction of one's sexual interest or an individual's natural preference toward members of the same sex, the opposite sex, both sexes, or other sexes.

STEALTH

A term used to describe an LGBTQ person who can pass for straight, or who fits heterosexual norms when it comes to gender identity/expression. Sometimes used in a pejorative sense.

STONEWALL

Refers to the political unrest and riots that took place at the Stonewall Bar in New York City on June 27, 1967. This event is often identified as the starting point for modern queer activism and civil rights initiatives.

STRAIGHT

Refers to a person of heterosexual sexual orientation.

THIRD GENDER

Term used by those people who believe that they are neither male nor female in their gender identity and/or expression and believe that they are part of third gender altogether. (See Two-Spirit.)

TRANS

A generic term used to refer to a wide range of transgender people.

TRANNIE

An offensive term used to refer to transgender people.

TRANSDYKE OR TRANNYDYKE

A lesbian-identifying transwoman or MTF.

TRANSFAG OR TRANNYFAG

A gay-identifying transman or FTM.

TRANSFOLK

An encompassing term used to refer to members of the entire trans community.

TRANSGENDER

The state of one's gender identity (self-identification as male, female, both, or neither) not matching one's "assigned gender" (identification by others as male or female based on physical/genetic sex).

TRANSITIONING OR TRANSITION

The process of intentionally changing from one physical and social gender presentation to another by living and changing one's sex or gender. This multi-step process usually takes several years and may or may not include sexual reassignment surgery and/or hormonal supplements to alter one's body.

TRANS MAN

Slang or alternative term used for a FTM.

TRANSPHOBIA

Irrational fear of transgender people and/or alternative gender expressions.

TRANSSEXUAL

A person who self-identifies as a member of the gender opposite from the one assigned to them at birth.

TRANSVESTITE

Term (now considered offensive by most queer individuals) used to refer to people who self-identify with their birth sex and gender but who feel inclined to wear the clothing, jewelry, etc., of the opposite gender to fulfill emotional needs. Interestingly, the majority of these individuals are actually heterosexual men. Crossdresser is currently the most appropriate term to use to refer to such an individual.

TRANS WOMAN

Slang or alternative term used for a MTF.

Two-Spirit

Based on the trans-tribal concept of the "berdache," Two-Spirit refers to third-gender people, people who have both male and female spirits within their bodies. The term was originated in 1990 during the Third Annual Intertribal Native American/First Nations Gay and Lesbian Conference. While the term was originally used to refer to Native Americans who wanted an alternative to western labels, it has since been used by many queer people of various ethnic backgrounds who prefer a less restrictive term for gender expression.

World AIDS Day

Occurring every year on December 1st, this is an international day of action dedicated to raising awareness of the global AIDS epidemic.

Ze

A gender-neutral pronoun used by some individuals of trans experience who feel that "he" and "she" do not fully reflect all potential gender identities.

APPENDIX A

SCHOLARSHIPS AND FINANCIAL RESOURCES FOR LGBTQ STUDENTS

AUDRIA M. EDWARDS SCHOLARSHIP FUND

www.peacockinthepark.org

Established in 1987 by Audria Edwards' children, Woody Johnson (a.k.a. Lady Elaine Peacock) and Misty Waters, the Audria M. Edwards Scholarship Fund is administered by Peacock Productions Inc. and is available to the gay, lesbian, bisexual, and transgender community and/or the children of queer persons who reside in Oregon and/or Southwest Washington. Since 1987, the fund has awarded more than $152,000 in grants to LGBTQ individuals and/or their children to assist in their pursuit of postsecondary education.

THE LESBIAN LEADERSHIP SCHOLARSHIP PROGRAM

www.uncommonlegacy.org

Spearheaded by the Uncommon Legacy Foundation, The Lesbian Leadership Scholarship Program provides several $1,000 awards to undergraduate and graduate students who address lesbian social, cultural and, educational needs through their projects and/or course of study. The recipients awarded the scholarships must provide evidence of exceptional academic performance and demonstrate personal/financial hardship and a record of service to the lesbian/gay/bisexual/transgender community.

MATTHEW SHEPARD SCHOLARSHIP

Since 1999, The LEAGUE Foundation has offered the Matthew Shepard Scholarship with the support of the Shepard family. The Foundation has honored Matthew's memory by awarding at least one scholarship to a student who has demonstrated leadership in promoting diversity and understanding in the community.

MESSENGER-ANDERSON JOURNALISM SCHOLARSHIP AND INTERNSHIP

www.thetaskforce.org/aboutus/messenger.cfm

The National Gay and Lesbian Task Force offers a $240,000 scholarship program for undergraduate college students who plan to pursue a degree in journalism or communications at an accredited 4-year college or university. Messenger-Anderson scholarships are available at a rate of $5,000 the first year, followed by up to $2,500 the next two years for a total award of up to $10,000. Those applicants awarded Messenger-Anderson scholarships must re-apply and qualify for renewals each year. Scholarship winners are required to participate in the eight-week Messenger-Anderson Scholarship Intern Program at the Task Force office in New York City.

NGPA EDUCATION FUND

www.ngpa.org/education.html

The National Gay Pilots Association has established The NGPA Education Fund to provide educational assistance in the form of scholarships to members of the gay and lesbian community who have expressed an interest in an aviation career as a professional pilot.

PFLAG NATIONAL AND LOCAL SCHOLARSHIPS

www.pflag.org/Local_PFLAG_scholarships.344.0.html

$2,500 PFLAG SCHOLARSHIPS INCLUDE:

Palmer B. Carson-PFLAG "Sakia Gunn" Scholarship for LGBTQ Community Involvement

Palmer B. Carson-PFLAG "Esera Tuaolo" Scholarship for Athletic Achievement

Palmer B. Carson-PFLAG Scholarship for Nevada/Reno residents

Palmer B. Carson-PFLAG "Jeanne Manford" Scholarship for LGBTQ Leadership

Palmer B. Carson-PFLAG Scholarship for LGBTQ Advocacy

Gays, Lesbians, and Allies at Dow Scholarship for Allies in Honor of Kathleen Bader

PFLAG National Donor Scholarship

$1,000 PFLAG SCHOLARSHIPS INCLUDE:

Palmer B. Carson-PFLAG General Scholarships (13 students selected)

Scholarships for science, engineering, business or finance (13 students selected)

PFLAG National Donor Scholarship

QUEER ASIAN AND PACIFIC ISLANDER PRIDE SCHOLARSHIP FUND

www.apiwellness.org/youth.html

Since 1986, The Asian and Pacific Islander Wellness Center has served as the oldest and largest non-profit HIV/AIDS services organization in North America targeting Asian and Pacific Islander communities. In July 2000, they created the Queer Asian and Pacific Islander Pride Scholarship Fund. Each year since, they have awarded scholarships totaling $16,000 to deserving applicants. Executive Director John Manzon-Santos says: "The goal of this landmark scholarship program is to help eradicate the isolation, invisibility, homophobia, and heterosexism faced by thousands of Asian and Pacific Islander lesbian, gay, bisexual, transgender, queer, and questioning youth living in the Bay Area and beyond."

THE QUEER FOUNDATION'S EFFECTIVE WRITING AND SCHOLARSHIPS PROGRAM

http://home.comcast.net/~threepennynovel/queerfoundation/scholarships.html

The Queer Foundation is a nonprofit organization dedicated to improving the educational condition of lesbian, gay, bisexual, and transgender youth. The Foundation also raises funds to provide financial and administrative support for the Effective Writing and Scholarships Program. Each year, the Queer Foundation offers $1,000 scholarships to a select number of talented and gifted LGBTQ high school students who participate in an essay contest designed to promote queer studies and improve the educational condition of homeless queer youth. The Queer Foundation believes these scholarships "enable LGBTQ youth, by means of their studies and effective writing, to contribute to building a stable future for queer youth through business/community involvement and self-directed improvement."

TRANSGENDER SCHOLARSHIP AND EDUCATION LEGACY FUND

www.tself.org/index.html

The International Foundation for Gender Education was founded in 1987 to dismantle the intolerance of transvestitism and transsexualism brought about by widespread ignorance. Since then, IFGE has rededicated itself to outreach through education for the emancipation of all people from restrictive gender norms. The IFGE awards numerous scholarships to transgender-identified students through its collaborative Transgender Scholarship and Education Legacy Fund (TSELF) in the United States and Canada.

APPENDIX B
LGBTQ ACADEMIC RESOURCES

Since 1997, John G. Younger, Professor of Classics and Western Civilization at the University of Kansas, has diligently scoured the internet to compile and constantly update a comprehensive webpage detailing all of the Gay, Lesbian, Bisexual, Transgender, and Queer Studies programs available in the United States and Canada. According to his latest postings, the following schools offer undergraduate majors, minors, certificates, and/or concentrations in Gay, Lesbian, Bisexual, Transgender, and Queer Studies:

MAJORS

Brown University

Hobart and William Smith Colleges

University of Chicago

Wesleyan College

MINORS

Allegheny College

Bowdoin College

Concordia College

Cornell University

Hobart and William Smith Colleges

Hofstra University

Humboldt University

Kent State University

Ohio State University

San Francisco State University

Stanford University

State University of New York—Purchase

Towson University

University of California—Berkeley

University of California—Los Angeles

University of California—Riverside

University of Delaware

University of Minnesota

University of Nebraska—Lincoln

The University of North Carolina at Chapel Hill

University of North Texas

Western Washington State University

York University

CERTIFICATES OR CONCENTRATIONS

Arizona State University

Brandeis University

Denison University

Duke University

University of Colorado at Boulder

University of Maryland

University of Iowa

University of Wisconsin—Madison

University of Wisconsin—Milwaukee

Yale University

For more information, log on to People.ku.edu/~jyounger/ lgbtqprogs.html.

APPENDIX C
SUPPORT NETWORKS AND ADVOCACY

On-Campus Advocacy Resources

- Activism Training and Resource Materials
  www.actionpa.org/activism/index.html
- Human Rights Campaign Generation EQ
  http://hrc.org/generationeq
- National Youth Advocacy Coalition
  www.nyacyouth.org
- Publications on Student Activism
  www.soundout.org/organizinglibrary.html
- Southern Poverty Law Center: Teaching Tolerance
  www.splcenter.org/center/tt/teach.jsp

Suggested Transgender Internet Resources:

- Gender Crash
  www.gendercrash.com
- Live Journal Communities (includes many groups, such as FTM students, gender outlaws, genderqueer, MTF, partners of tg, transgender, transyouth)
  www.livejournal.com
- People in Search of Safe Restrooms (PSSR)
  www.pissr.org
- PFLAG's Transgender Network
  http://pflag.org/TNET.tnet.0.html
- Recommended Transgender Films
  www.umass.edu/stonewall/transhand
- Successful Trans Men
  http://ai.eecs.umich.edu/people/conway/TSsuccesses/TransMen.html
- Sylvia Rivera Law Project
  www.srlp.org

- Trans-Academics.org
  www.trans-academics.org
- Trans Family
  www.transfamily.org
- Transgender Care
  www.transgendercare.com
- Transgender Crossroads
  www.tgcrossroads.org
- Transgender Law and Policy Institute:
  www.transgenderlaw.org
- Transgender Youth Resources
  www.youthresource.com/living/trans.htm
- Trans Health:
  www.trans-health.com
- The Transitional Male
  www.thetransitionalmale.com
- Trans Proud:
  www.transproud.com
- Transsexual Women's Successes
  http://ai.eecs.umich.edu/people/conway/TSsuccesses/
  TSsuccesses.html
- University of Massachusetts—Amherst Transgender Guide
  and Training Resources
  www.umass.edu/stonewall

AIDS RESOURCES FOR COLLEGES AND UNIVERSITIES[1]

Below is a listing of organizations and universities that have published information on AIDS and safer sex. Before developing your own AIDS education materials or AIDS policies, you should obtain samples of existing flyers, booklets, and training materials. Why "reinvent the wheel" when there are already some outstanding AIDS/HIV publications already in existence?

- AIDS Project Los Angeles (APLA) is a nonprofit, community-based organization dedicated to supporting and maintaining the best possible quality of life for persons affected by, infected by, and at risk for HIV in Los Angeles County. APLA also works to reduce the incidence of HIV infection by providing risk reduction, prevention education, and information to the general public. Write or call: AIDS Project, Los Angeles 1313 North Vine Street, Los Angeles, CA 90028, 213-993-1600.

- AIDS Healthcare Foundation provides all services to people with AIDS from the initial clinic screening through hospice care. There are over a dozen treatment and service sites in the greater Los Angeles area. For more information contact: AHF Executive Offices, 6255 West Sunset Boulevard, 16th Floor, Los Angeles, CA 90028-7403, 213-462-2273 or 800-AHF-2101.

- American College Health Association (ACHA): ACGA publications include: "AIDS on the College Campus: An ACHA Special Report." This booklet examines AIDS from a campus perspective, and includes information on housing, testing, confidentiality and education. ACHA educational flyers include "Making Sex Safer," "Safer Sex," "The HIV Antibody Test," and "AIDS: What Everyone Should Know." For more information, contact: ACHA, 15889 Crab Branch Way, Rockville, MD 20855, 301-963-1100.

1   Excerpt. Outcalt, Charles; Curtis F. Shepard, PhD; and Felice Yeskel, EdD. *Lesbian, Gay, Bisexual, & Transgender Campus Organizing: A Comprehensive Manual.* National Gay and Lesbian Task Force. 1995. www.thetaskforce.org/downloads/reports/reports/CampusOrganizingManual.pdf.

- American Red Cross: Red Cross publications include: "AIDS, Sex and You," "If Your Test for Antibody to the AIDS Virus is Positive," "AIDS and Your Job—Are There Risks?," "Caring for the AIDS Patient at Home," "Facts About AIDS and Drug Abuse," "Gay and Bisexual Men and AIDS." Films and posters on AIDS and AIDS prevention are also available. To obtain materials, contact: The American Red Cross, 2025 East Street NW, Washington, DC 20006, 202-737-8300.

- California AIDS Information Clearinghouse: Based at the Los Angeles Gay and Lesbian Community Service Center, the Clearinghouse offers resource information about AIDS service organizations, prevention education materials and brochure distribution. Contact: California AIDS Information Clearinghouse, 1625 North Schrader, Hollywood, CA 90028, 213-993-7415.

- Gay Men's Health Crisis (GMHC) publishes a wide range of brochures and booklets on AIDS. Publications include: "Safer Sex Guidelines," "Medical Answers about AIDS," "Women and AIDS," "Condom Guide for Men and Women, " "Legal Answers about AIDS," "Infection Protection Guidelines for People with AIDS," "GMHC Volunteer Training Manual," "Eroticizing Safer Sex Workshop Manual," "Safer Sex Comix," and more. Some publications are available in Spanish and Mandarin Chinese. Various posters and buttons on safer sex and AIDS can also be purchased. To obtain a publication order form or to place an order, contact: GMHC, Box 274, 132 West 24 Street, New York, NY 10011, 212-807-7517.

- Health Education and Resource Organization (HERO) publications include: "Safe Sex Guidelines for Men and Women Concerned About AIDS," and "AIDS Precautions for the First Responder." For more information contact: HERO, 101 West Read Street, Suite 812, Baltimore, MD 21201, 301-945-AIDS.

- San Francisco AIDS Foundation publications available for sale include: "AIDS Lifeline," "Straight Talk About Sex and AIDS," "Women and AIDS," "Your Child and AIDS," "When A Friend Has AIDS," "Fact vs. Fiction: Ten Things You Should Know About AIDS," "AIDS Antibody Testing at Alternative Test Sites," "Lesbians and AIDS: What's the Connection?," "AIDS: A Self Care Manual," "Coping with AIDS," "The Family's Guide to AIDS," "AIDS Medical Guide," "AIDS and Your Legal Rights," "Information for People of Color," "Reaching Ethnic Communities in the Fight Against AIDS," "AIDS Safe Sex Guidelines," "Can We Talk?," "The Hot 'N Healthy Times," "Safe Sex Guidelines for Women at Risk for AIDS Transmission," "AIDS in the Workplace," "Alcohol, Drugs & AIDS," "Shooting Up and Your Health," "Poppers and AIDS," "The AIDS Hotline Training Manual," and "Designing an Effective AIDS Prevention Campaign Strategy." Some of these publications are available in Spanish and Chinese. The SF AIDS Foundation also sells resource guides for health care personnel and educators, as well as AIDS videos, posters, pins, and condoms. To obtain an order form or sampler packet, contact: The San Francisco AIDS Foundation, Materials Distribution Department, 333 Valencia Street, 4th Floor, San Francisco, CA 94103, 415-861-3397.

- Whitman Walker Clinic (Washington DC): Publications available from the Whitman Walker Clinic include: "Safer Sex: You Don't Have To Do It Alone," "Staying Healthy: AIDS Information for Gay Men," and "Alcohol, Drugs, AIDS and Your Health." For more information contact: The Whitman Walker Clinic, 1407 S Street NW, Washington, DC 20009, 202-332-6483.

APPENDIX D

CAREER INFORMATION WEBSITES AND ORGANIZATIONS

A bevy of resources currently exist for aiding in your online job search. LGBTQ-specific services like the ones listed below will continue to flourish as more and more people across the country continue to come out at work. If you're LGBTQ and you're looking for a job, take advantage of the following websites and services specifically devoted to helping you find your perfect career match.

JOB SEARCH RESOURCES FOR LGBTQ PEOPLE

GAYJOB.BIZ

www.gayjob.biz/index.cfm

GayJob.biz is an online community operated by Here! Interactive Media (H.I.M.) and is designed for gay and lesbian individuals looking for jobs, as well as the global business community seeking diverse job applicants. Employers can place job listings, search a database of resumes, or advertise on their website. GayJob.biz doesn't charge you to post your resume and search their database of jobs. GayJob.biz is also part of the Gay Web Monkey network and provides a good number of articles about queer college news at GayJob.biz/page.cfm?sectionid=2.

GAY FINANCIAL NETWORK'S CAREER CENTER CHANNEL

http://career.gfn.com/channel_cc.cfm

Launched by Walter B. Schubert in 1998, a third-generation financier and the first openly-gay member of the New York Stock Exchange, The Gay Financial Network is the first Internet media company devoted to financial services whose sole business is to address and satisfy the unique financial and legal needs and concerns of the American LGBTQ community. Gfn.com takes the form of a web-based finance magazine and currently enjoys a broad readership; it has become the definitive source of financial information for the LGBTQ community. GFN's Career Center Channel offers a wealth of information for job hunters as well as wide-ranging queer professional, corporate, and alumni directories.

GLPCareers

www.glpcareers.com

Founded in September 2000, the Gay and Lesbian Professionals Career website is the preeminent Internet search engine providing employment opportunities and resources to LGBTQ job seekers in the United States. The mission of GLPCareers is to promote excellence in employment services for the gay community by matching highly qualified LGBTQ employees with a gay-friendly environment.

GLPCareers is aggressively positioning itself to be the leading job search engine for the LGBTQ community. In order to achieve this goal it seeks out the most LGBTQ-friendly employers and matches them with the highest caliber of candidates. The ultimate goal is to provide gay job seekers with a work environment which values the diversity LGBTQ people contribute.

HireDiversity

www.hirediversity.com

HireDiversity.com is the nation's leading online service for diversity recruitment and career development, providing top quality services and networking opportunities while linking underrepresented candidates with *Fortune* 1000 corporations, government agencies, and non-profit/educational institutions. Hire Diversity supports the career development and success of job candidates with all levels of experience, from seasoned professionals to recent college graduates and interns. HireDiversity.com also offers career advice, information on diversity events throughout the country, resume distribution, competitive salary information, and interviewing tips and tactics. Many of HireDiversity's clients operate in global economy or industry sectors that seek highly skilled, multicultural, and/or bilingual professionals who can best represent them in their respective target markets.

HRC Workplace Project

www.hrc.org/Template.cfm?Section=Work_Life

The Human Rights Campaign Workplace Project maintains this website as a national source of information on workplace policies and laws surrounding sexual orientation and gender identity. According to the HRC, it's the nation's most comprehensive, accurate and regularly updated database of corporate policies and workplace laws:

The Human Rights Campaign also develops and releases an annual Corporate Equality Index that measures major corporations on a scale from 0 to 100 based on criteria regarding issues of fairness for LGBTQ employees. The Corporate Equality Index is a great resource for queer job-seekers, investors and consumers seeking information to help them make more informed decisions about how the companies they work for treat the LGBTQ community. In 2006, an unprecedented 138 major U.S. companies earned the top rating, a tenfold increase in the 4 years since the index was introduced in 2002.[1]

PLANETOUT MONEY AND CAREERS

http://planetout.com/money

Planet Out's Money and Careers section offer tons of tips on "queer careers," articles on gay issues in the workplace, and comprehensive job listings. It also offers an innovative search engine to help you find an LGBTQ-friendly company of interest, as well as provide ongoing editorials with a queer slant about relevant workplace issues.

PROGAYJOBS

www.Progayjobs.com

ProGayJobs is an organization dedicated exclusively to the employment needs of the LGBTQ professional workforce. ProGayJobs' mission is two-fold:

- To assist the LGBTQ workforce in finding satisfying, enriching jobs with companies that offer freedom from discrimination and harassment due to their sexual orientation and/or gender, equal benefits for the partners of LGBTQ employees that are comparable with those offered to the spouses of married employees, and equal opportunity for advancement and career development.

- To assist diversity-focused employers and recruiters in recruiting and retaining highly qualified, talented LGBTQ employees for their companies and clients.

---

1   Echelon. "As Black Friday Approaches, Human Rights Campaign Releases Buying for Equality 2007." www.echelonmagazine.com/news_hrc10.htm.

LGBTQ Professional Groups

Financial Services Industry Exchange

www.f-six.org

The Financial Services Industry Exchange is a leading global networking and professional services organization specifically for gay and lesbian financial services professionals.

Lesbian and Gay Veterinary Medical Association

www.lgvma.org

Provides support for individuals, education for the community, and a forum for information exchange and social interaction.

National Lesbian and Gay Journalists Association (NLGJA)

www.nlgja.org

The National Lesbian and Gay Journalists Association is an organization of journalists, online media professionals, and students that works from within the journalism industry to foster fair and accurate coverage of lesbian, gay, bisexual, and transgender issues. NLGJA opposes workplace bias against all minorities and provides professional development for its members.

National Lesbian and Gay Law Association (NLGLA)

www.nlgla.org

National Lesbian and Gay Law Association is a national association of lawyers, judges, and other legal professionals, law students, and affiliated lesbian, gay, bisexual, and transgender legal organizations. Established in 1988 and an affiliate of the American Bar Association, NLGLA sponsors year-round regional and local networking events throughout the United States. NLGLA has rapidly become a national voice for lesbians, gay men, bisexuals, and transgender people in the legal profession. The association exists to promote justice in and through the legal profession for the lesbian and gay community in all its diversity.

NATIONAL ORGANIZATION OF GAY AND LESBIAN SCIENTISTS AND TECHNICAL PROFESSIONALS (NOGLSTP)

www.noglstp.org

The National Organization of Gay and Lesbian Scientists and Technical Professionals (NOGLSTP) is a national organization of LGBTQ people (and their advocates) employed or interested in scientific or technological fields. NOGLSTP's goals include educating the scientific and general communitys about LGBTQ issues in science and the technical workplace; educating the queer community about relevant topics in science; dialogue with professional societies and associations; improving members' employment and professional environment; opposing queer phobia and stereotypes by providing role models of successful LGBTQ scientific and technical professionals; and fostering networking and mentoring opportunities among members.

OUT PROFESSIONALS

www.outprofessionals.com

With over 1,100 members, Out Professionals is one of the biggest and most influential gay and lesbian professional organizations. From useful workshops and in-depth seminars to celebrity lectures and informal socializing, Out Professionals is the must-have membership for anyone seeking social and networking contacts in the New York area. OP members work in advertising and public relations, banking and finance, communications and marketing, computers and new media, entertainment and television, film and video, journalism and publishing, and dozens of other fields.

OUT IN TELEVISION AND FILM

www.outintvandfilm.org

Out in Television and Film is a national professional organization that promotes the visibility of lesbian, gay, bisexual, and transgender professionals in the film and television industries; helps LGBTQ professionals achieve their highest professional goals; and fosters corporate cultures that provide equal opportunities and benefits for "out" professionals.

POPCORNQ FILM AND VIDEO PROFESSIONALS

http://groups.yahoo.com/group/pqprofessionals/join

The PopcornQ Film and Video Professionals List is an e-group for film and video professionals (makers, distributors, exhibitors, festival programmers, bookers, journalists, etc.), with an emphasis on the genre of gay, lesbian, bisexual, and transgender motion pictures and events. The list is also open to critical discussions of issues in queer cinema, info about queer film festivals, job announcements, and items of interest to film professionals.

POWER-UP

www.power-up.net

Power-Up promotes the visibility and integration of gay women in entertainment, the arts, and all forms of media.

CONSORTIUM CONTRIBUTORS:

We would like to sincerely thank the following members of the National Consortium of Directors of LGBT Resources in Higher Education for their guidance and thoughtful contributions to this book:

Debbie Bazarsky is the Lesbian, Gay, Bisexual, Transgender Center Director at Princeton University and serves on the Executive Board of the National Consortium of Directors of LGBT Resources in Higher Education. Previously, Bazarsky served as the first coordinator of the Queer Resource Center at the University of California—Santa Barbara and worked at The Ohio State University's Lesbian, Gay, Bisexual Student Services. She is currently working towards her doctorate in human sexuality at Widener University with a focus on lesbian sexuality.

Brett-Genny Janiczek Beemyn, PhD is the Director of the Stonewall Center at the University of Massachusetts—Amherst; co-chair of the National Consortium of Directors of LGBT Resources in Higher Education; and a board member of the Transgender Law and Policy Institute. A trans activist and historian, Beemyn has spoken and written widely on transgender issues, particularly the experiences of transgender college students and trans-inclusive campus policies. Beemyn is currently writing a book with Sue Rankin entitled *The Lives of Transgender People*, which is based on the results of their research—the first large-scale, national study of transgender people in the U.S.

Matthew Carcella is the Assistant Director of the LGBT Center at Princeton University.

Saralyn Chesnut is the Director of the Office of LGBT Life and Adjunct Professor of American and Women's Studies at Emory University.

Daniel Coleman is the program coordinator for the GLBT Student Support Services at Indiana University where he is a graduate student in the Jacob's School of Music working on a Master of Music in trumpet performance. Coleman is also an adjunct professor of trumpet at Indiana State University. He holds a Bachelor of Music in performance from Capital University's Conservatory of Music. At Capital, he was president of and held many other leadership positions in PRIDE, the undergraduate GLBTQA group, for three consecutive years. While in Columbus, Ohio he volunteered for the Human Rights Campaign, Equality Ohio, and Stonewall Columbus. Coleman's diverse performing background includes soloing and competing in National Competition as well as winning the concerto competition at Capital University.

Jeremy P. Hayes, MS, is the Assistant Director in the Office of Diversity Services at Suffolk University. He previously was the coordinator of LGBT Student Services at Iowa State University where he completed his undergraduate degree and his MS in higher education. He has been a member of the National Consortium of Directors of LGBT Resources in Higher Education since 2002 and is a former board member. He also serves on the executive board of the Society Organized Against Racism in New England Higher Education.

Andrea D. Domingue is the Assistant Director for New York University's Office of LGBT Student Services. She graduated from NYU with a MA in Higher Education Administration and received a BA in Mathematics from The University of Texas at Austin. Andrea also serves as an Executive Board member for the National Consortium of LGBT Directors in Higher Education.

Jami Grosser currently serves as the Assistant Director for the Lesbian, Gay, Bisexual, Transgender Resource Center at the University of California—Riverside. She has been active as a student affairs professional for the past 6 years in roles with admissions and residential life. She currently serves on the Executive Board of the National Consortium of Directors of LGBT Resources in Higher Education. She received her BA in Life Science and Women's Studies from Kansas State University, and a master's degree in Higher and Postsecondary Education from Arizona State University.

Adrea Jaehnig is the founding director of the Syracuse University LGBT Resource Center. Prior to assuming this position in 2001, she was the Associate Director of the Office of Residence Life. She has her MA degree in Higher Education and Student Affairs Administration from the University of Vermont and is a doctoral candidate in Higher Education at Syracuse University. Jaehnig is co-chair of the National Consortium of Directors of the LGBT Resources in Higher Education, and a member of the American College Personnel Association and the National Association of College Student Personnel Administrators.

David Kessler earned a BA with a double major in English and History at Texas A&M University and a MEd degree in Higher Education Administration at the University of Texas at Austin. As a student and professional, David has collaborated with students, faculty, and staff in efforts to improve the campus climate for LGBTQ individuals at a small, religiously-affiliated institution and public, four-year universities. He continues to be an advocate for the LGBTQ population in higher education with his service to the University of Texas at San Antonio and NASPA.

Lis Maurer is the founding Coordinator of The Center for Lesbian, Gay, Bisexual and Transgender Education, Outreach, and Services at Ithaca College in Ithaca, New York. The American Association of Sex Educators, Counselors, and Therapists has designated Maurer a Certified Sexuality Educator and Counselor. Maurer is also a member of the Editorial Advisory Board of the American Journal of Sexuality Education, and a Certified Family Life Educator through the National Council on Family Relations. Maurer's written work on sexual orientation and gender identity has appeared in a variety of publications.

Camaron Mikio Jimenez Miyamoto is the Coordinator of Lesbian, Gay, Bisexual, Transgender, and Intersex Student Services at the University of Hawaii at Manoa.

Jessica Pettitt is a member of CAMPUSPEAK (campuspeak.com) as a professional speaker and consultant focusing on transgender inclusion and white privilege. She has worked extensively with ACPA's SCLGBTA and currently serves as treasurer for the National Consortium of Directors of LGBT Resources in Higher Education. For more information, visit www.jessicapettitt.com.

Terri Phoenix is the Assistant Director of the LGBT Center at The University of North Carolina at Chapel Hill.

Kerry John Poynter is currently employed in the Office of Multicultural Affairs at Columbia University where he coordinates LGBTQ programming and community building. He was employed at the Duke University Center for Lesbian, Gay, Bisexual, and Transgender Life from 1999–2006 where he managed and coordinated events and programs including the LGBT Safe Space Ally Program known as SAFE on Campus (Students, Administrators and Faculty for Equality). He received his MA in Administration of College Student Affairs from Western Michigan University. His writing interests include the development of heterosexual allies of LGBTQ people, the use of technology in multicultural education, and LGBTQ people of multiple cultural identities.

Ronni Sanlo, PhD is the director of both the UCLA MEd in Student Affairs and the UCLA Lesbian, Gay, Bisexual, Transgender Center. Before going to UCLA, Sanlo was the LGBT Center Director at the University of Michigan. Sanlo currently holds the Professional Standards Chair on the board of NASPA, and is the founding chair of the National Consortium of LGBT Campus Resource Center Directors. She is a frequent presenter and author. Her most recent book, *Gender Identity and Sexual Orientation: Research, Policy, and Personal Perspectives: New Directions for Student Services*, is published by Jossey-Bass. Dr. Sanlo resides on the campus of UCLA as a Faculty-in-Residence. She is the proud grandmother of two little girls and the daughter of outrageous PFLAG parents.

Heidi Adielia Stanton works in higher education as the Director for the Gender Identity/Expression and Sexual Orientation Resource Center at Washington State University where she actively advocates for students. Her passions include rocking the boat, changing the world, and painting the stories of her soul onto her canvasses.

Amit Taneja is the Assistant Director of the LGBT Resource Center at Syracuse University, where he is also pursing his PhD in Higher Education. He is the co-chair elect for the National Consortium of Directors of LGBT Resources in Higher Education. He has also served as a teaching assistant for courses in the LGBT Studies program at Syracuse University, and facilitates a monthly discussion group for LGBTQ students of color. His research focuses on the impact of college on the identity development of LGBT Students of Color.

Michelle D. Vaughan, PhD is a Counselor at the Longwood University Counseling Center.

CONTENT PARTNERS

The following organizations have partnered with us on this guide, and we are truly grateful for their endorsement and support:

- **The National Consortium of Directors of LGBT Resources in Higher Education** seeks to critically transform higher education environments so that lesbian, gay, bisexual, and transgender students, faculty, administrators, staff, and alumni/ae have equity in every respect through three major goals: Providing support to colleagues serving lesbian, gay, bisexual, and transgender communities in higher education; consulting with higher education administrators in the interest of improving campus climate and services for lesbian, gay, bisexual, and transgender faculty, staff, students, administrators, and alumni/ae; and advocating for institutional policy changes and program development that recognize the needs of lesbian, gay, bisexual, and transgender people. For more information about the National Consortium of Directors of LGBT Resources in Higher Education, visit LGBTCampus.org.

- **Parents, Family, and Friends of Lesbians and Gays (PFLAG)** promotes the health and well-being of gay, lesbian, bisexual, and transgender persons, their families, and friends through: support, to cope with an adverse society; education, to enlighten an ill-informed public; and advocacy, to end discrimination and to secure equal civil rights. Parents, Families, and Friends of Lesbians and Gays provides opportunity for dialogue about sexual orientation and gender identity, and acts to create a society that is healthy and respectful of human diversity. For more information about PFLAG, go to PFLAG.org.

The following organizations contributed their expertise, resources, and content to the development of this book:

- **Campus Pride** serves student leaders of lesbian, gay, bisexual, transgender, queer, and ally campus organizations by providing access to accurate and consistent resources that demonstrate support, education, and visibility on college and university campuses. Campus Pride envisions a safer campus environment free of homophobia, biphobia, transphobia, heterosexism, and genderism at colleges and universities and works to develop student leaders, campus networks, and organizations to create such positive change. For more information about Campus Pride, go to CampusPride.org.

- **The Gay and Lesbian Alliance Against Defamation (GLAAD)** is dedicated to promoting and ensuring fair, accurate, and inclusive representation of people and events in the media as a means of eliminating homophobia and discrimination based on gender identity and sexual orientation. GLAAD's Youth Empowerment Media Program specifically deals with college-age LGBTQ youth to make sure they are fairly represented in the media, along with issues important to them. GLAAD offers media training to campus groups to help students become better equipped to share their stories, and to help ensure they have the tools to reach out to local and school media outlets to get their voices heard. For more information about GLAAD, go to GLAAD.org.

- **Horizons Foundation** exists to mobilize and increase resources for the LGBTQ movement and organizations that secure the rights, meet the needs, and celebrate the lives of LGBTQ people; empower individual donors and promote giving as an integral part of a healthy, compassionate community; and steward a permanently endowed fund through which donors can make legacy gifts to ensure the LGBTQ community's capacity to meet the future needs of LGBTQ people. For more information about the Horizons Foundation, visit HorizonsFoundation.org.

- **The Human Rights Campaign (HRC)** is America's largest civil rights organization working to achieve gay, lesbian, bisexual, and transgender equality. By inspiring and engaging all Americans, HRC strives to end discrimination against LGBTQ citizens and realize a nation that achieves fundamental fairness and equality for all. HRC seeks to improve the lives of LGBTQ Americans by advocating for equal rights and benefits in the workplace, ensuring families are treated equally under the law, and increasing public support among all Americans through innovative advocacy, education, and outreach programs. HRC works to secure equal rights for LGBTQ individuals and families at the federal and state levels by lobbying elected officials, mobilizing grassroots supporters, educating Americans, investing strategically to elect fair-minded officials, and partnering with other LGBTQ organizations. For more information about HRC, visit HRC.org.

- **The Lambda 10 Project** works to heighten the visibility LGBTQ members of college fraternities and sororities by serving as a clearinghouse for educational resources and educational materials related to sexual orientation and gender identity/expression as it pertains to the fraternity/sorority experience. For more information about The Lambda 10 Project, visit Lambda10.org.

- **Lambda Legal** is a national organization committed to achieving full recognition of the civil rights of lesbians, gay men, bisexuals, transgender people and those with HIV through impact litigation, education, and public policy work. For more information about Lambda Legal, visit LambdaLegal.org.

- **The National Gay and Lesbian Task Force** builds the political power of the lesbian, gay, bisexual, and transgender community from the ground up by training activists, organizing broad-based campaigns to defeat anti-LGBT referenda and advance pro-LGBT legislation, and by building the organizational capacity of the LGBT movement. The Policy Institute, the movement's premier think tank, provides research and policy analysis to support the struggle for complete equality. As part of a broader social justice movement, the Task Force works to create a nation that respects the diversity of human expression and identity and creates opportunity for all. For more information about The National Gay and Lesbian Task Force, visit TheTaskForce.org.

- **The Point Foundation** provides financial support, mentoring and hope to meritorious students who are marginalized due to sexual orientation, gender expression, or gender identity. For more information about The Point Foundation, visit ThePointFoundation.org.

- **Soulforce:** The purpose of Soulforce is freedom for lesbian, gay, bisexual, and transgender people from religious and political oppression through the practice of relentless nonviolent resistance. For more information about Soulforce, visit SoulForce.org.

- **Transgender Law and Policy Institute** is nonprofit organization dedicated to engaging in effective advocacy for transgender people in our society. The TLPI brings experts and advocates together to work on law and policy initiatives designed to advance transgender equality. For more information about the Transgender Law and Policy Institute, visit Transgenderlaw.org

- **The Trevor Project** is a nonprofit endeavor established to promote acceptance of gay and questioning teenagers, and to aid in suicide prevention among that group. The project's Trevor Helpline is the first national 24-hour toll-free suicide prevention hotline aimed at gay and questioning youth. The Trevor Project also reaches teens through The Trevor Educational Package. Designed from the start to be a teaching tool for school and institutional use, the package combines the Academy Award winning short film TREVOR—a comedy/drama about a gay 13-year old boy named Trevor who, when rejected by friends and peers because of his sexuality, makes an attempt to take his life—with teaching guides and support materials created by Intermedia, Inc., an award-winning educational media company with a long history of bringing difficult subjects into the classroom. Since its completion in 1995, The Trevor Educational Package has been disseminated to hundreds of schools, universities, community groups, and professional organizations around the country. For more information about The Trevor Project, visit TheTrevorProject.org.

- **Women's College Coalition:** Founded in 1972, the Women's College Coalition is an association of women's colleges and universities—public and private, independent and church-related, 2- and 4-year—in the United States and Canada whose primary mission is the education and advancement of women. The Coalition collects and disseminates information relating to the education of women and gender equity in education. Other priority areas are the issues of recruitment and retention of women in math, science, and engineering, and the development of women's leadership. For more information about the Women's College Coalition, visit WomensColleges.org

FINDING THE FUNDS

What you should know about paying for your college education

A year attending a public college on average costs $12,796. Going to a private one will cost you $30,367 per year. Laying down what could be as much as $120,000 if not more over four years is a lot. That's the equivalent of almost 500 iPods, 12,000 movie tickets, or 444,444 packs of instant noodles.

Your parents have a tough job ahead of them. Just about everyone needs some kind of financial assistance. Fortunately, you have many different options, including grants, scholarships, work-study, federal loans, and private loans. Read on to learn about these options and share this with your parents.

OTHER PEOPLE'S MONEY

Scholarships and Grants • These are the best forms of financial aid because they don't have to be paid back. Scholarships are offered to students with unique abilities that the school is seeking to infuse into the student body, such as exceptional talent in music, art, or athletics. However, most scholarships require that you pass and maintain a minimum GPA requirement and some grants may not extend through all four years of your undergraduate education.

Federal grants for undergraduate study include Pell Grants, Federal Supplemental Educational Opportunity Grants (FSEOG), Academic Competitiveness Grants (ACG), and national SMART grants. Pell Grants are the most common type of federal grant awarded to undergraduate students, and form the base upon which supplemental aid from other financing sources may be added. Moreover, Pell Grant recipients receive priority for FSEOG awards, which are provided to students with exceptional financial need, and for National SMART Grants for math and science students.

Academic Competitiveness Grants (ACG) are a brand new kind of grant that began in the 2006–07 academic year. They are for students who have attended secondary school programs that have been qualified by the government as achieving a high standard of academic rigor. As with Federal Supplemental Educational Opportunity Grants, ACG awards are generally provided as a supplement to students already receiving Federal Pell Grants.

Additionally, your state residency or the state where the school you wish to attend is located also opens you up to state-funded grants and scholarships. Remember to check out the state grant application deadlines found on the FAFSA website mentioned below.

Note that as you advance through your undergraduate education, that progress itself makes you eligible for additional federal, state, and private grant and scholarship opportunities.

Maximize your eligibility for free money by completing the Free Application for Federal Student Aid ("FAFSA") online annually at http://www.fafsa.ed.gov. Visit the Department of Education's student aid portal at http://studentaid.ed.gov for the latest information on federal aid available to students like you. According to the National Center for Education Statistics, approximately 63% of all undergraduates receive some form of financial aid. There is approximately $80 billion in federal grants, loans and work-study funds available out there. Even if you don't think you'll qualify, it is worth it to fill out this form.

Work-study • Federal work-study is another way to lessen the burden of college tuition. Work-study is an actual part-time job, with pay of at least the current federal minimum wage— sometimes higher depending on the type of work you do.

Another advantage of federal work-study is that the program can sometimes place you in jobs related to your field of study. So, while you might be able to get equivalent wages working at a local restaurant or retail store, with work-study, you can sometimes gain resume-building experience related to your degree – in a school laboratory or research center, for example.

How much work-study you receive depends on your level of financial need and the funding level provided by your school. Be aware that work-study alone isn't going to be enough to pay for your education. But, it can be a good way to lessen the sting.

LOANS

When scholarships, grants, and work-study don't cover the full cost of attendance, many students take out loans to help out with the rest.

Avoid loans if you can. A loan can best be described as renting money. There's a cost and it may not be an easy cost to bear.

Here's an interesting anecdote. Many students graduate college without knowing what types of loans they received, who the lender was, and how much they owe. The first time many students become aware of the scope of their obligation is when they receive their first bill—six months after graduation.

This is often because students are passive participants in the financial aid process and do not educate themselves or ask questions. Most students receive a list of "preferred lenders" from their financial aid office and simply go with the lender recommended to them. Over the course of the previous year, relationships between financial aid offices and lenders have been called in question by State Attorneys General, the Department of Education and regulators. Financial aid offices in certain cases received revenue from lenders in exchange for being placed on the "preferred lender list." Some schools have even rented out their name and logo for use on loan applications. These practices occur without disclosure to parents and students.

It is important to know that the "preferred lenders" may not offer the best deals on your loan options. While your financial aid office may be very helpful with scholarships and grants, and is legally required to perform certain duties with regard to federal loans, many do not have staff researching the lowest cost options at the time you are borrowing.

Remember that your tuition payment equals revenue for the school. When borrowing to pay tuition, you can choose to borrow from any lender. That means you can shop for the lowest rate. Keep reading. This will tell you how.

TYPES OF LOANS

The federal government and private commercial lenders offer educational loans to students. Federal loans are usually the "first resort" for borrowers because many are subsidized by the federal government and offer lower interest rates. Private loans have the advantage of fewer restrictions on borrowing limits, but may have higher interest rates and more stringent qualification criteria.

Federal Loans • There are three federal loan programs. The Federal Perkins Loan Program where your school lends you money made available by government funds, the Federal Direct Loan Program (FDLP) where the government lends its money directly to students; and the Federal Family Education Loan Program (FFELP) where financial institutions such as MyRichUncle lend their own money but the government guarantees them. While most schools participate in the Federal Perkins Program, institutions tend to favor either the FFELP or FDLP. You will borrow from FFELP or FDLP depending on which program your school has elected to participate in.

> The government only lends money directly to you under the Federal Direct Loan Program. Lenders provide loans guaranteed by the federal government in the Federal Family Education Loan program.

The Federal Perkins Loan is a low-interest (5%) loan for students with exceptional need. Many students who do not qualify or who may need more funds can borrow FFELP or FDLP student loans. Under both programs, the Stafford loan is the typical place to start. The Stafford loan program features a fixed interest rate and yearly caps on the maximum amount a student can borrow. Stafford loans can either be subsidized (the government pays the interest while the student is in school) or unsubsidized (the student is responsible for the interest that accrues while in school). Starting July 1, 2007, the maximum amount an independent freshman student can borrow is $7,500.

It is often assumed that the government sets the rate on student loans. The government does not set the rate of interest. It merely indicates the maximum rate lenders can charge. The lenders are free to charge less than the specified rate of 6.8% for Stafford loans. There is also an origination fee of up to 2% dropping to 1.5% on July 1, 2007. In some cases you may also be charged up to a 1% guarantee fee. Any fees will be taken out of your disbursement.

Historically lenders have hovered at the maximum rate because most loans were distributed via the financial aid office whereby a few lenders received most of the loans. The end result was limited competition. At 1,239 institutions, one lender received more than 90% of the number

Stafford loans in 2006.

Certain lenders offer rate reductions, also known as borrower benefits, conditioned on the borrower making a certain number of on-time payments. Unfortunately, it is estimated that 90% of borrowers never qualify for these reductions.

Last year, MyRichUncle challenged this process by launching a price war. The company cut interest rates on Stafford loans and introduced widespread price competition. These interest rate cuts are effective when students enter repayment and do not have any further qualification requirements. In addition, students only lose the rate reduction if they default.

Parents can also borrow a PLUS loan. The Parent PLUS Loan program allows the parents of dependent students to take out loans to supplement the aid packages of their children. The program allows parents to borrow money to cover any cost not already met by the student's financial aid package up to the full cost of attendance. Unlike the Stafford Loan, eligibility for the Parent PLUS loan is not determined by the FAFSA. A parent fills out a loan application and signs a master promissory note. Eligibility is contingent upon whether the parent has an adverse credit history. Adverse credit history is defined as being no more than 90 days delinquent on any debt, having not declared bankruptcy in the last five years, and having not been the subject of a default determination on a foreclosure, a repossession, a tax lien, a wage garnishment, or a write-off of Title IV debt in the last five years.

The maximum rate a lender can charge for Parent PLUS loans is 8.5%. PLUS loans also have an origination fee of up to 3%, and a guarantee fee of up to 1%. Any fees will be taken out of your disbursement.

Your financial aid office is legally required to certify for lenders that you are enrolled and based on your financial aid package, the amount in Federal loans you are eligible to borrow. You are free to choose any lender even if the lender is not on your financial aid office's preferred lender list.

To shop for low cost Federal loans, call a number of lenders before applying to determine their rates and fees. This is an effective approach because your application will not impact the price. Once you are comfortable that you have the lowest cost option, apply and submit the Master Promissory Note to your lender of choice.

Private Loans • Private student loans can make it possible to cover the costs of higher education when other sources of funding have been exhausted. Additionally, when you apply for federal loans, you can borrow up to what your institution has pre-defined as the annual cost of attendance. If your anticipated expenses are above and beyond this pre-defined cost because of your unique needs, it will take a series of appeals before your institution will allow you to borrow more federal loans. Private loans help you meet your true expectation of what you will need financially. Private loans can pay expenses that federal loans can't, such as application and testing fees and the cost of transportation.

When you apply for a private loan, the lending institution will check your credit history including your credit score and determine your capacity to pay back the money you borrow. For individuals whose credit history is less than positive, lenders may require a co-borrower: a credit-worthy individual who also agrees to be accountable to the terms of the loan. While private loans do not have annual borrowing limits, they often have higher interest rates, and interest rate caps are higher than those set by Federal loans. Generally, the loans are variable rate loans, so the interest rate may go up or down, changing the cost.

To shop for a private loan, after you've researched several options, apply to as many of them as you feel comfortable. Once you are approved, compare rates. Pick the lowest cost option.

EXTRA LESSONS

Borrow the minimum • Just because someone is offering to lend you thousands upon thousands of dollars doesn't mean you should necessarily take them up on that offer. At some point, you'll have to repay the debt and you'll have to do it responsibly. Wouldn't it be better to use your money for something more worthwhile to you?

Know your rights • Currently, student lending is an industry that is under heavy scrutiny. It is important, now more than ever, for parents and students to have an active voice and to make educational and financial choices that are right for them. Some schools work with "preferred lenders" when offering federal and private loans. You are not required to choose a loan from one of these lenders if you can find a better offer. With respect to Federal loans the financial aid office has a legislated role which is to certify for the lending institution that you the borrower are indeed enrolled and the amount you are eligible for. They are not legally empowered to dictate your choice of lender and must certify your loan from the lender of your choice. You have the right to shop for and to secure the best rates possible for your loans. Don't get bullied into choosing a different lender, simply because it is preferred by an institution. Instead, do your homework and make sure you understand all of your options.

Know what you want • When it's all said and done, you will have to take a variety of factors into account in order to choose the best school for you and for your future. You shouldn't have to mortgage your future to follow a dream, but you also shouldn't downgrade this opportunity just to save a few bucks.

An out-of-the-box approach • Community colleges are a viable option for those ultimately seeking a four-year degree. Articulation agreements between community colleges and major four-year institutions allow students to complete their general education requirements at community colleges and have them transferred to a four-year institution. If you are really keen on graduating from that fancy four year college of your choice, transferring in from a community college is a cheaper path to getting that same degree. At an average cost of $2,272 per year, it is a thought worth exploring.

MYRICHUNCLE

NOTES

NOTES

NOTES

NOTES

More expert advice from The Princeton Review

Guide to College Majors, 2007 Edition
978-0-375-76596-4 • $22.00/$28.00 Can.

More than 350 profiles of the most popular majors with:
- An overview of the major
- Career options and salary potential information
- Tips on the best high school prep work
- Sample college curriculum for the major
- Fun facts and interesting trivia

Paying for College without Going Broke, 2007 Edition
978-0-375-76567-4 • $20.00/$27.00 Can.

Selected by *The Washington Post's* "Color of Money" book club.

Thoroughly revised and updated to take the stress, confusion, and guess-work out of applying for financial aid.

Parents' Guide to College Life
978-0-375-76494-3 • $13.95/$21.00 Can.

The market is saturated with college admissions guides, but this is the only one that gives parents *honest answers* to the *real questions* they have when they send their children to college.